ULYSSES, DANTE, AND OTHER STORIES

Cultural Inquiry

EDITED BY CHRISTOPH F. E. HOLZHEY
AND MANUELE GRAGNOLATI

The series 'Cultural Inquiry' is dedicated to exploring how diverse cultures can be brought into fruitful rather than pernicious confrontation. Taking culture in a deliberately broad sense that also includes different discourses and disciplines, it aims to open up spaces of inquiry, experimentation, and intervention. Its emphasis lies in critical reflection and in identifying and highlighting contemporary issues and concerns, even in publications with a historical orientation. Following a decidedly cross-disciplinary approach, it seeks to enact and provoke transfers among the humanities, the natural and social sciences, and the arts. The series includes a plurality of methodologies and approaches, binding them through the tension of mutual confrontation and negotiation rather than through homogenization or exclusion.

Christoph F. E. Holzhey is the Founding Director of the ICI Berlin Institute for Cultural Inquiry. Manuele Gragnolati is Professor of Italian Literature at the Sorbonne Université in Paris and Associate Director of the ICI Berlin.

ULYSSES, DANTE, AND OTHER STORIES

ELENA LOMBARDI

ISBN (Hardcover): 978-3-96558-056-5
ISBN (Paperback): 978-3-96558-57-2
ISBN (PDF): 978-3-96558-058-9
ISBN (EPUB): 978-3-96558-059-6

Cultural Inquiry, 28
ISSN (Print): 2627-728X
ISSN (Online): 2627-731X

Bibliographical Information of the German National Library
The German National Library lists this publication in the Deutsche
Nationalbibliografie (German National Bibliography); detailed
bibliographic information is available online at http://dnb.d-nb.de.

© 2023 ICI Berlin Press

Cover design: Studio Bens
Cover photograph: © Ray Charles White Archives

Except for images or otherwise noted, this publication is licensed under a
Creative Commons Attribution-ShareAlike 4.0 International License. To
view a copy of this license, visit:
http://creativecommons.org/licenses/by-sa/4.0/.

In Europe, volumes are printed by Lightning Source UK Ltd., Milton
Keynes, UK. See the final page for further details.

Digital editions can be viewed and downloaded freely at:
https://doi.org/10.37050/ci-28.

ICI Berlin Press is an imprint of
ICI gemeinnütziges Institut für Cultural Inquiry Berlin GmbH
Christinenstr. 18/19, Haus 8
D-10119 Berlin
publishing@ici-berlin.org
www.ici-berlin.org

For my mother, Lucia (1928–2023)

For Seryozha (1971–2023)
Эх раз, ещё раз, ещё много много раз

Contents

List of Figures viii

Incipit 1

1. *Lectura* 13

2. Sing me, o Muse, again 47

3. To Pursue Virtue and Knowledge 91

4. '... And Maybe Sometime' 125

5. It Was Sunset 173

6. All In One Place 213

Colophon 265

A Narrated Bi(bli)ography Preceded by a Postface
and Interspersed with Notes that Lack Superscript.
Also Illustrated, for that Matter. With the Addition of
a One-word Glossary. 273

A List of Primary Sources 307

List of Figures

1. Jean-Baptiste Carpeaux, *Ugolino and his Sons*, 1865–67 (detail).
   Image credit: The Metropolitan Museum of Art, New York. Purchase, Josephine Bay Paul and C. Michael Paul Foundation Inc. Gift, Charles Ulrick and Josephine Bay Foundation Inc. Gift, and Fletcher Fund, 1967 119

2. Abraham Ortelius, *Theatrum Orbis Terrarum. Descriptio Maris Pacifici* (detail), British Library, 009025, Maps.C.2.d.6, 6.
   Image credit: British Library 131

3. The Hereford Mappa Mundi, *c.* 1300.
   Image credit: © Hereford Cathedral 148

4. Pietro Vesconte, Portolan chart of Western Europe and the Mediterranean, with the principal powers indicated by means of flags, *Maps for the Liber Secretorum Fidelium Crucis*, *c.* 1320–25, additional MS 27376, ff.180v–181.
   Image credit: British Library 149

5. Isidore of Seville, *Etymologiarum libri XX* (detail), MS Latin 7585, 164v.
   Image credit: Bibliothèque nationale de France 150

6. Rembrandt Van Rijn, *A Woman Making Water*, 1631, etching.
   Image credit: © The Trustees of the British Museum. In the open access versions, the image is shared under a Creative Commons Attribution-NonCommercial-ShareAlike 4.0 International (CC BY-NC-SA 4.0) licence 219

7. MS Strozzi 150, c. 32r (detail).
   Image credit: Biblioteca Medicea Laurenziana, Florence. Permission granted by the Ministry of Culture. Any form of further reproduction by any means is forbidden for the print versions. In the open access versions, the image is shared under a Creative Commons Attribution-NonCommercial-NoDerivs International (CC BY-NC-ND) licence 235

8. MS Plut.40.13, c. 25r (detail).
   Image credit: as Figure 7 237

9. MS Conv.Soppr.204, c. 96r (detail).
   Image credit: as Figure 7 238

10. MS Plut.40.20, c. 78r (detail).
    Image credit: as Figure 7 239

11. MS Egerton 943, c. 63r (detail).
    Image credit: British Library 242

12. Mermaid, object number 97-39-70/72853.
    Image credit: courtesy of the Peabody Museum of Archaeology and Ethnology, Harvard University. Gift of the Heirs of David Kimball, 1897 261

13. Sirena, Museum of Natural History, Milan.
    Image credit: photograph by Andrea Cherchi 262

14. My mother. Image credit: the author 290

15. Enrico Pazzi, *Monument to Dante*, 1865, Piazza Santa Croce, Florence.
    Image credit: photograph by Jörg Bittner Unna. 294
16. Ameca, 2021. Image credit: Engineered Arts Ltd . . . 301

Incipit

'*Inferno* 26, the canto of Ulisse, is one of the highlights of Dante's *Commedia*. A daring rewriting of Homer's Odysseus, it becomes in turn a mandatory passage for many authors of the Western canon and beyond. For the reader it is an episode fraught with confusion. Am I supposed to love Ulysses or criticize him? Is he the "innocent" [two hands gesture in the air, the top of the index and middle fingers flexing, to signify the speaker's intention to accentuate innocence and to put it at a vague yet friendly distance] Is he the "innocent" victim of an overwhelming desire for knowledge, or a liar, a manipulator? In shaping Ulysses' mad flight past the pillars of Hercules into the unknown world, has Dante created an exceptionally modern character, indeed the "quintessential human being" [*idem*; double bunny ears signifying a rather ironic detachment in this case], or is he being very medieval, condemning sternly the excesses of antiquity? There is no straight answer to these questions, but they have been posed by hosts of readers since the middle ages [short pause; the speaker and the group allude to pondering].

As postmodern readers, all we can do is read this text together and point out its ambiguities, contradictions, and tensions.'

~

And so begins my lecture on Dante's Ulysses, year in, year out, in lecture rooms across the world. Those who have listened to this prologue for the first time are now past their midlife, others are still students in the making.

Year in, year out, the next hour or so becomes for me, and hopefully for my students, a fast and tight navigation over an agitated sea strewn with words and concepts — poetry, world literature, philosophy, geography, some (very rudimentary) economics, the meaning of writing.

Since you, reader, might not be a twenty-year-old student of Italian in an anglophone country (though that is a lovely, and rare, thing to be), here are a couple of A4s with bullet point tips on how to read the *Comedy*, and on its author. The manual I never dared to write.

- Dates? Really? As in 'the *Comedy* was written sometime between the birth and the death of its author', followed by all sorts of historical truths (them documents, they never lie), erudite beliefs, and educated guesses. You probably need to know only one date, and a fictional one for that matter. Easter 1300, somewhere near the beginning of April. This is when Dante sets his *Comedy*, which he actually starts writing a few years later. It makes sense: a new century, the first official Jubilee convened by the Pope, midlife (ah, see? this helps you figure out when he was born, roughly). And hindsight. Since

Dante starts writing his poem most likely in 1307, dating it to 1300 allows him to send messages from the afterlife he is writing about, to 'foresee' events that had already happened, and to present such happenings as willed by 'god', with the strange consequence that he ends up sounding like a prophet (and some readers think he is).

- The equally drastic and novel stunt whereby Dante casts himself as the main character of his poem. As teachers, then, we often remind our students to distinguish between Dante-poet and Dante-character (also known as D-traveller, or even D-pilgrim). This distinction is a bit pedestrian, not always valid, but for the most part useful. D-poet imagines himself lost in a forest, which leads to a journey in the afterlife. He gives himself-as-character two guides, also fictionalized historical people: the Latin poet Virgil and a poetic creature from his youth, his beloved Beatrice.

- Aside. 'Prophet' and 'pilgrim' are, of course, the denominations of one of the possible interpretations of the poem, the Christian reading; by some considered the only reading, by me avoided like the devil, because it is as ugly as sin. (Don't look at me strangely — a medieval poem on the Christian afterlife needs to be read in a Christian way no more than an epic poem requires a military reading. Priests and generals make bad readers, I think.)

- Yes, it is a poem about the Christian afterlife, consisting of three parts, or canticles — *Hell, Purgatory,* and *Paradise* — in turn divided into 33 cantos of various length + one proemial canto (= 100). Numbers are neat in this story. And, yes, they do suggest trinity, but more in a three-to-tango type of way. D-character, alive and embodied, is given the dubious privilege of witnessing Punishment, Atonement, and Blessedness across various sections of the three realms: circles (hell), terraces (purgatory), and heavens (paradise). The characters he encounters are embodied too, enveloped in a strangely conspicuous 'aerial body'.

- The genius invention is the metrics. This poem is written in *terza rima* (or *terzina*, tercet), a core of three hendecasyllables (lines of 11 syllables), 'enchained' by a system of rhymes that moves back and forth like a tide: ABA, BCB, CBC, etc. The middle rhyme-word of one tercet becomes the outer rhyme of the following. It needs to take a step back to go forward. You retreat and then you jump. You are scared and then bold. Nostalgic and driven. You got the point. It is an incessant embracing of otherness through the familiar. A living together; until the poet tears this plot apart by artificially inserting a full stop and thus ending the canto. A rhyme is always left unfinished. There is always someone left out in the cold.

- From a very practical point of view, the *terza rima* is very hard to interpolate and mess up. Thus, we have a pretty stable text, in terms of both language and content, which is not a given for ancient and medieval works, perennially submerged in the sea of variance. Thanks, 'god', for that! (and apologies for what I said above about your followers making bad readers).

- This text is written in a vernacular of the Italian peninsula, a Florentine/Tuscan version, which today we roughly recognize as Italian. Back then it was an unruly, ungrammatical, and quite obscure language, with a small and rather monological literary tradition. A mother tongue without prestige or palette. [And, no, Dante was not the 'father' of the Italian language; at best, he was its wet-nurse.] Dante moulds his vernacular to forge a polyglot, plurilingual work, in which language knows no limits, fear, or shame.

- The *Comedy* is a swear word that has become canon. A giant raised middle finger to all the niceties, conveniences, politenesses, genres, styles, and traditions. It became canon out of the power of language alone. The *Comedy* entered the canon slamming the door loud. It sat there, looking all tough and surly. 'Got a problem with me, man?' They let it stay. Many have tried to smooth it or tame it, but no one has succeeded yet.

- [The canon is unfashionable, I know, but each of us has a complicated relation to it. I am not ready to divorce it yet. I probably never will. I am staying for the children.]

- Please forget the adjective 'divine'. It was added two hundred years later. *Comedy*, *Commedia*, or, if you want to be a real snob, *Comedìa* is the only approximation to the title of the poem. In a letter written by Dante or by someone very close to him, *Comedy* is explained in a very straightforward way, as the opposite of tragedy: it has a stinky beginning (hell) and a happy ending (paradise). Difficult to argue with that. 'Comedy' also means dialogism, plurilingualism, an extraordinary variety of styles and of voices, unfathomable depths of expression, scratching, or soothing, rhymes, the vitality of open and generous bodies, the maddening thrust of desire, and some funny toilet humour.

- Please keep in mind instead the materiality of this text. It was written in ways that are both familiar and foreign to us. A cream-colour page made of goat's skin, on which writers used to trace lines to guide their hand; carbon or plant-based inks that took a while to dry and blotched a lot; the writer holding a quill in one hand and a small knife to sharpen it in the other (a bit like the way today we hold knife and fork) and using a pumice stone to smooth the page out.

- Not a single line written by Dante's hand has reached us, but the *Comedy* was copied by countless scribes, each manuscript a different adventure of writing.

To the author, now. What do you need to keep in mind? Little or nothing.

- Perhaps, as customary, a parenthesis containing digits and a dash: (1265–1321). Round brackets like little hands gesturing at opening and closing, containing the variety, complexity, and banality of a life. So obvious that we tend to gloss over it, until the parenthesis refers to someone we love, and then it is atrocious, or to ourselves, and then it is unthinkable.

- A list of other, or 'minor', works: I will spare you that one, reader.

- A crisis: 1302, the year our poet was exiled from his native Florence and began wandering through Italy. The years during which the *Comedy* is written are times of hardship, disillusion, exclusion, and loneliness, but also of a productive homelessness, of disorientation, of writhing away from the grips of localism. There is no *Comedy* without exile.

– And this beautiful quote by Russian poet Osip Mandelstam: 'The question occurs to me — and quite seriously — how many sandals did Alighieri wear out in the course of his poetic work, wandering about on the goat paths of Italy.'

A note on reading Dante. It does take three to tango, and this time it has nothing to do with the trinity: it takes a writer, a reader, and a text, and the transformative encounter that follows. You choose what kind of reader of the *Comedy* you want to be. Maybe a reader-student, who requires much more information than what I gave above. Or you might well like to imagine yourself as one of the first readers of the poem, and dive into it without quite knowing the what, the when, and the how. 'The *Comedy* contains its own footnotes', one of my teachers used to say. I do repeat this statement to my students, year in year out, with a conviction that is somewhat proportional to the sceptical look on their faces. 'But you need to be patient' — I add. Don't rush through an ancient text. Don't expect a quick fix, this is obvious, but also don't expect to understand it at a first reading, or second, or even tenth. And accept that this is the thrill of it. The journey of interpretation, the postponement of satisfaction, is so much more exciting than the landing of a stable meaning.

An old text needs time and space.

With an internal ruler, measure the space that you need around yourself and inhabit it with silence. Place yourself, as comfortably as you can, in it. As lightly as you wish. But place yourself. Reading, this profoundly intellectual experience, is also one of the greatest physical pleasures you can encounter.

Be a little bit like Machiavelli: find a room of your own in your inner self's house: a quiet, safe place. And then populate it; be in conversation.

> Venuta la sera, mi ritorno a casa ed entro nel mio scrittoio; e in sull'uscio mi spoglio quella veste cotidiana, piena di fango e di loto, e mi metto panni reali e curiali; e rivestito condecentemente, entro nelle antique corti delli antiqui huomini, dove, da loro ricevuto amorevolmente, mi pasco di quel cibo che solum è mio e ch'io nacqui per lui; dove io non mi vergogno parlare con loro e domandarli della ragione delle loro azioni; e quelli per loro humanità mi rispondono; e non sento per quattro hore di tempo alcuna noia, dimentico ogni affanno, non temo la povertà, non mi sbigottisce la morte: tutto mi transferisco in loro (Letter to Francesco Vettori, 10 December 1513).

> When evening comes, I return home and enter my study; on the threshold I take off my workday clothes, covered with mud and dirt, and put on the garments of court and palace. Fitted out appropriately, I step inside the venerable courts of the ancients, where, solicitously received by them, I nourish myself on that food that alone is mine and for which I was born; where I am unashamed to converse with them and to question them about the motives for their actions, and they, out of their human kindness, answer me. And for four hours at a time, I feel no boredom, I forget all my troubles, I do not dread poverty, and I am not terrified by death. I absorb myself into them completely (translation by J. B. Atkinson and David Sices).

Or do like Augustine and shut down all things around you; and then silence yourself too.

> Si cui sileat tumultus carnis, sileant phantasiae terrae et aquarum at aeris, sileant et poli et ipsa sibi anima sileat et transeat se non se cogitando, sileant somnia et imaginariae revelationes, omnis lingua et omne signum et quicquid transeundo fit si cui sileat omnino ... (*Confessions* 9, 10, 25).
>
> If someone can achieve a state in which the turmoil of the flesh is silent, silent are the phantasies of earth, waters, and air, silent the poles, and silent the soul itself, able to go beyond itself by not thinking of itself [apologies for the many 'it-selves', but that's the text's point I am afraid — so fricative, and voiceless, but such must be the soul; it is spirant after all]. Silent the dreams and imaginary revelations, silent every tongue and every sign and everything that is transitory ... if only ... if only one could ... (my rather free translation. The sweet detail is that Augustine figures this out in conversation with his mum).

Well, Augustine is not talking about reading, is he? He is describing the steps of some mystical rapture toward the contemplation of the divinity. Shush! Augustine says, in a very hypothetical way, and listen to 'H'im. Shush! (this is how I understand it) and listen to the voice of your text.

Reading, for me, is the greatest form of comfort and solace. [Not consolation, no. Consolation is not for books and readers, consolation happens only between embodied humans, one of whom is a mother, or mother figure (I learned this from reading Rilke, though).]

Especially reading the classics. To calm myself, I read Plutarch. I know, it sounds pretty lame when you write it down. Give it a try though. At first, it does not work. It is difficult even to get to the end of one sentence. A residue of daily concerns still looms around like space debris. I spend the first minutes of my reading mostly with my eyes closed, stroking the page with the back on my hand. Nothing fancy or satisfying there (it is just paper), maybe just the sound of the caress, imperceptible, like sand slipping through the fingers. But then something squares inside. It is perhaps the incessant vocatives in the speeches ('O Caius Crassinius, which hopes do we have?' ... 'We will splendidly win, o Caesar'), or the awkward sentences ('By Hercules! May Pyrrhus and the Sannites follow this code until they are at war with us!'), or the archaic, long-forgotten names ('Eupatrids, Gheomorois and Demiurges', 'Terpander, Taleta, Pherecydes'), the flat, still semi-true, proverbial dictum ('the luxury that, due to their lack of taste, they reputed happiness'), or just the Greek letters dancing on the facing page, and I am in — a world of crystal calm, where sometimes I can hear the writer's stylus scratching on the papyrus. I soon find the time and the space for reading, a capacity that dilates my hours, abduction from every-day concerns, and an antidote to the toxicity of the 'devices'. The obstacle and the plateau (and being worthy of rereading every five years): this, and nothing else, is what makes a 'classic' to me. This is the free yet especial ticket to my canon.

A note on the translation. Choosing the English version of a poet that is widely translated like Dante ends up being a matter of affection. I am attached to Charles Singleton's 1970 translation, which I have used for my academic dealings with Dante since I was a graduate student. It is (mostly) exact, very literal, prosaic, aseptic, actually antiseptic (the germs of strangeness cannot flourish there), analgesic (the grating pain of Dante's language is put to rest), anaesthetic, sedate, and even soporific. It is my way to ask you, reader, to glance at the original, to taste its sound, to chase meaning, even if it is a matter of one word, and to realize that, at heart, we are all linguists. Sometimes you will see me making fun of this translation — like when I tease some of its adverbial choices, such as 'therewithin' and 'therefrom' — but it is meant to be good-natured.

The very few footnotes that you will encounter are mostly expansions of the main text. Scholars do not fear, though: there is a section with bibliographical references, but I have chosen to narrate it, and to weave it with reflections on the operation of this little book and on the meaning of scholarship itself. You will find it at the end. At the very end, you will also find a more restrained list of primary sources and of the translations I have employed throughout the text (unless the translation is mine, in which case I note it). I have arranged them in order of appearance, rather than in alphabetical order. As such, they look like a forlorn chorus line, or a jolly *danse macabre*, and they tell yet another, independent story.

And what about me? After all you are reading my reading of Dante. And with a good portion of me in it. Think of me as a scribe, of the kind that tends to wander off. An academic, profoundly in love with their subject matter, who has reached the age of irony. Think of me as a voice, as an idiolect. Or rather, voices, in the plural, as I randomly and sometimes inadvertently inhabit the characters I am trying to explain or mimic the genres that I am reading. Often, I try to contain myself in parentheses or square brackets, but most of the time I am roaming free.

Think of me as a renter of the English language: it lets me inhabit its space and I pay it back with monies of strangeness and bagloads of typos.

Sometimes, I also feel a bit like Ulysses. An oar-less, sail-less Ulysses, stranded around Gibraltar, half perplexed and half intent. Less hardy but equally ardent. An underground type of Ulysses (here meaning 'Dostoevskyian', 'self-defeating' rather than 'cool' and 'young'). A female

Ulysses, for that matter, but I refuse to be called Penelope or Siren.

When asked who my audience may be, I am at a pleasurable loss. A bit like Ulysses too, a curious and patient reader, is my answer. Of you I know nothing but this.

1. *Lectura*

To properly introduce the episode of Ulysses, I will practice a time-honoured exercise in Dante studies: the *lectura*. Somewhere between a lecture and a reading, it is a private reflection that is also a public performance, a deceptively erudite display that conceals the distinctive desire to leave one's own dent in the text. The practice began in semi-private form as early as the *Comedy* started circulating in the mid-fourteenth century, alongside a very early (and also uninterrupted) tradition of written commentary, yet its inaugural date is 23 October 1373, when the old and ailing Giovanni Boccaccio began his reading in the church of Santo Stefano di Badia in Florence, upon public request. This being Italy in a medieval nutshell, a killer amount of bureaucracy was involved: a petition to the Priori of the Arts (the leaders of the guilds who were ruling Florence) and to their military chief, the 'Gonfaloniere di giustizia', was then approved by both 'chambers', first the 'Consiglio del capitano del popolo' (186 votes against 19), and then the 'Consiglio del podestà e del comune' (114 votes against

7). I suspect it killed Boccaccio, who only got to read as far as canto 18 of *Inferno* in the course of sixty lectures. Another remarkable moment for the *lectura* is the late sixteenth century, when readers like Galileo Galilei gathered around Dante's text in the Accademia Fiorentina, in an act perhaps of resistance against the religious and political strictures that soon would relegate Florence and Italy to a secondary role in Europe.

Long story short: the tradition of the *lectura* has been uninterrupted since the late middle ages, and it is the little-big quirkiness of my own academic discipline: we read. We read Dante constantly, obsessively, relentlessly, mostly repeating the same things over and over, until, almost by inertia, the weight of boredom and repetition becomes momentum, a detail is explained, a new vein of the text appears, an original approach eventually surfaces. Today, there are several *lecturae* ongoing at the same time. We read canto by canto, horizontally, vertically, diagonally, tangentially. We read. And then we print ourselves reading. We are a machine. Some kind of Terminator of reading.

This habit then trickles down to our academic writing and teaching. In the following pages you will see how I read the canto of Ulisse in my university lectures. Always in the same way in the last twenty-plus years, yet with those little deviations and digressions that have made this reading profoundly different from that first handwritten canvas of a lecture that I jotted down in October 2000 in Montreal. Luckily, the students change every year. This time, I shall also take several tempting detours that role, pedagogy, and decorum do not usually allow.

The canto begins with a retrospective gaze, which helps to briefly contextualize it. We are in the *Malebolge*, the 'Evil Pouches' that constitute the circle of Fraud, the largest and most characteristic of the nine circles of hell. We have just left the seventh pouch (cantos 24 and 25), where the thieves are gathered — those robbers of property that are now deprived of the most cherished belonging, one's identity, and are continuously turned into snakes and back to humans in a relentless metamorphosis adhering to the fearful law of *contrapasso* (counter penalty, or punishment that fits the crime). Before we venture into a strange new zone, the pouch of the 'evil counsellors', a little retrospection on the characters encountered among the thieves allows the poet to address for the nth-time his arch-nemesis: the city of Florence that recently exiled him. Having met, he says, five of his fellow citizens among the thieves, he is ready to lash out with a sarcastic apostrophe against the community that has generated them.

>   Godi, Fiorenza, poi che se' sì grande
>   che per mare e per terra batti l'ali,
> 3   e per lo 'nferno tuo nome si spande!
>   Tra li ladron trovai cinque cotali
>   tuoi cittadini onde mi ven vergogna,
> 6   e tu in grande orranza non ne sali.
>   Ma se presso al mattin del ver si sogna,
>   tu sentirai, di qua da picciol tempo,
> 9   di quel che Prato, non ch'altri, t'agogna.
>   E se già fosse, non saria per tempo.
>   Così foss'ei, da che pur esser dee!
> 12 ché più mi graverà, com' più m'attempo.

> Rejoice, O Florence, since you are so great that over sea and land you beat your wings, and your name is spread through Hell! Among the thieves I found five of your citizens, such that shame comes to me — and you rise thereby to no great honor. But if near morning our dreams are true, you shall feel ere long what Prato, as well as others, craves for you. And if it were already to come, it would be not too soon. Would it were, since indeed it must, for it will weigh the more on me the more I age.

Florence, by then the most florid and fast-expanding city-state (*comune*) of central Italy, was swollen with ambition and aggression. Dante turns it into a giant bird of prey. The story goes that these lines ironize an inscription on a public building dated 1255, where the city was flaunted as 'she who owns the sea, the land, and the entire world' ('quae mare, quae terram, quae totum possidet orbem'). But its pride, Dante says, is only felt in hell, so heavily is it populated by his fellow citizens.

Then he goes all prophetic. He can do so, we have seen, thanks to the stunt of setting the fictional date of his *Comedy* in 1300, while he started writing it in 1307, so it is all hindsight for him, and projection for us. Florence has enemies (the city of Prato is one of many, and the closest spatially). Florence will pay soon – she will – she is a bitch – she is my bitch – I love her – oh god I hate this – I am getting old. This is a rough translation of the strange last lines of this passage (10–12), where the predictive fervour turns into a *cupio dissolvi*, the death drive of the poet himself, rage stuck in his throat, overwhelming, tragic, roaring between the optative, the present, and the future (it were … it would … it must … it will).

Get hold of yourself.

We realize at this point that Dante and his guide are crossing from one pouch to another, a passage that is both physically and linguistically taxing. Listen to the quarrelling sound of the rhymes (-ee; -ia; -oglio) and to the crackling of the line 'tra le schegge e i rocchi de lo scoglio', or look at the strange word 'iborni', which could equally mean 'i borni' (the boulders, like our cautious translator understands) or a strange rendition of the Latin *eburneus* (ivory colour), meaning that the poet and his guide are turned pale by fear [or by excessive erudition].

        Noi ci partimmo, e su per le scalee
    che n'avea fatto iborni a scender pria,
15 rimontò 'l duca mio e trasse mee;
        e proseguendo la solinga via,
    tra le schegge e tra ' rocchi de lo scoglio
18 lo piè sanza la man non si spedia.

> We departed thence, and by the stairs which the jutting rocks had made for our descent before [or: which made us pale in our descent before], my leader remounted and drew me up; and pursuing the solitary way among the jags and rocks of the ridge, the foot could not advance without the hand.

While his avatar (D-traveller) is stretched in this rock-climbing act, the poet is wrapped in a similarly rocky thought, which testifies to his involvement in what is to come. He vents a strange quasi-appeal to the reader on the necessity of restraining his talent, in order not to waste it. There is something very painful at stake. Notice the first construction: I grieved then, and I grieve now. The rock climber and the poet are one, involved in the same dolorous feeling. Watch! Curb. Restrict, restrain! Do not fall.

        Allor mi dolsi, e ora mi ridoglio
    quando drizzo la mente a ciò ch'io vidi,
21 e più lo 'ngegno affreno ch'i' non soglio,
        perché non corra che virtù nol guidi;
    sì che, se stella bona o miglior cosa
24 m' ha dato 'l ben, ch'io stessi nol m'invidi.

> I sorrowed then, and sorrow now again, when I turn my mind to what I saw; and I curb my genius more than I am wont, lest it run where virtue does not guide it; so that if a kindly star or something better has granted me the good, I might not grudge myself that gift.

In plain translation: I am about to write one of the peaks of my poem, the story of an unguided intellectual endeavour, so I will bridle my own bright mind. I shall not run, I will be cautious, I will not mess up. Won't jinx it.

Hey, but you can't do that, his genius seems to argue. And what follows is a sudden rise of style, a precious, ambitious double simile to describe the pouch of the evil counsellors. Seen from afar it looks like a valley at dusk, in which suddenly the fireflies light up. There is something classical in this — it makes one think of Callimachus or Virgil, and of that miracle whereby the classics turn the most common, everyday natural occurrence into a string of the finest language. There is a lyricism to it, a sudden heightening of poetry and its retreating away from story into painting, 'photography', or, if we can envision it, into a frameless visual image. A picture so perfect, and yet so natural, that the reader feels at home in it.

>   Quante 'l villan ch'al poggio si riposa,
>   nel tempo che colui che 'l mondo schiara
> 27 la faccia sua a noi tien meno ascosa,
>   come la mosca cede a la zanzara,
>   vede lucciole giù per la vallea,
> 30 forse colà dov'e' vendemmia e ara:
>   di tante fiamme tutta risplendea
>   l'ottava bolgia, sì com'io m'accorsi
> 33 tosto che fui là 've 'l fondo parea.

> As many as the fireflies which the peasant, resting on the hill — in the season when he that lights the world least hides his face from us, and at the hour when the fly yields to the mosquito — sees down along the valley, there perhaps where he gathers grapes and tills: with so many flames the eighth ditch was all agleam, as I perceived as soon as I came where the bottom could be seen.

But there is something else in this image. The fireflies. If you have seen it, reader — a valley lighting up with fireflies — you will know what I mean. An utterly unrealistic natural phenomenon that opens, joyfully, the gates of the beyond. I saw it only once. I was well into my twenties, visiting a friend's acquaintance, who lived rather solitarily on some wild hills in Tuscany. A bottle of wine, the vista; that kind of simplicity. And then, the valley below lit with fireflies. Some close, some near. I started jumping like a little child. The fireflies! Do you see the fireflies? 'Poor city girl' was the laconic comment of the host. And that was it. The friend, the friend-of-the-friend, the solitary cottage, the view, all have now slipped out from the weavings of memory, but the excitement is still here, 'now again', like Dante's renewing pain in reverse.

The second image is a biblical simile, less exciting than that of the fireflies, yet intellectually intriguing. If, from afar, the pouch looks like a valley full of fireflies, up close these appear like big flames that might hide something. While the first simile is all exquisite lightness, the second one is convoluted in its preciousness.

> E qual colui che si vengiò con li orsi
> vide 'l carro d'Elia al dipartire,
> 36 quando i cavalli al cielo erti levorsi,
> che nol potea sì con li occhi seguire,
> ch'el vedesse altro che la fiamma sola,
> 39 sì come nuvoletta, in sù salire:
> tal si move ciascuna per la gola
> del fosso, ché nessuna mostra 'l furto,
> 42 e ogne fiamma un peccatore invola.

> And as he who was avenged by the bears saw Elijah's chariot at his departure, when the horses rose erect to heaven, for he could not so follow it with his eyes as to see aught save the flame alone, like a little cloud ascending: so each flame moves along

> the gullet of the ditch for not one shows its theft,
> and each steals away a sinner.

Let's face it: this is not the passage in the Bible to which we run for instruction and comfort. Except for me, that is. I return to it every year just five minutes before the lecture, because somehow I always forget what this whole business of bears and chariot and vengeance is about, and what the hell these people are called in English. Elisha and Elijah! that's what they are called — I burst every time I go back to read the second book of Kings (2. 23–24). And year after year I get a little fonder of the story of such a prickly and petty god that would send two bears to wolf down (please allow the mixed metaphor) no less than forty-two little boys who had taken the piss out of one of his prophets, calling him 'baldy'. Sounds more Brothers Grimm than Logos to me. Still, the word of god this is:

> And he [Elisha] went up from thence to Bethel. And as he was going up by the way, little boys came out of the city and mocked him, saying: Go up, thou bald head. Go up, thou bald head. And looking back, he saw them, and cursed them in the name of the Lord: and there came forth two bears out of the forest, and tore of them two and forty boys (Douay Bible).

A story like this cannot but baffle readers. It makes Elisha a troubled character in the Jewish tradition, some interpreters imagining that he is eventually punished for this incident and others viewing the children like some bad-boys gang. In some interpretations, the Little Boys are a gang of water polluters, which makes of Elisha and his bears the first eco-warriors. It is not entirely surprising that Christian exegesis, perennially preoccupied to bring stories together, interprets the slaughter of the boys as an act of 'rightful vengeance' and Elisha's baldness (*calvities*) as no less than a prefiguration of the supreme bald patch: the Calvary (skull).

Or maybe it is just a matter of lack of training: until shortly earlier Elisha was actually an under-prophet, a trainee, who had just witnessed his master Elijah being rapt to heaven in a flaming chariot (II Kings 2. 11–12). In this case, the interpretation is smoother, as Elijah's rapture was read as the image of the elevation of the soul to god.

The *contrapasso* is as captivating as it is clear: in life the evil counsellors used their speech to give treacherous advice to people, always hiding the truth from others, so they are now forever trapped in and stolen away by giant tongues of fire.

> Io stava sovra 'l ponte a veder surto,
> sì che s'io non avessi un ronchion preso,
> 45 caduto sarei giù sanz'esser urto.
> E 'l duca, che mi vide tanto atteso,
> disse: 'Dentro dai fuochi son li spirti;
> 48 catun si fascia di quel ch'elli è inceso.'

> I was standing on the bridge, having risen up to see, so that if I had not laid hold of a rock I should have fallen below without a push; and my leader who saw me so intent, said, 'within these fires are the spirits: each swathes himself with that which burns him.'

The traveller's attention is attracted by a twin flame. I do not quite know why, but often the great episodes of Dante's *Hell* involve two (think of Paolo and Francesca in *Inferno* 5, Farinata and Cavalcanti in canto 10, or Ugolino and Ruggieri in 32), of which one usually ends up telling the story while the other listens. I suspect it is about a tragic, toxic togetherness, how being together is the supreme form of loneliness and, perhaps, of storiness.

The classical world makes a curious entrance, intertwined yet divisive. The two-pronged flame reminds the traveller of a quintessential ancient tragedy: the nefarious, impeccably dead-end story of Thebes, beginning with Oedipus's incest and ending in the funeral pyre of his sons, Eteocles and Polynices, whom the father cursed to such enduring enmity that, after killing each other, they could not even bear to be in the same pyre, the flame parting into two. The tale of Thebes is one of the core narratives of antiquity: Dante wisely employs it only as a side story in his poem, as if to distance his clever, new, lively comedy from highbrow, no-future tragedy.

> 'Maestro mio', rispuos'io, 'per udirti
> son io più certo; ma già m'era avviso
> 51 che così fosse, e già voleva dirti:
> chi è 'n quel foco che vien sì diviso
> di sopra, che par surger de la pira
> 54 dov'Eteòcle col fratel fu miso?'

> 'Master', I replied, 'I am the more certain for hearing you, but already I thought it was so, and already I wanted to ask: who is that fire which comes so divided at its top that it seems to rise from the pyre where Eteocles was laid with his brother?'

The next series of tercets is key to understanding the canto. Introducing the dwellers of the twin flame as Ulysses and Diomedes, Dante also clearly spells out for his readers the reason why they are in hell, three notorious fraudulent misgivings spanning from the tragic to the comic: the wooden horse that caused the destruction of Troy and the beginning of the Roman genus; the theft of the Palladium, the great statue of Athena that dominated the citadel of Troy; and, finally, the deception of Achilles who, dressed in female clothes and hiding away from war while romancing a certain Deidamia, was startled into action (and break-up) when the deceiving duo started banging swords and shields around him.

> Rispuose a me: 'Là dentro si martira
> Ulisse e Dïomede, e così insieme
> 57 a la vendetta vanno come a l'ira;
> e dentro da la lor fiamma si geme
> l'agguato del caval che fé la porta
> 60 onde uscì de' Romani il gentil seme.
> Piangevisi entro l'arte per che, morta,
> Deïdamìa ancor si duol d'Achille,
> 63 e del Palladio pena vi si porta.'

> He answered me, 'Therewithin [therewithin??] are tormented Ulysses and Diomedes, and they go together thus under the vengeance as once under the wrath; and in their flame they groan for the ambush of the horse which made the gate by which the noble seed of the Romans went forth; within it they lament the craft, because of which the dead Deidamia still mourns Achilles, and there for the Palladium they bear the penalty.'

Why such digging in the past? These are, incidentally, pre-*Odyssey* stories. And why such a proliferation of reasons? Psychoanalysis teaches that the accumulation of excuses is tantamount to an admission of guilt, or at least a sign of unease with one's narrative. Dante's wealth of explanations indeed foresees (or perhaps instigates) a very strange consequence: the fact that many readers choose to ignore these three reasons and adamantly believe that the sin of Ulysses is crossing Hercules' pillars. But this is plainly impossible because, as we shall see, there is no fraud in the trespassing. [There is trespass in the trespassing.] So then these oblivious readers will say: his sin is the oration he gives to his sailors, which, once again, is hardly deceitful. It is a very strange case of textual lobotomy, of the disabling of someone's capacity for critical reading and for textual memory. I am forever unsure whether it is Dante's text that produces such voids, or if it is due to the subsequent mainstream commentary tradition, trying even in our time to uphold the impossible, i.e., the 'orthodoxy' of the poem (also known as: All That Dante Places In Hell Must Be Shit. Period. Otherwise, god is cross). So please, reader, stay with me in this instance, and throughout your reading of Ulisse (it is, ultimately, yours and not mine) repeat this mantra: the sin of Ulysses and Diomedes is the threefold fraud spelled out in lines 55 to 63. The sin of Ulysses is the Trojan horse, the theft of the Palladium, the deception of Achilles (ungrammatical, but true; it is a threefold yet singular matter). The sin of Ulysses and Diomedes is ... The sin ... In other words, try enjoying the trespassing for what it is.

I always wonder if I should spend some words on Diomedes. I hardly ever do in class. I feel for him, though. Great Achaean king, brave and merciless warrior, with a rather spacious role in the *Iliad* and an interesting afterstory that brings him to found several cities in Italy, and yet always a secondary character, not well written, never in the 'alone' mode. [Perhaps this has to do with his rather one-dimensional figure in Homer — he fights, and fights, and fights some more; he even wounds Aphrodite, and ends up unloved.]

Homeric Ulysses and Diomedes are a pair also in a famous episode from the tenth book of the *Iliad* (which, like the *Odyssey*, Dante did not read in its original version), the so-called 'Doloneia', a night sortie in the no-man's land between the two warring lines, which combines deception (by Odysseus) and slaughter (by Diomedes) of a certain Dolon, a Trojan who in turn had left his camp to spy on the Greeks. In this episode, Diomedes makes a rather prophetic declaration. 'I want Odysseus as my companion in this deed', he says. 'He is so smart, that, with him, I feel I could escape even a blazing flame' (10, 246–47; my rendition). Really? muses Dante, sharpening his pen.

Upon hearing about the two heroes in the flame, the traveller goes all childish. Please, may I speak to those people? Please, pl-e-a-se, p-lease, pretty please, pleeeease, mummy, PLEASE! I am going to throw a tantrum:

> 'S'ei posson dentro da quelle faville
> parlar', diss'io, 'maestro, assai ten priego
> 66 e ripriego, che 'l priego vaglia mille,
> che non mi facci de l'attender niego
> fin che la fiamma cornuta qua vegna;
> 69 vedi che del disio ver' lei mi piego!'

> 'If they can speak within those sparks', I said, 'master, I earnestly pray you, and pray again, that my prayer avail a thousand, that you deny me not to wait until the horned flame comes hither: you see how with desire I bend towards it.'

There is more than childish plea, however. There is the utter excitement of a poet who is about to blow new life into a great poetic creature. This is best understood in comparison to what happened earlier in the poem. In canto 5 of the *Inferno*, in the circle of lust, the traveller had met two unknown characters, Paolo and Francesca. Two provincial lovers, whose tragic yet banal story of adultery and death was perhaps just courtly gossip, are about to be turned into one of the archetypes of modern love poetry. Dante stages the attraction between himself and these new poetic creatures: they look, he says, 'as doves called by desire' ('quali colombe dal disio chiamate'; *Inferno* 5, 82). They leave behind the ranks of the other lovers, whose story had been told many times already, glide through the toxic air of hell and bend, full of desire, towards Dante's commandeering yet loving appeal. The lovers' headlong impulse is compulsion to poetry, it is lust for Dante's poetic authority, which will subsume their flimsy and inconsistent historical status into a powerful text. In canto 26, however, in front of the massive and rather secure poetic figures of antiquity, the new medieval vernacular author acts the compulsion out. He bends in desire toward Ulysses and Diomedes. It then takes the (classical, established) authority of Virgil to negotiate the dialogue.

> Ed elli a me: 'La tua preghiera è degna
> di molta loda, e io però l'accetto;
> 72 ma fa che la tua lingua si sostegna.
> Lascia parlare a me, ch'i' ho concetto
> ciò che tu vuoi; ch'ei sarebbero schivi,
> 75 perch'e' fuor greci, forse del tuo detto.'

> And he to me: 'Your prayer deserves much praise and therefore I accept it; but do you restrain your tongue: leave speech to me, for I have understood what you wish — and perhaps, since they were Greeks, they would be disdainful of your words.'

It also takes a language enigma. What is it that 'the Greeks' have with Dante's speech? The Italian 'schivi' (shy or averse) and 'detto' (language, utterance, expression) are rather ambiguous in this instance. Is this a matter of language or of style? Is Virgil showing off his Greek, as the ancient commentators held (and perhaps the poet letting us know that he was not able to read that language), or is he flaunting his rhetorical prowess (as moderns tend to think)? This riddle is best enjoyed in relation to what happens in the subsequent canto.

Bear with me. We need to take a tangent into a short, fun, inconclusive aside; my favourite kind of detour. The 'disdain of the Greeks' looks indeed like a matter of both language and style. In the next tercets, we will see Virgil addressing the heroes with all the trimmings of high ancient rhetoric, beginning with a lofty *captatio benevolentiae*, the part of the speech where the orator attracts the sympathy of the audience with some well-placed compliment crafted in captivating and empathic language. No, they were not a bunch of hypocritical snobs: *captatio benevolentiae* is the part of our everyday socializing routine that comes just after the greeting; hello, how are you, how was your weekend, a lovely jacket you are wearing today. We too precede our dealings with others with a stab at empathy, codified as it may be. My favourite and utterly incomprehensible one is the British 'how do you do' or 'how are you', a questionless typification of the other as the 'encountered person to whom I show interest', to which one is supposed to answer with the same suspensive 'how are you' (whereas I, to the horror of my interlocutor, answer 'I am well, thank you, had a great weekend, do you like my jacket? I bought it second hand in that shop, on that street, on the left' … until they cringe away). Now you see my inclination to tangents.

Likewise, the end of a social interaction codified by the art of rhetoric would be a polite and ornate send-off; that equally suspended moment at the close of an encounter when we let go of each other, usually with gentleness and care, because it is a vulnerable instant, a leave-taking that retains somewhere an element, a micron of the big farewell. A splinter of death. In life, where we are all writers and readers of our occasions, it sounds like: 'lovely to see you, have a good weekend, really like that jacket.'

Dante leads us to imagine that Virgil voices a lofty leave-taking at the end of Ulisse's speech. At the beginning of canto 27, we see the twin flame walk away 'with the consent of the gentle poet' ('con la licenza del dolce poeta';

Inferno 27, 3). If we were to infer Virgil's epic send-off from his greeting in the previous canto, we would imagine something like: 'O Argives! May Athena powerful in arms protect you in the underworld, may Apollo's lyre uphold your fame all over Hellas.' Instead, we are faced with a paradox. Another flame in the pouch, containing the rustically vernacular soul of the cunning politician Guido da Montefeltro, overhears Virgil speaking to Ulysses not in Greek or Latin, not even in the Tuscan variety of the medieval Italian vernacular in which the *Comedy* is written, but in a version of the medieval Lombard dialect, a vernacular utterly void of social or literary prestige, which is imagined to be Virgil's native Mantuan. [Very concisely: Dante believed that languages were the instinctual product of the post-lapsarian, post-babelic human being. Most tongues remained messy and vital vernaculars, others, such as Latin and Greek, having acquired political and intellectual prestige, were made artificial by a series of grammatical rules and thus became 'universal' and authoritative languages, called 'grammars'. The *Comedy*'s vernacular is both ambitious and unruly. In the language enigma of cantos 26 and 27, then, Dante inscribes in a parodic way the complex interaction between grammatical and vernacular languages.]

> O tu a cu' io drizzo
> la voce e che parlavi mo' lombardo,
> dicendo 'Istra ten va, più non t'adizzo'
> (*Inferno* 27, 19–21)

> O you to whom I direct my voice and who just
> now spoke Lombard, saying 'Now go your way, I
> do not urge you more'

That is, Virgil's grand (and potentially Greek) leave-taking sounds to Guido as something like 'off ya go, dude', uttered in a lackluster Lombard dialect and in a rather flat wording.

Guido manages to annoy Virgil to the point that he elbows Dante forward: 'Parla tu; questi è latino' (you speak: he is Italian; 27, 33). The reason for this riddle and its reflection on the episode of Ulisse is still mysterious, but it does tinge with a grotesque hue the issue of style and language in the previous canto, as if there were another ghostly text, where the great epic poet and the great epic character converse at the edge of expression. As if Dante were inviting his reader to imagine that other speech, the speech not written.

Back to canto 26 now, where Dante's turmoil-cum-tantrum on the subject of literary and linguistic authority not only produces the language enigma that is then brought into relief in the comic pastiche of the next canto, but also engenders a trenchant, and equally confusing, irony in the way Virgil addresses the ancient heroes. He basically tells them: 'In return for all the nice things I said about you in my (elitist, epic, grammatical) poem, please tell us your story.' Readers conversant with the *Aeneid* are surprised at good-natured, let-me-do-the-talking Virgil: with mounting suspicion they deconstruct his *captatio benevolentiae* and see it for what it is, a pack of lies. As we shall see in the next chapter, Virgil is not an excited cantor of Ulysses. Not in the least. Virgil loathes Ulysses, he reduces him to a cynical trickster, the con-artist of speech ('fandi fictor'; *Aeneid* 9, 602). Virgil, not Dante, stigmatizes Ulysses as an evil counsellor. I need to contradict myself here: this particular *captatio benevolentiae* is, in fact, a hypocritical piece of linguistic snobbery (notice how he sweeps everything under the carpet with a light-touch admission of guilt: 'if I deserved of you much or little'). Which makes of Virgil a false counsellor himself. How clever! But then, another dilemma rises: was Dante writing for the educated readers? Or was he trying to gaslight them?

> Poi che la fiamma fu venuta quivi
> dove parve al mio duca tempo e loco,
> 78 in questa forma lui parlare audivi:
>> 'O voi che siete due dentro ad un foco,
>> s'io meritai di voi mentre ch'io vissi,
> 81 s'io meritai di voi assai o poco
>> quando nel mondo li alti versi scrissi,
>> non vi movete; ma l'un di voi dica
> 84 dove, per lui, perduto a morir gissi.'

> After the flame had come to where it seemed to my leader the time and place, I heard him speak in this manner: 'O you who are two within a fire, if I deserved of you while I lived, if I deserved of you much or little when in the world I wrote the lofty lines, move not; but let one of you tell me where he went, lost, to die.'

... If only this tongue could speak in a rustic style and language like its Italian counterpart in the next canto! It would say: 'You deserve nothing of us, you bastard!'; 'you *** liar!'; 'You, cantor of an emasculated hero, the Gods' pet, whom everyone likes because he is sooo boring' ... 'Pious, they call him, Diomedes, pi-o-us!' 'Fuckwit! That's what I call him. A dull bureaucrat, a cynical lover ... Yeah, yeah, he lost his wife and killed his lover, but never was his fault ... I — I ...' (and here the burning tongue starts stuttering and gets even more inflamed) 'I came back to my missus ... well in some version of the stupid story ... and was true to all them lasses I met, Circe, Calypso, even the young'un, what was she called again?' ... 'A half warrior, he sang, Diomedes! A bloody coward.'

But the classics were urbane people, civilization and all. So the flame gurgles within itself all these insults (I imagine) and after a long, painful internal rumination, starts answering the question politely. The question being — *attenzione*! — not what was your sin [we know what the sin is: start the mantra here], but 'how did you die?'. The furious desire for knowledge, the journey, the trespassing — I shall repeat this until I am blue in the face — are the cause of death, not of damnation. They are, beautifully and exclusively, of this earth.

It takes a while for Ulisse's voice to find its way out of the tongue of fire. This monstrous device for speaking is cruelly ironic, considering that the sin punished in the area is 'fraud by words'. In the next canto, we learn that these huge burning tongues are indeed language torture-machines. They are compared to the Sicilian bull — a cruel brass cast built by the Athenian artisan Perillus for Phalarys, the tyrant of Agrigento: when heated around the victim, it transformed human screams into the bellowing of a bull. The doleful words of the damned wander ineffectually and painfully through the fire. They sound like fire, crackling and hissing until they manage, with a desperately athletic wriggle ('guizzo'; *Inferno* 27, 17), to force the tongue to speak.*

After the slow description of the torturous utterance, the first word spoken by Ulisse (the heavy-sounding

---

* I promised very few footnotes, but this one is worth having; the description of the language torture machine in the next canto, *Inferno* 27, 7–19: 'Come 'l bue cicilian che mugghiò prima | col pianto di colui, e ciò fu dritto, | che l'avea temperato con sua lima, | mugghiava con la voce de l'afflitto, | sì che, con tutto che fosse di rame, | pur el pareva dal dolor trafitto | così, per non aver via né forame | dal principio nel foco, in suo linguaggio | si convertïan le parole grame. | Ma poscia ch'ebber colto lor vïaggio | su per la punta, dandole quel guizzo | che dato avea la lingua in lor passaggio, | udimmo dire [...]' (As the Sicilian bull (which bellowed first with the cry of him — and that was right — who had shaped it with his file) was wont to bellow with the voice of the victim, so that, though it was of brass, yet it seemed transfixed with pain: thus, having at first no course or outlet in the fire, the doleful words were changed into its language. But after they had found their way up through the tip, giving it the same vibration that the tongue had given in their passage, we heard it say [...]).

'Quando') is craftily displaced at the end of the line, and the pause that follows allows the reader to fully appreciate, and indeed to experience if reading aloud, the fatigue involved in the act of speaking.

> Lo maggior corno de la fiamma antica
> cominciò a crollarsi mormorando,
> 87 pur come quella cui vento affatica;
> indi la cima qua e là menando,
> come fosse la lingua che parlasse,
> 90 gittò voce di fuori e disse: 'Quando

> The greater horn of the ancient flame began to wag, murmuring, like one that is beaten by a wind; then carrying to and fro its tip, as if it were a tongue that spoke, it flung forth a voice and said: 'When

When we finally get to that 'Quando' we almost feel that the tongue of fire will never talk, that its secret will forever be buried in the torture machine. But when it does finally manage to utter, its words take flight. And we forget we are in hell.

> Quando
> mi diparti' da Circe, che sottrasse
> me più d'un anno là presso a Gaeta,
> 93 prima che sì Enëa la nomasse,
> né dolcezza di figlio, né la pieta
> del vecchio padre, né 'l debito amore
> 96 lo qual dovea Penelopè far lieta,
> vincer potero dentro a me l'ardore
> ch'i' ebbi a divenir del mondo esperto
> 99 e de li vizi umani e del valore;

> When I departed from Circe, who had detained me more than a year there near Gaeta, before Aeneas had so named it, neither fondness for my son, nor reverence for my aged father, nor the

> due love which would have made Penelope glad,
> could conquer in me the longing that I had to gain
> experience of the world, and of human vice and
> worth.

There we are. The end of the ancients' Ulysses, and the beginning of the modern one. The moment antiquity rockets into modernity through the pen of a disgraced medieval poet. When the circular turns linear, into a mad and genius tangent of desire heading towards the unknown.

'Redefining *in medias res*' one could say of these lines. The new hero emerges from the middle of the story, from the magma of a narration that at this point had implicated every infinitesimal bit of him. In the ancient story, this would be truly in the middle (in the *Odyssey*, which Dante did not read first hand, this would be books 9–12), when the pace of adventure accelerates and peaks — battles and drugs, Cyclops, storms and giants, metamorphosis, a good amount of lust, a crucial trip to the underworld, followed by sirens, monsters, more storms, mutinies and shipwreck — to slow down suddenly into a slumber (the seven years spent in the arms of sweet Calypso, after which the bow of the ship starts pointing home). Dante's Ulysses emerges, to put it in other words, from some kind of orgasm of the original story.

And from now on it is a whole brand-new adventure. Like never before. Or after.

This new character, and his author, say 'no' to everything. Neither … nor … nor, which in Italian sounds even sharper and more definitive: Né … né … né. Only the 'Wild Rover' — the protagonist of a British folk song whose utter capacity for negation (no, nay, never, no more) I first encountered to my shock and amusement through a quasi-Greek choir of ten-year-olds at my son's school — is more of a rejecter than Dante's Ulysses. (And, in his own little way, the rover, although he does come home, is a figure of perennial roaming in the sea of addiction.)

The idea of return itself is Ulisse's target. First, the family unit, neatly organized into son, father, wife; and, beyond that, the familiar. The sweetness, the reverence, the love that builds homes and countries. All thrown away, and rather hurriedly; there is no indulging in the snapping sound of these three lines (94–96). Even poor Penelope, whose long name could have provided some space for lingering, for sitting just once more, just a second longer on that familiar sofa, for cocooning in those vowels that are thick as body and warm as an embrace ... even poor Penelope is turned into the hastily accentuated, already-left-behind, Penelopè: she becomes, in a subtle way, the very 'né' of her abandonment.

What is the burning ('ardore') then, the ardent desire that diverts our hero? Simple: experience. *Ex-periri*, to see it for yourself, to test, to prove, to acquire first-hand knowledge. To be there. With your body, with your senses. To believe no one else's story. To make your own. Not 'to strive, to seek, to find, and not to yield': although a memorable line, to which my series of infinitives is unconsciously indebted as I realized during my first re-reading, Tennyson's sequence does not quite catch this moment for me. Dante forges a productive yet succumbing human being, not an unyielding hero.

Two are the big attractions out there. In a very modern fashion there is the world ('il mondo') in its physical and geographical dimension, and in a very classical fashion there is the human being in its ethical aspect, in its being a creature of vice and virtue, as Aristotle and Cicero saw it, for instance.

It is the latitude of geography that kicks in first. And individuality. Strangely, excitingly, they are one:

100 ma misi me per l'alto mare aperto
   But I put forth on the deep open sea

Mr Me ('Ma-me', But-me) and the deep blue sea are one in the slippery yet rhythmic sound of this portentous line. Mmmm we are sliding with him in the blue. Aaaa it is beautiful. To-to: why do I feel like I am flying? Like I am falling?

Mr But-Me and few resources and people. One boat, a select group of sailors; and 'forwards backwards we go over the (Mediterranean) sea'. [Don't ask: it is inexplicable why Dante's Ulysses should call to my memory every weird children's song through which I, having just moved from North America to the UK and a stranger to both places, sat perched on an uncomfortable plastic chair in some school hall, the faint and simultaneous smell of feet and bleach tucked away in the unheated room, thinking … this country is strange … primary school children should not be singing about vice and addiction … and bottles of rum in their tums.]

   sol con un legno e con quella compagna
102 picciola da la qual non fui diserto.
      L'un lito e l'altro vidi infin la Spagna,
   fin nel Morrocco, e l'isola d'i Sardi,
105 e l'altre che quel mare intorno bagna.
      Io e' compagni eravam vecchi e tardi
   quando venimmo a quella foce stretta
108 dov'Ercule segnò li suoi riguardi
      acciò che l'uom più oltre non si metta;
   da la man destra mi lasciai Sibilia,
111 da l'altra già m'avea lasciata Setta.

   with one vessel only, and with that small company
   which had not deserted me. The one shore and
   the other I saw as far as Spain, as far as Morocco,
   and Sardinia, and the other islands which that sea

> bathes round. I and my companions were old and slow when we came to that narrow outlet where Hercules set up his markers, that men should not pass beyond. On the right hand I left Seville, on the other I had already left Ceuta.

The beginning is still very much *Odyssey* — a long, curious, Mediterranean cruise with stretches of deep sea, and islands to circumnavigate. But there is one place that attracts him. The centre of gravity of the known universe. Gibraltar.

The story of Hercules' pillars is as straightforward as it is vague: Hercules, en route to his tenth labour, the acquisition of the cattle of the monster Geryon in the farthest west, planted two columns on the two sides of the strait. It is unclear why he did that, and whether these are two natural headlands (such could be the rock of Gibraltar itself) or two actual pillars erected by the hero, as they are often represented in the afterlife of this notorious landmark with the addition, so the modern story goes, of a little sign: *Nec plus ultra*. No further. The modern story might well have originated in Dante's wording itself, the injunction that 'human beings should not pass beyond': the famous Latin motto would be no less than the translation into Latin of Dante's 'più oltre non'. The postponement of the negation, a mere and automatic poetic device, is sheer ingenuity. 'Further' and 'further not' are one and indistinguishable in this simple equation. Plus ('più', more, there, go!) and minus ('non', less, here, stop!) cancel each other out. What is left is the 'oltre', the great beyond. The trick of this perfect game is the 'plus'. 'Oltre' already means 'further'; it is not correct to say 'more further', or 'more beyond'. But you need the 'more' to balance the 'not'.

The human being in a nutshell. Good and evil. Don't do this. I will. Just because you said not to. The forbidden fruit. Borders, limits, trespassing — we will look at these later. For now, let us turn to the text again, to notice that this happens at a strange moment of Ulisse's life, when he and his sailors are old and tired. Interesting. And somewhat refreshing. This is not the usual story of youth and boldness, having life in front of you, daring, and staking the future. This is about maturity and experience, fatigue, and loss: this *is* Tennyson's Ulysses, 'made weak by time and fate'.

These men are old and slow, they are a small crew ('compagna picciola'; 102), hardly filling one boat (the implication being that the rest of the fleet was lost adventure by adventure, in line with Homer's tale). They have little left to live ('picciola vigilia'; 114), and also brief is the speech that Ulisse gives to his companions ('orazion picciola'; 122). I always found this adjective — the 'small' that connotes the crew, the oration, and life — rather disconcerting. Ulisse minimizes. But why? The All-Hell-Is-Shit readers have a ready answer: Ulisse minimizes because he is a liar and a manipulator. But I told you already that I am not one of them, at the risk of being naïve and oblivious to the medieval religious context in which this story is written. Also, if Ulisse had said 'grande' — big crew, big life, big speech — they would declare he is a liar and a manipulator. They would believe the same had he said 'medium', or 'extra small'. Or nothing. They will say he is a liar and manipulator, period. So, what is the point of reading? They would attach 'bad' to everything that happens in Dante's *Hell*, like 'in bed' to the message in the fortune cookies (is that still a thing in the new Millennium?).[†] End of small

---

† Apparently, it is not; and after the seventh reader noted 'you have lost me here', I decided to add an explanatory note. More than once (twice perhaps) in the final decades of the last brave millennium I heard the rather lame joke that one ought to interpret the message in the fortune cookies one used to eat at the end of a meal in Chinese restaurants in

rant. Which is my own tiny diversion to hide the fact that I still am not quite sure about why Ulisse keeps on saying 'small'.

What I do know, however, is that the small oration is one of the most moving passages that you might read. Exciting (thousands of dangers!), touching (he calls them 'brothers'), sad (they have little left to live), severe (you are not brutes!). Full of dignity, yet still naughty. As you read it, it feels like when you are a little child playing in the waves. So scary, so grave, so much fun, when you see the 'big one' mounting far from the shore; it swells, it forms a menacing white crest — please please, don't break just yet, I am here, I am waiting for the blow. I am scared. Take me with you. I am swept away. The sweet undertow. Pebbles so smooth they hardly hurt. This is how I feel every time I read this speech.

> 'O frati', dissi, 'che per cento milia
> perigli siete giunti a l'occidente,
> 114 a questa tanto picciola vigilia
> d'i nostri sensi ch'è del rimanente
> non vogliate negar l'esperïenza,
> 117 di retro al sol, del mondo sanza gente.
> Considerate la vostra semenza:
> fatti non foste a viver come bruti,
> 120 ma per seguir virtute e canoscenza.'

> 'O brothers', I said, 'who through a hundred thousand dangers have reached the west, to this so brief vigil of our senses that remains to us, choose

---

the West as solely valid 'in bed'. 'You will be lucky' ... in bed; 'don't hold onto things' ... in bed; 'be slow to speak and quick to act' ... in bed. It is silly, you see, not particularly funny, and a little vulgar but not enough to snap you out of your comfort zone, which sometimes a crass vulgarity does. A trivial and lacklustre gloss, just like saying that all the characters in Dante's *Inferno* are bad because this is a medieval poem about the Christian hell. [In sum: in hell + bad = in bed.]

> not to deny experience, following the sun, of the
> world that has no people. Consider your origin:
> you were not made to live as brutes, but to pursue
> virtue and knowledge.'

If we do insist on contextualizing this speech within the medieval system of values, though, we will find there is nothing wrong with it, nothing 'fraudulent'. Ulisse is simply repeating the quintessential ancient and medieval refrain that human beings differ from animals precisely because of their desire to pursue 'virtue and knowledge', to exercise their intellectual side. This is ethics for beginners, bouncing from Aristotle's *Nicomachean Ethics*, to Cicero, to Aquinas. And to Dante himself, who in a previous work, the *Convivio* (*The Banquet*, written around 1304–07), had stated, following Aristotle, that the desire to know is natural to the human being ('Sì come dice lo Filosofo nel principio della Prima Filosofia, tutti li uomini naturalmente desiderano di sapere'; *Convivio* 1, I, 1) and that for the human being 'to live is to use reason' (whereas for animals to live is to feel: 'manifesto è che vivere nelli animali è sentire — animali, dico, bruti, vivere nell'uomo è ragione usare'; *Convivio* 4, VII, 11; translation by Richard Lansing). If not yet suggesting a fully-fledged Christian ethics, Ulisse is rehearsing its foundations, the seeds, indeed, of the Western reflection on what it is to be human. (Not that there is nothing troubling with such reflection, as we shall see, but this is not horribly 'sinful' either. It is human-istic [hyphen to point out the fracture, or maljunction, between the two concepts].)

Ulisse is not trying to cheat them either. He does not say that beyond Gibraltar there are bounties to take, women to rape, lands to occupy, or battles to win (in short: 'glory'). We are old, he says, we might die there. He says:

there is nothing there; emptiness, desert, pure cosmos. And yet ...

> Li miei compagni fec'io sì aguti,
> con questa orazion picciola, al cammino,
> 123 che a pena poscia li avrei ritenuti;
> e volta nostra poppa nel mattino,
> de' remi facemmo ali al folle volo,
> 126 sempre acquistando dal lato mancino.

> With this little speech I made my companions so keen for the voyage that then I could hardly have held them back. And turning our stern to the morning, we made of our oars wings for the mad flight, always gaining on the left.

The power of words alone transforms an old and tired crew into a machine. Into an 'us'. They are made sharp, pointed. The desire for the great unknown is penetrating, lancinating. They ache for it. 'Acuto' is an adjective that in Latin and Italian has a huge span. A small angle, a smart observation, a sharp knife, a shrill sound, a stabbing pain, a piercing sensation, a clean cut, an intense sentiment, an incisive perception, an acute illness. It cuts and cuts and cuts across language. It tears and punctures and you only feel it when it is inside, when it is too late. It stirs, it makes you mad. 'It spurs on.' (It has always baffled me how 'encouragement' can take the shape of a sharp stick, or a pointed metal star attached to someone else's boots and cutting into your flesh.)

And off they go, they start rowing in unison: wood, body, and rhythm are one. They can hardly be stopped. Hardly ('a pena') — magnificent detail. He could still retain them; they are not out of his control. He holds them. Yet his power over them diminishes at each oar stroke, at every shrieking sound of the wood against the rowlock (which, I have learned today, is also called 'spur').

There is more terrible subtlety in this image. We feel, as readers, that we are going towards some dazzling brightness, the fresh, inebriating clarity of a perfect morning, but we are not — it is the back of the ship that turns toward morning, while the front, 'we', are going west, towards the night. Moreover, in this supreme moment of weightlessness, the moment of the leap, there is no wind whatsoever (and how could it be there? It would mean that other forces, call it nature, or call it god as you like it, were seconding this journey). Just oars. It is an unnatural flight, but oh, so much more exciting. I guess the best approximation for us moderns is the moment when a plane takes off, when even people like me — the permanently terrified of flying — feel the hit of anticipation. Readers, my flight assistants, please get ready for take-off. Get ready for *the* line:

de' remi facemmo ali al folle volo.

There is something fateful about its perfection. You cannot but pronounce it: 'emi – emmo – ali – al – olle – olo'; a supreme melody prefaced by a brisk staccato (de'); a coarse caress, a grave flight (oxymora oxymora, where would I be without you?). It sticks to your memory, like some kind of internal engraving that forever changes your poetic constitution. We-made-of-our-oars-wings. We. Ulysses, the crew, and us readers.

And, indeed, in the night we fall.

> Tutte le stelle già de l'altro polo
> vedea la notte, e 'l nostro tanto basso,
> 129 che non surgëa fuor del marin suolo.
> Cinque volte racceso e tante casso
> lo lume era di sotto da la luna,
> 132 poi che 'ntrati eravam ne l'alto passo

> The night now saw the other pole and all its stars,
> and ours so low that it did not rise from the ocean

> floor. Five times the light beneath the moon had
> been rekindled and as many quenched, since we
> had entered on the passage of the deep

In this night, there is the excitement of the so far unseen stars of the other hemisphere. As with fireflies earlier on, here too some inexplicable textual finesse brings the reader, this reader at least, to a comfortable closeness with the ancient text. Some of you will share this emotion with me. The first time when, already an adult, I travelled to the southern hemisphere. It was the stars that did it for me. The unseen stars of the other pole that flashed an exhilarating smile, the thrill of being so human and so small, so scared, and yet so cosy. For some of you it was perhaps the other way round. For others, just a shrug, or nothing. For Dante, it was a wild stretch of imagination. Reading is situated. Reading has stars.

Here you can also see for yourself how one of the often-repeated prejudices on the 'medievals' is not true — they did not think the earth was flat. The credence simply was that there was nothing in the southern hemisphere, just water. In those waters, Ulisse tells us almost casually, they navigated for five moon cycles. Time takes the form of an austere, abstract, almost absurd fast-forward succession of white crescents and white circles on a black canvas. We hear nothing of these five months — we can only imagine them. Empty and equal, day after day, just water and the sky, sky and the water. Sun, perhaps, and even dead calm. Or winds and storm. Pallid dawns and violent bloody sunsets. The vitreous sea under the boat. Turquoise. Bluesilver. *Glas*. Aquamarine. Grey. Snotgreen. *Oltremare*. The tiny ruffle of the boat's wake. Saltwhite. The voices of the crew, exchanging orders or a brief joke. Ulisse's silence, his eyes forever lost on the horizon. Some strange fish or marine creature jumping out of the water. A large, indolent albatross tailing or leading the inflated sails (or even a humbler seagull, I figure, less likely to be revered, or mocked). [I even have more puerile questions on the five moons: what did they eat? Did they have enough water? But epic, it is known, is not about stomach and intestines. It is about guts. And this is why we are perennially unable to identify ourselves with 'characters'; they never have to go to the loo.]

The nervous traveller in me does identify, however, with the next frantic, joyful cry. 'Terra! Terra!' Though a very timid sailor myself, I fully understand the excitement of the sighting of the land, first spotted by someone high up on the mast, and then by everyone on the ship.

>   quando n'apparve una montagna, bruna
>   per la distanza, e parvemi alta tanto
> 135 quanto veduta non avëa alcuna.
>   Noi c'allegrammo

> when there appeared to us a mountain dark in the
> distance, and to me it seemed the highest I had
> ever seen. We rejoiced

This land is out of proportion, though — too tall, ominous, and dark. It is the mountain of purgatory that Dante places at the edge of the southern hemisphere. The cheerful assurance of the crew becomes despair in the course of a line.

>   Noi ci allegrammo, e tosto tornò in pianto;
>   ché de la nova terra un turbo nacque
> 138 e percosse del legno il primo canto.
>   Tre volte il fé girar con tutte l'acque;
>   a la quarta levar la poppa in suso
> 141 e la prora ire in giù, com'altrui piacque,
>   infin che 'l mar fu sovra noi richiuso.

> We rejoiced, but soon our joy was turned to grief,
> for from the new land a whirlwind rose and struck

> the forepart of the ship. Three times it whirled her round with all the waters, and the fourth time it lifted the stern aloft and plunged the prow below, as pleased Another, till the sea closed over us.

Who is the 'other' who is pleased to sink the ship? 'H'im — as everyone hurries to capitalize? Makes sense. Either Ulisse gentlemanly accepts defeat by a stronger power, with just a hint of understatement (the positive reading), or he is so daft that he is not able to realize the existence of god after such evidence (the negative reading).

I am intrigued by the storm, though: a tornado, a vortex, or a waterspout moving swiftly from the new land, whirling and unsteadying the boat three times (of course) into some kind of giant eddy. Meteorologically, it is not entirely sound: don't storms normally move from sea to land and not vice versa? [well, this is god, and god can do everything, settles the puny Dantist. Wait and see, though, I have a totally implausible but much more fun idea about this shipwreck].

May we suppose that the boat whirls clockwise? We are at the antipodes after all, and the Coriolis effect is my version of god. Why three times? The trinity might be involved, sure, but a boat bumping three times before sinking is also an epic staple (see, for instance, Virgil's retelling of Homer's episode of Scylla and Charybdis in *Aeneid* 3, 566–67. [What a mess! We need to talk about intertextuality soon]).

Ultimately, what do we acknowledge as readers? That he almost got there, by human means alone, or that he never reached the shore? He nearly gets there; he does not get there. Whatever context we might choose for our reading, our appreciation of Ulisse's flight is forever trapped in the platitude of the glass half full or half empty.

'Until the sea closed over us.' Without necessarily espousing the virtues of disaster — intellectual, poetic, metaphysical, or otherwise — we need, readers, to inhabit this submerged perspective. We need to dive and hold our breath; we need to look up at the keel of the boat tracing a hypothetical line of a bluer blue than the water surrounding it. We need to swim up to discover that the surface of the sea is like an imperceptible film made of light, concealing under its apparent calm volumes and volumes of profundity. When you pierce it, it is thrust, it is elation, it is pain, it is also nostalgia.

'Until the sea closed over us.' The secret of our reaction to this canto forever lies in that last line, under the firm yet fluid hold of the water.

2. Sing me, o Muse, again

The simplicity of it never fails to surprise and amuse me. That at the twin beginnings of what we often consider the first, most representative (even the — ouch — original) texts of Western culture, we should find in order: some rather lethal masculinity (wrath, the man), 'song' (now that I find beautiful, and, as much as I have issues with Western culture, I also love it just for this appeal to music, poetry, and voice), a fortified female presence, and, in the second case, 'me' (mememe). To top up the line, the fearsome, patrilinear identity of Achilles, and Odysseus's versatility.

> Μῆνιν ἄειδε θεὰ Πηληϊάδεω Ἀχιλῆος
> οὐλομένην
>
> The wrath sing, o Goddess, of Achilles son of Peleus,
> ruinous
>
> Ἄνδρα μοι ἔννεπε, μοῦσα, πολύτροπον
> The man, sing me, o Muse, of many places
> (my literal translations)

Virgil, with a powerful combination of self-importance and minimalism, vaporizes the now rickety lady from the first line, organizing wrath into an army and stripping the man of his quirkiness (he will shortly reclothe him with piety).

> Arma virumque cano.
>
> The arms and the man I [memememe] sing
> (my translation)

It is a long journey, that of the proem of the epic poem, and it travels outside of the layout of this essay, but let me at least recall the narrative genius of Ludovico Ariosto, who, at the height of the Italian Renaissance, brings the ladies back (and an army, for that matter) and ties epic and romance in a masterful, witty knot:

> Le donne, i cavalier, l'arme, gli amori,
> Le cortesie, le audaci imprese io canto.
> (*Orlando Furioso* 1, I, 1–2)
>
> The women, the knights, the arms, the loves,
> The courtesies, the audacious adventures I sing.
> (my translation)

We are interested in the second Homeric proem; but let us linger on the first, for a moment, and indulge ourselves in the unfailing pen of Philip Roth, with the first undergraduate class of his formidable Classics teacher, Coleman Silk:

> 'You know how European literature begins?' he'd ask, after having taken the roll at the first class meeting. 'With a quarrel. All of European literature springs from a fight.' And then he picked up his copy of *The Iliad* and read to the class the opening lines. '"Divine Muse, sing of the ruinous wrath of Achilles . . . Begin where they first quarreled, Agamemnon the King of men, and great Achilles." And what are they quarreling about, these two violent, mighty souls? It's as basic as a barroom

brawl. They are quarreling over a woman. A girl, really. A girl stolen from her father. A girl abducted in a war. *Mia kouri* — that is how she is described in the poem. *Mia*, as in modern Greek, is the indefinite article 'a'; *kouri*, or girl, evolves in modern Greek into *kori*, meaning daughter. Now, Agamemnon much prefers this girl to his wife, Clytemnestra. "Clytemnestra is not as good as she is", he says, "neither in face nor in figure." That puts directly enough, does it not, why he doesn't want to give her up? When Achilles demands that Agamemnon return the girl to her father in order to assuage Apollo, the god who is murderously angry about the circumstances surrounding her abduction, Agamemnon refuses: he'll agree only if Achilles gives him *his* girl in exchange. Thus reigniting Achilles. Adrenal Achilles: the most highly flammable of explosive wildmen any writer has ever enjoyed portraying; especially where his prestige and his appetite are concerned, the most hypersensitive killing machine in the history of warfare. Celebrated Achilles: alienated and estranged by a slight to his honor. Great heroic Achilles, who, through the strength of his rage at an insult — the insult of not getting the girl — isolates himself, positions himself defiantly outside the very society whose glorious protector he is and whose need of him is enormous. A quarrel, then, a brutal quarrel over a young girl and her young body and the delights of sexual rapacity: there, for better or worse, in this offense against the phallic entitlement, the phallic *dignity*, of a powerhouse of a warrior prince, is how the great imaginative literature of Europe begins, and that is why, close to three thousand years later, we are going to begin there today ...' (*The Human Stain*, pp. 4–5).

Twenty-four books of war, and war, and more war ensue. Siege, skirmish, brawl, night forays, duels under the midday sun, close combat, spear throwing, hollow thuds! on large shields, fateful chill invading the men's limbs, and souls receding towards Hades with cavernous screams. The wide-open eyes of the dead stare at us from the page. The greatest homosexual love ever narrated, and the best figure of a grieving father ever drawn. A child, half scared and half excited at the sight of a shining helmet, its terrible crest waving in the air.

The second beginning is less incendiary, but no less dramatic and full of consequences. It contains a most exciting adjective: πολύτροπος (*polytropos*), made up of the words *polys* (much/many) and *tropos* (way, turn, manner, place, both literal and figurative). English translations vary widely: the man 'of many turns', 'many devices', 'many wiles', 'skilled in all ways of contending', 'ingenious', and more. A recent translation uses the word 'complicated': of this interpretation, I like the etymology (*con-plicare*; to fold together, to produce several folds). The oldest Latin translation calls Odysseus *versutus*, from *vertere*, to turn. Someone who is *versutus* has the capacity to 'turn around' self and events. The core of this adjective is *versus*, a preposition that means 'toward', 'in the direction of', and a noun meaning 'row', 'range', and, therefore, 'line of writing', verse. Changeability, momentum, and poetry; this might be Ulysses' make. And journey. The most honest translation of the first adjective of the *Odyssey* might well be 'the man of many journeys'.

This capacious adjective makes of Ulysses a theme rather than a character: a slang, a name for something, a dimension, a gadget. The theme of Ulysses is peculiar in that it is not exclusive of literature or art, but it has turned, since the beginning, into a cultural issue, a philosophical example, a historical refrain, an anthropological milestone, even the illustration of some kind of human behaviour.

A story. Written over and over again in a sinuous, serendipitous manner, similar to the hero's vagrant journey. It stretches genres, characters, plots, and narratives to make them resemble, strangely, 'life'. Life that is epic, and a fable, and comic, a lyric arpeggio, and a metaphysical tale. Life that explores the edges of death, and then comes back. Life that is at once populated and lonely.

'Made beautiful by fame and adversity' ('bello di fama e di sventura'): as such Ugo Foscolo, an Italian Romantic poet, once defined Ulysses. Beautiful and profoundly fallible, Ulysses is tied to the narrative of being human in small and big ways. In everyday speech an 'odyssey' is a particularly complicated journey, and Ulysses is everybody and everything that is cunning, independent, original, and explorative. In history and literature, Ulysses stands for the desire for knowledge that breaks limits and borders open, often with little regard for consequences: Renaissance navigators, nineteenth-century explorers, cosmonauts of the modern era are all 'Ulysses' in our narratives. While she, of course, waits home.

Not being much of a sailor myself, I hesitated to surf the *mare magnum* of the web in search of the multiple significances of Ulysses, just to find that 'the algorithm' (what/who-ever they are) is one step ahead of me and knows that I only search for books and cultural elucidations. So no surprises there: my open sea is actually just a pond (and so is yours). A bit polluted, for that matter, but not so much that I don't dive in: the ubiquitous Wikipedia, some rather uninteresting books and pseudo-cultural websites. The only remotely not-me reference is also very puzzling: the 'Ulysses App', promising that it 'Helps You Focus on What You Want to Say Ulysses Organizes All Your Projects in One Place'. Why all the robotic capital letters, I ask myself? All in One Place? So dreadfully not Ulysses; the very opposite of this character's expansion! What were they thinking at Apple? Can they even read? I wonder, and quickly retreat into my chartaceous domains.

POLYTROPOS

The man of many ways, Ulysses is both wandering and multifaceted. A multidimensional tramp. He is also a multiform character, who always exceeds itself.

To me, *polytropos* means also 'the man of many versions'.* In this adjective, I find, Homer embeds not only the qualities, but also the afterlife of his Odysseus; the limitless possibilities of the human mind and those of rewriting and re-creation. The *polytropos* is a character always bigger than representation, it is the multiple Ulysses that have been sung since antiquity, the myriad of rewritings, each relaunching the journey. The many incarnations of Ulysses of which literature and beyond is populated are all *tropoi*, 'turns' of the Homeric Ulysses, and there are still more turns to take. Ulysses is probably the most rewritten character of all times [I proudly announce in my lectures. As I put it in writing, I realize that I need either to pull out stats or to say something generically common-sense like 'second perhaps only to Jesus Christ', but I have not done the maths and lack a good second option. Christ is much repeated and little rewritten, now that I think of it. Do not trust me on this one, then. The most rewritten character of all times may well be Topo Gigio].

---

*   *Polytropos* is not the only way in which Odysseus is poly-. The prefix of abundance abounds around our hero, with notable epithets being πολυμήτις, *polymetis*, the man of many counsels, or many deceptions; πολυμήχανος, *polymechanos*, the man of many ingenious devices; πολύαινος, *polyainos*, the man of many stories, much praised; and πολύτλας, *polytlas*, meaning resistant, patient, even much-suffering.

Tropos is also the ancestor of trope — a truly capacious word in the field of literary studies and beyond: a figure of speech, a way of style, a variation on an established theme, an embellishment, a twist and a turn. Ulysses has many such tropes, from antiquity to our days: some monuments (Dante! Joyce!), expansions (ex.: Kazantzakis), contractions (ex.: Tennyson), challenges (ex.: Walcott, Atwood), but also just beautiful moments (Chaudhuri). [Feel free to change the examples in parenthesis with your own journey into Ulysses. The first parenthesis, however, has become canon: you might have to dislodge it with a lightsaber.]

The Ulysses thread is, I promise, the juiciest, most exciting string you can possibly follow in world literature and art. It is something you can do solo, or with the help of scholars and writers who have done so already. My own Italian literature is full of incarnations of Ulysses, some big and some small, some fun and some on the fascist side of things, some heroic and some decadent, soft spoken, cried out, bent, punched. Again, I will resist the temptation of listing them all, and leave you with my own favourite, a short poem by Umberto Saba, a homosexual Italian-Jewish writer with a touch of Slovenian heritage, a proper *polytropos*, someone for whom troping was a subtle way of life, a matter of survival. The poem, written in 1946, is called *Ulisse*:

> Nella mia giovinezza ho navigato
> lungo le coste dalmate. Isolotti
> a fior d'onda emergevano, ove raro
> un uccello sostava intento a prede,
> coperti d'alghe, scivolosi, al sole
> belli come smeraldi. Quando l'alta
> marea e la notte li annullava, vele
> sottovento sbandavano più al largo,
> per fuggirne l'insidia. Il porto
> accende ad altri i suoi lumi; me al largo
> sospinge ancora il non domato spirito,
> e della vita il doloroso amore.

> In my youth I sailed | the Dalmatian coast. Tiny islands | rose from the surface of the waves, covered | with algae, slippery, beautiful as emeralds in the sun, | where an occasional bird paused searching for prey. | When the high tide and night submerged them, | sails under wind dispersed offshore | to escape the peril. Today my kingdom | is that no man's land. The port | lights its lamps for others; still driving me on | to the open sea, my unbroken spirit | and the aching love of life (translation by George Hochfield and Leonard Nathan).

It is the sombre first-person voice, although not unique, that does it for me. The old age that says 'in my youth', the metamorphosis of the siren, now fully naturalized into a bird. The no man's land. The skidding and the peril. The wetness and amazing greenness of the viscid rocks. A tiny corner of the Mediterranean in topographical detail. The day and the night. And, of course, the painful love of life.

We give it many names. Some are metaphors like 'source' ('root', 'sprout', 'echo'), too often implying a unidirectional relation between texts. Some are old frills like 'fortune'. Others are neologisms, like 'intertextuality', at the verge of wearing out but still my favourite; or cute understatements like 'reception'; or grand statements like 'influence'. It is post-structuralist, post-Oedipal, postmodern. It is an endless game, vast, lonely, and populated like Ulysses' sea. To me, it is the magic of the great theatre of literature, the childish excitement at the recollection, the pang that redoubles the pleasure of reading.

An old essay by the Italian critic Giovanni Nencioni calls it 'the pleasure of agnition' ('Agnizioni di lettura', 1967). There is a plain and gratuitous pleasure, Nencioni says, in recognizing the pattern of a text within another, even if it is only a rhythm, or a single word. Technically, agnition is the moment in ancient drama or novel where, with a spasm of excitement, the spectator/reader finds out what they sensed since the beginning, that the shepherd who wandered suspiciously at court and is about to be executed because he was mistaken as a thief is actually the estranged son of the king, actually the daughter who was cross-dressing as a man in order to rescue her lover (or: … No-I-am-your-father … [I am wondering whether Darth Vader's black head-thingamabob is nothing else than an image of the dark side of rewriting; whether I have sat endlessly boring hours in front of a TV screen actually watching a saga about the canon. Either way, I did it for the children.]).

Agnition, to me, is not only the identification of another being, the acknowledgement of their significance, or the appreciation of a resolution; it is mutual recognition. It is self-perception. 'Hey there, I know you', I think with a soft smile, when I discover a pre-existing fragment in a text I am reading. 'I know you, and this makes me feel better, happier, more me.' Or: 'I know you are there, even though I have not met you yet. This is comforting.' 'Of course you are here! It cannot be otherwise', as you run through a crowded square to hug a loved one you had not seen in ages.

Call it and study it what you want, rewriting (let's call it this) relies on a simple fact: the subject is not original. Someone, perhaps many, have already written Ulysses — the man of many versions.

What is the attraction? Not sure. In olden times it was more of an obligation: you wanted to call yourself an epic poet, you needed to confront certain passages, to have them in your portfolio. But today? Is it a matter of passion or confrontation?

Whence does it spring forth, where does it flow? Amit Chaudhuri, reflecting on his conversation with Joyce's *Ulysses*, calls it 'the confluence of alienness and intimacy'. It is merging then; influx and outflow. Perhaps the mobile landscape of a delta.

What is the payback? Landing a triple axel? [Yes, I am sucker for figure skating, minus the costumes.] Sneaking into the canon (that menacing, choking headgear) from the backdoor? Or is it a gentler immersion in the great sea of literature?

No matter how you look at it, you will agree that Dante's agitation in front of Ulysses appears well founded. That buzz in the air, crease in the text, twinge of nervousness (please please please, master, let me talk to him!) is nothing else than the acknowledgement of the enormous task of rewriting Ulysses. This recognition makes Dante the first modern writer, doesn't it? The writer of the last epic and the first novel, as György Lukács called him — truly somewhere between Homer and Joyce, a wonderfully lonely and absurd place to be for a poor Florentine exile in 1307.

Dante's incarnation is, at the same time, utterly new and astonishingly old. An entirely new story is born from the sameness of each textual detail, from the play of multiple sources. Like a patchwork seen from afar, or those pictures that are made of thousands of little photographs — often to mean something truly tautological like 'we are us', 'you are me', difference is good, but we also like unity, we are liberal but do not worry, this is not too radical, we will not ask you to share your wife (or, worse, your car) with your neighbour. Yet the Dantean manifestation of Ulysses is somewhat more hypnotic than a picture of President Obama made by thousands of different little pics of Americans — if only because it is brought together not by some haphazard technology, but by a fine weaver of stories, powered by a chaotic, mysterious, and centuries-long cultural memory.

A crucial piece of information is that, as you will read routinely in Dante scholarship, 'Dante did not read the *Odyssey*.' Of course; he didn't read Greek, as hardly anybody else did in thirteenth and early fourteenth century Italy. Dante did not read the Homeric poems in the original language, but it sounds like he knew the story (and, importantly, the plural stories) of Ulysses very well. He might not have known the *Odyssey* first-hand, but he is somewhat more Homeric than Homer. The sync of his own narration is simply perfect:

> Quando
> Mi diparti' da Circe,
>
> When
> I departed from Circe

When ... The blank at the end of the line, a pause, we have seen, coming after so arduous an attempt to speak that it almost feels like the hero will never be able to utter past this word, and this story will stop here in the agonizing and ineffectual attempt at overcoming the sadistic dictature of language ... 'Quando' is literature's hiatus, the turning of a page in its infinite book.

The second plain fact about rewriting is that each rewriting involves both the new text and the original one, not only in the mind of the reader, but in the teeming flow of literature itself. This is what T. S. Eliot called the 'present moment of the past', the place of the impersonal emotion of art. You simply can no longer read Ulysses without its rewritings. Case in point, which has partially, if not entirely, to do with Dante's rewriting, is the fact that we tend to think of the *Odyssey* as a poem about sea voyage. Homer's Ulysses is an accidental navigator, Dante's is a real one.

AMETRETOS PONOS: A LABOUR WITHOUT MEASURE

Strange as it sounds, the *Odyssey* is not technically, or not entirely, a travel book, or a book about the sea. What most of us call 'odyssey' is actually less than half of the twenty-four books that make up the *Odyssey* — namely books 5–13 (or, if we want to be really strict, books 9–12). The beginning (1–4) is about his son Telemachus's own travel to find news of his missing father, and the end (13–24) is about Odysseus returning to Ithaca, reconnecting with Penelope, and slaughtering her suitors. We tend to forget that the *Odyssey* is very much about son and wife and home. Here too they say Dante did not know the *Odyssey*, and yet he dismisses it so well. Neither father, nor son, nor wife (né …né …né): I will not address the beginning or ending of the story that (you say) I have not read.

Odysseus is after all not born a navigator; he is a farmer, a shepherd king of a small, forsaken rocky island. He is impelled to travel not by curiosity but by a pseudo-voluntary military draft: he is one of the many small-time kings who must offer help to the revenge war of the more powerful Achaean kings, Agamemnon and Menelaus. [You know the story: the Trojan Paris abducts Menelaus's wife, a thousand ships are launched, war, and war, and more war ensues, Troy falls after many years of siege.] Although there is no historical trace of the Homeric Trojan war, this is a repeated pattern in Greek history: independent kingdoms or cities forging alliances into larger federations under the influence of dominant entities and living in a constant state of instability and war (think Athens and Sparta, for instance, and that endless skirmish or local scuffle that we are used to calling, rather grandiosely, the 'Peloponnesian Wars').

Odysseus is cunning and puts himself in trouble. He is punished (not rewarded) with an adventurous return and a reputation for curiosity.

As many readers have pointed out, at the ideal centre of the *Odyssey* there are deep roots, those of a mighty olive tree. In book 23 we read that young Odysseus had carved his nuptial bed from this tree, leaving its roots intact, then built his bedroom around it, and then the palace. Odysseus is strangely yet enormously rooted. French poet Paul Claudel puts it with particular grace. Anchor and root, sailor and poet, tree and poetry, Penelope and the Muse, are all implicated in an inextricable plant-like dream:

> La racine de l'Odyssée, c'est un olivier.
>
> Cet olivier, Homère, j'en suis sûr, l'a rencontré dans un de ses voyages, et pourquoi pas à Ithaque même? Quel bel arbre! Aussi fier, aussi pur, aussi radieux, j'allais dire presque aussi saint, dans la force de sa fibre tendue, que l'un de ces êtres parfaits, de ces irréprochables plants humains, dont l'art hellène a perpétué au milieu de nous le témoignage. On parle d'un marin qui jette l'ancre, dit le poète, et moi, je vois ici un être vivant qui est capable de m'enraciner pour à jamais avec lui à ce coin de propriété. De quelle intensité il est attaché à ce qu'il aime et quelle éloquence de ce feuillage d'argent dans la lumière à parler de ses racines! Arbre sacré, enfant de Zeus, médiateur entre la substance et l'azur, ah! je le sens! désormais ce n'est plus à une autre industrie que la tienne que je demanderai cette grâce qui est l'huile! Ah! si les dieux m'avaient accordé une autre épouse que celle-ci invisible, la Muse, en qui m'est dénié tout ce qui fait la vie des autres hommes, c'est à ton fût, immortel, que je voudrais amarrer la couche nuptiale. De tes branches je ferais mon toit et j'en enclorais l'ombre par un mur. Nul dans ce sanctuaire dont tu es l'âme ne serait admis à pénétrer que moi seul et celle que j'aurais choisie. Et si le sort, un jour, pèlerin d'un rêve inextricable, ne refusait pas au bâton de l'aveugle ce qu'il accorda à la rame du navigateur, c'est là que

m'attendrait, inviolablement fidèle entre les prétendants à l'époux, Pénélope, ma patrie! (Preface to the 1949 Gallimard edition of the *Odyssey*).

The root of the Odyssey is an olive tree.

Homer saw this olive tree, I am sure, in one of his voyages; and why not in Ithaca itself? What a beautiful tree, as proud, as pure, as radiant, almost saintly, I would say, in the force of its tense bark, as one of these perfect beings, of these irreproachable plant-humans, of which Hellenic art has brought witness to us. We are talking about a sailor who throws the anchor and I, says the poet, I see here a living being that has the capacity of rooting me with itself, forever in this corner of land. With such intensity it is attached to what it loves, and such is the eloquence of this foliage, silver in the light, when it speaks of its roots! Sacred tree, child of Zeus, mediator between matter and the blue, ah! I can feel it! From now on, I shall not ask for the grace of oil from any other trade but yours! Ah, had the gods given me another bride than this invisible Muse, in which the life of other people is denied to me, I would have liked to moor my wedding bed to your immortal trunk. I would make my roof with your branches and enclose their shadow with a wall. No one but me, and she whom I would have chosen, would be allowed to enter this sanctuary of which you are the soul. And if one day fate, wanderer of an inextricable dream, were not to refuse to the blind man's stick what it conceded to the navigator's oar, it is here that she would wait for me, inviolably faithful to the husband among the suitors, Penelope, my homeland! (my translation).

If the root of the *Odyssey* is the olive tree, its heart is, undeniably, the travelling. It begins with a solitary island, the dwelling of a sorrowful goddess in the middle of the sea, the colours blinded by the sun (book 5). To me, it begins almost with a haze, which has to do with her name and attribute, the Luminous Hider. Like the scorching sun hides, so is she too much light. Too much, that is the curse of dear Calypso.

Sounds familiar, does it not? Hiding and dazing with all sorts of artful blandishments a lover who wants to leave, who stays in the insular diorama just out of boredom and lack of a better prospect. Sleeping next to her at night, and sitting on the beach during the day, with his dour little face forever looking out at sea. Eventually she allows her lover to depart on a makeshift raft (she helps him build the raft, for god's sake!), we see him becoming a point on the horizon, he is gone. With a sigh we walk back with Calypso, her steps now heavy on the deserted beach, a silent tear shining like a liquescent diamond, a poor gem disappearing in the burning sand.

Another woman waits on another beach. A girl indeed. The amazement of one's first love. The fear, and attraction, and estrangement of young sexuality. It is like a game, isn't it? Carefree, the girls, Nausicaa and her maids, are playing ball. One missed shot and the ball falls into the sea — they scream, playfully, and awake the naked hero. How old is Nausicaa? Maybe twelve or thirteen, or even younger. About to disappear in a culture that wants her married as soon as possible to satisfy genealogies and alliances. She is sensible and will not counter the tide. She will let go and be subsumed by it. She is not one of those mad maidens who haunt ancient myth or tragedy by wanting something or someone else, or refusing to comply, and being forever cursed. He is not the hideous older man who takes advantage of an innocent girl. This is just a marvellous impasse.

She is pliable, Nausicaa. Odysseus compares her to a young palm shoot, one he saw, he says, in Delos —

for a long moment, he says, he just stopped to admire it, forgetful of past and future, and of the war he was leading. Spellbound, because that plant did not look of this earth. Its charm, I imagine as I pause my reading, fulfils all the senses: supple, yet firm, it is cold and smooth to the touch, the rustle of its leaves almost inaudible; bright and dewy, I sense its warm scent, like fresh bread, and even a particle of its unripe taste in my mouth.

The episode of the beach of the Phaeacian island is, like the vision of the palm sprout, a suspenseful and enchanted moment. The young girl and the old hero facing each other, each confronting some tangled internal turmoil. The old male battered and naked — he barely reaches for a branch to cover his crotch (and, no, strangely it is not comic) — the girl not knowing why she is not scared. They both know that there is something wrong in this encounter, and they let it go. In doing so, they forever remind us that there is something divine in one's first love, in one's last.

The extended episode that follows — the long sleepless nights that Odysseus spends hearing and telling his story at the court of Alcinous, Nausicaa's father — is like an incision in the *Odyssey*, a long recess full of pleasures.

I am not, normally, one of those people who idealizes the old or 'other' times, but if there is one thing I am terribly sad not to have witnessed it is entertainment before the media. But my mother did. Born in rural Piedmont she spent her early years living with her family in a watermill in the countryside. In the thirties, it was still common for a *cantastorie*, a wandering storyteller (literally storysinger), to stop by farmsteads at night and entertain several families with improvised narrations in exchange for dinner and a little change. They would all gather in the barn, lie down comfortably in the hay, and listen to stories that had very remote roots, some of them old as the *Odyssey*.

Stories of battle, journey, love, and marvellous creatures encountering deities from the local folklore, the horror genre and the native dialect mixed to an estranging comic effect. Thrillingly (to me, who still owns a speck of that experience through my mother's own storytelling) this is roughly the same ritual that happened for millennia around the world, in humble homes as well as palaces and, indeed, in those perfect nights at the palace of Alcinous.

Long, infinite nights (11, 373), ambrosial nights (11, 330), nights that you don't want to end. It is the beauty, and wisdom, and artifice of story (11, 367–69) that weaves their voluptuous darkness, their splendid impenetrability. These nights remind me of the 'vantablack', the ur-dark I once saw in a museum: a tone so rich that it makes the spectators want to dive into it, surrounding them with a velvety desire.

In one such night, we meet Demodocus, the blind bard (after encountering him, does the 'Homeric Question', the issue of the historicity of the blind poet Homer, matter at all? I sometimes wonder). In one such night, Odysseus narrates 'the odyssey' that we know, the story of sea adventures that becomes then the type of the *Odyssey* itself. The ill-advised raid on the island of the Ciconians; lotus eaters; the Cyclops and the man-eating Polyphemus; the land in sight!; Aeolus's wineskins releasing the winds; more anthropophagy with the giant Lestrygonians; Circe, the beautiful weaver-pharmacist who turns them all into pigs (I never quite understand why) but then becomes Odysseus's best ally (here too I do not quite understand why — to be sure, he has a way with women); [...]; the sirens; Scylla and Charybdis (do you know they really exist? They are facing currents in the Strait of Messina, between mainland Italy and Sicily: swimming there is some sort of dangerous and exhilarating dance); the Sun's untouchable cattle.

[...]: the ellipsis in the previous sentence is the *nekyia*, or the evocation of the dead (book 11). An enormous parenthesis in the story, perfectly reclined in the space of one book, a bullet-perfect hole, a *lacuna*, but literally so: a pool of blood where stories surface and dive. A voyage at the end of the world that is also the beginning of the return.

For the reader of Homer, the *nekyia* is a hair-raising passage. We are still in the warm night of Alcinous's court, smelling of spices and myrtle, of humid stars and ambrosia, the perfume of sweet dreams bygone that never came true. The tone suddenly veers from adventurous drama to horror. The colour no longer the healthy blue of the Mediterranean sea and the luxuriance of its islands, but fog, and dirty darkness, black and fuming blood, icy crying, and a fear that makes you so pallid you look green. Odysseus reaches the land on the far side of Oceanus, whose inhabitants, the Cimmerians, live in eternal night (sounds north to us); he digs with the sword a pit of one cubit (18 × 18 inches or 45.7 × 45.7 centimetres: I love the detail), and fills it with blood from sacrificial victims. As in a horror story, the zombie-like dead appear. Some kind of mad desire impels them to drink the blood; only then can they talk. But Odysseus keeps them at bay with the sword, he does not allow them near the pit. In a scene that mixes horror as the genre and horror as the intolerable, the hero meets his own mother, whom he had last seen alive in Ithaca, and yet he can't let her approach. He must chase her away with the sword, because he needs to talk to someone else first, another blind man, Tiresias, the great diviner who will foretell his future. Only after talking to Tiresias will Odysseus allow his own mother to drink the blood, only then will he talk to her, try to embrace her. After her, a rank of women and men come by, all famous, and glorious, and tragic; he still protects the pit with the sword and only allows one at a time to drink. Here a scowling Agamemnon tells the blood-tinged story of his death; here heroes and heroines come to die for real. The *nekyia* is not only a non-place at the end of the world; it is also the end of all previous words, it is heroism gone bad, it is Achilles telling us: 'I'd rather be a farmer, a slave, a nobody on earth, than the king of these threadbare shades' (11, 488–91; my translation). It is the end of glory. The beginning of story.

For the reader of Dante, the *nekyia* is an amazing hall of mirrors where Odysseus narrates the *Comedy* (a journey to the underworld) that produces its own Ulisse, a new incarnation of himself. Now this does sound complicated but let me explain.

The *nekyia* is, after all, a journey in the land of the dead, although technically Odysseus only does part of the journey, from Circe's island to the end of the world, while the dead do the other part from the depth of Erebus to the bloody pit, where, summoned by the hero's prayers and offerings, they put up their show. The *Odyssey*'s *nekyia* may not be the first but it is certainly a crucial early narrative of the *katabasis*, the journey to the underworld, a fundamental epic and narrative staple, and a tradition that peaks in Dante's *Comedy*. Homer's *nekyia* is the basis for Virgil's *Hades*, which is in turn the 'source' (allow me) of Dante's *Comedy*, almost literally so at the beginning of *Hell*, where the borrowings from Virgil are most evident. So popular was the genre of the descent to the underworld (*descensus ad inferos*) that even Jesus Christ was made to do a *nekyia*, in a time, that between death and resurrection, when he was surely tired: the apocryphal, but hugely entertaining episode of the Harrowing of Hell. Up to the present day, literature, popular culture, and film are packed with (mostly male) heroes going to a scary and dangerous place below/on/above earth to achieve renovation for themselves and salvation for others. Lately, evil is often portrayed as a faceless, humid, hairy, [mortally boring and horrendously obvious] gaping cut. In ancient and early modern katabases, though, there seems to be more fear, more fun, and more trust in embodiment and disembodiment.

In the first major take on the narrative of the underworld, then, a blind (appropriately so) prophet opens up the story of Odysseus to its future incarnations. Once you have killed all the suitors (i.e., at the end of the *Odyssey*, book 24), Tiresias tells him, you will need to depart again. You need to take an oar (unclear whether to navigate or just to carry on his shoulder — the latter looks goofy, I know, but please hang on) until you come to the people who do not know the sea, do not eat salt with their food, and do not know about ships (so he must be walking quite a bit with the thing on his shoulders). There, a very clear sign will be given to you: a passer-by will look at you and say that you are actually carrying a winnowing fan (the tool used to separate grain from chaff — if you, like me, were wondering. It looks, to me, like a larger version of the equally enigmatic lacrosse stick). At this point, you need to plant the oar in the ground. Only then you can celebrate sacrifices, come home (again!), and finally encounter a sweet death in your old age … a sweet death … *ex halòs*: meaning either 'from' or 'away from' the sea. Un-be-lie-va-ble!

To make sure that readers are shackled to this absurd story, Odysseus retells it *verbatim* to his wife (*Odyssey* 23, 248–84), merely changing the 'you' of Tiresias to his 'I'. He calls his future a labour without measure (*ametretos ponos*): he is right; the feat, or toil, of Ulysses' after-story is still incommensurable today. Re-reading the prophecy away from the madness of the *nekyia* and within the domestic context of Penelope's anxiety (whaat? you're leaving again!

[she is right too]) we notice a couple more things. The emphasis on the transition between the world of the sea and that of the land. The irrationality of the guy seeing someone with an oar and thinking winnowing fan (when it was, throughout, a lacrosse stick), the absurdity of planting the oar in the ground: these details colour the story with the hue of a dream and make it strangely human.

With our heads still spinning from the sweeping arc of the prophecy, let us be amazed at what this means to us as readers of Dante: the story writes itself within the story. Within an eschatological context (read: from hell) Odysseus tells the story of Tiresias telling him that he must leave again and will die at sea. He tells, in other words, the story of the death of Dante's Ulisse. Maybe. Maybe a future me will die at sea, says Odysseus. The elusiveness of *ex halòs* is the element that at once binds and disconnects the Greek and the Italian Ulysses.

Remember Dante's own ambiguity? His Ulisse actually gets to see land, and '*from the new land* a whirlwind rose' that tosses and turns the boat according to the will of *another*. Can this be classified as a land or a sea death? Who is 'another'? ... I know, I know, it is god ... but for the reader of the third millennium, it might as well be the god of story, endlessly playing variation.

Incidentally, that god is the god of story is not too far-fetched, even for the ancients and the medievals. Augustine, for one, envisaged the story of the universe as a poem (*magnum carmen*, a great poem, or *musicum carmen*, a song) and god as its endless, unrelenting moderator. Like a writer or a musician, god knows 'what and when to give, to add, to take away, to withdraw, to increase, or to diminish' ('novit ... quid quando impertiat, addat, auferat, detrahat, augeat, minuatve'; *Letters* 138, 1, 5). [A great reading of this theme, from which this quote is taken, is Leo Spitzer's

Classical and Christian Ideas of World Harmony. Spitzer was an Austrian-Jewish critic who, facing the tragic whirlwind of twentieth-century history, upheld relentlessly the continuity of antiquity and the middle ages, notwithstanding the logical and spiritual madness that both ages were at risk to evoke. I hope to return to this, but if not, please read Spitzer. And Auerbach. And Curtius. Please.]

The ambiguity of the *Odyssey*, vast like the sea, becomes in Dante the uncertain vastity of god itself, the ever equivocal story of god's existence.

And there is more. In the very text that he didn't read, Dante even finds his super-line. 'We made our oars wings in a mad flight', the apogee of canto 26, was already partially written in *Odyssey* 11, 125 (and 23, 272), 'oars [...] that are wings to the boats'. The context, however, couldn't be more different: you will arrive, says Tiresias, to people who don't know the sea, don't eat salt in their food [is he heading to Florence, wonders Dante?],† know absolutely nothing about boats with minium-stained cheeks (a beautiful way of saying that the prow was painted with vermilion), nor of handy/handsome oars that are wings to the boats ('ἐυήρε' ἐρετμά, τά τε πτερὰ νηυσὶ'; 11, 125).

Neither (Telemachus) ... nor (Laertes) ... nor (Penelope) says Dante .... No (sea) ... no (salt) ... no (boats) ... no (oars-as-wings) answers Homer from the bottom of the bloodstained pit. I win! (H. also says).

---

† One of the most touching moments of the entire *Comedy* is the verse in which Dante prophesies his own exile in the words of his ancestor Cacciaguida (*Paradiso* 17, 55–60). 'You shall come to know how salt is the taste of another's bread' (58–59). Still today, bread in Florence is baked without salt, which is a real pain in the palate for non-Florentines, and yet it is also poetry come alive every morning in bakeries.

I am sure there are many other direct contacts between the unread *Odyssey* and the unknown *Comedy*. They are not sources, or references; they are conversations. This morning, I entertained myself with a stunning play on the chessboard of literature: the face-off between the angry divinity from the island and the tiny human offshore in the final lines of *Inferno* 26 and in the episode of the Cyclops in book 9 of the *Odyssey*.

'No-one blinded me' — cries Polyphemus, the angry divinity, from the shore of the island, while the men hurry to lift the anchors and row away.

'I am Odysseus who blinded you!' — laughs the tiny human. The angry divinity throws a boulder in the sea, unsteadying the boat.

'Some-one is sinking me' — moans the tiny human, his ship just offshore, nearing the island of Purgatory.

'I am God, for Christ's sake!' — shouts the angry divinity from the shore of the island, throwing a whirlwind at sea, capsizing the boat.

SIC NOTUS ULIXES?

It is true that Dante did not read the *Odyssey* first-hand. Or second hand, for that matter: there is no such thing as the 'translation' of a text in the middle ages, but only endless retelling, expanding, modifying. Homeric stories find their ways into medieval ones in the most eclectic and sometimes absurd ways. The stories of Troy are more popular than those of Odysseus, as if the feudal middle ages were more comfortable with stationary battle than travel. No need to read the rather dull *Roman de Troye*: the *Chanson de Roland*, after all, is the medieval *Iliad*, complete with a raging alpha male and touches of homoeroticism. This time, however, it is not about goddesses bickering and some lucky prick winning the love of the most destructive beauty of all times, but about those darn infidels invading Spain.

Unless, of course, the entire *Comedy* is the new *Odyssey*. This is a bit of a stretch, I admit, but it is the same stretch that binds navigation and space voyage. The *Comedy* is, in other words, the *Odyssey* (one curious hero, fallen in divine disgrace, finds his way home) rocketed below and above the plane of the earth. With one important difference. The *Comedy* is firmly, irremediably, on foot, with some levitation at the end. Its text navigates, though. Oh it does; you will be amazed.

If you play the game of 'source' in the millennia that run between the *Odyssey* and the *Comedy* you will find that there is nothing new in Dante's incarnation — and this is also the greatness of it. In order to find the tesserae from which Dante's splendid new image of Ulysses is built, we need to look into the Latin reception and imagination of Ulysses. First, however, let us listen to the silences that proverbially speak volumes.

Dante himself announces one omission-cum-distortion in a comic way. As we have seen in the initial reading, he has his Virgil address the ancient heroes with some truly devious lines — 'if I deserved of you while I lived, if I deserved of you much or little when in the world I wrote the lofty lines' (*Inferno* 26, 80–82) — the word 'deserved' repeated twice, as to underline that ... no ... Virgil did not deserve any credit from the ancient heroes, his version of Ulysses in the *Aeneid* being a flat picture of a manipulator. Which fits well with Dante's placement of Ulysses in the pouch of the evil counsellors, but not with the story itself.

Remember the proem of the *Aeneid*? 'I sing the man and the arms': with it, Virgil announces that his poem will section, summarize, and bind together the two ancient epics whilst writing their sequel, the maritime and adventurous journey from burning Troy (the 'Odyssean' books 1–6), and the war in the new and fateful homeland to found the city of Rome (the 'Iliadic' books 7–12): a whole new Roman epic that will astonish the literary world. His hero of choice, the traveller-warrior Aeneas, is neither Achilles nor Odysseus. In putting down the ancient heroes, Virgil rages especially against the latter, gathering an anti-Odysseus tradition that was already live in ancient Greece, especially among the tragic poets. [In a haste; soon after Homer, the *polytropos* finds a fork in the road, either as the poly-clever or the poly-devious.]

We read of Ulysses mostly in the second book of the *Aeneid*, in the context of the tragic story of the fall of Troy. The adjectives 'durus' (harsh; 2, 7) and 'dirus' (sinister; 2, 762) open and close a truly damning portrait: he is insidious (2, 90; here we read of the 'envy of insidious Ulysses'; 'invidia pellacis Ulixi'), intimidating and belligerent in words and deeds (2, 97–99), an inventor of crimes ('scelerum inventor'; 2, 164), and again, lethal ('dirus'; 2, 261; he is later seen wounding an enemy; 2, 436). And on and on we go. Almost at the close of the poem, Virgil coins for him the cruel alliteration 'fandi fictor' (9, 602); 'liar', but literally 'fabricator of speech'.

Virgil's stance towards Ulysses is, however, more intriguing than it appears, in that his Ulysses is repeatedly reported. We never read about Ulysses, but about Ulysses in the words of Aeneas, reporting in turn Laocoon, Sinon, and Achaemenides. Even the 'fandi fictor' label is placed in the rather unexpected and far remote mouth of Numanus, the brother-in-law of Turnus, the king of the Latins conquered by Aeneas. It is a really strange scene (9, 590–637). Numanus, a rather fascist character, extols the toughness and uber-masculinity of his people: why did these effeminate foreigners come to challenge them? What madness made these faggots think that they can steal Latin wives? There are no Greeks here, no Ulysses inventor of words ('non hic Atridae neac fandi fictor Ulysses'; 9, 602) — as if Ulysses were some kind of universal figure for the limpness of the Easterners (Greeks and Trojans alike). Needless to say, he is shot down with an arrow by young Ascanius, Aeneas's son. Like Ascanius's fellow Trojans, we cheer and cry out in joy and lift our hearts to the stars, thankful for this textual vengeance.

'Sic notus Ulixes?' (*Aeneid* 2, 44). This is how you know Ulysses to be? Or, more cursorily, Don't you know Ulysses? — this is the only genuine question about the Greek hero in the whole *Aeneid*, and it is uttered by a 'just' character, the Trojan priest Laocoon, while trying to convince his citizens not to bring the Trojan horse inside of the city walls. The fact that he ends up gobbled up with his children by two monsters stirred from the sea suggests that ... no, actually, we do not know Ulysses.

The largest Virgilian defamation of Ulysses takes place just before the demise of Laocoon, in the context of Aeneas's retelling of the fall of Troy at Dido's court (like Ulysses at Alcinous's, here too the hero turns momentarily into a bard). Here (*Aeneid* 2, 57–198) we meet the Greek Sinon, the quintessential traitor, whose mission is to convince the Trojans to bring the horse within the walls. To gain their confidence, he gives himself up to the Trojans like a scared and scruffy fugitive and tells the story of how Ulysses first plotted to have his friend Palamedes killed, and then persecuted Sinon himself relentlessly to the point of forcing the priest Calchas to choose him as sacrificial victim for the smooth departure of the Greek fleet. Sinon's depiction of Ulysses as a violent, deceitful, and impious bully ultimately convinces the Trojans to allow the horse inside the city and causes the destruction of Troy; what ten years of war and a thousand ships could not accomplish, Aeneas remarks bitterly.

Thus, in the words of a 'pious' (and ultimately Latin) character, a Greek liar and manipulator talks about a Greek liar and manipulator, creating a distortion in which two main questions arise: 1) was Ulysses an insidious bastard to begin with? and 2) is this perhaps a matter of the need, on the part of Virgil, who is indeed rewriting both *Odyssey* and *Iliad*, to downgrade his 'source' as fictitious? (as in: my fiction is better [longer, harder] than your fiction; a lesson that Dante learned very well and inflicts on Virgil at several points of the *Comedy*).

There is only one semi-positive adjective attached to Ulysses in the *Aeneid*: 'infelix' (unhappy; 3, 614 and 690 — hold on to this adjective, please). While in book 2 Aeneas tells the story of the end of the *Iliad*, in the following book he retells his own odyssey, his torturous journey from Troy to the shores of Carthage. In the course of this agitated navigation, Aeneas encounters Achaemenides from Ithaca, one of the companions of 'unhappy' Ulysses, whom Ulysses and his mates carelessly abandoned in the Cyclopes' island (*Aeneid* 3, 588–691). This is some kind of take 2 on the episode of Sinon: the Trojans meet a dishevelled and scared Greek, but this time he is honest and has no intention to harm them. Through the encounter with Achaemenides Virgil revisits, in shorthand, the episode of Polyphemus from the ninth book of the *Odyssey*. Virgil's rewriting is rather faithful, if more condensed and slightly gorier — just a tad more blood spattered on the Cyclops's cave's walls, more burping, and more regurgitation of half-chewed human limbs. More gore and less of the 'modernity' (if I may ...) of the *Odyssey* and its portrayal of the hero's relentless curiosity in spite of danger and risk, less of the primacy of intelligence over brute force, and none of the cleverest trick in the history of narrative: Odysseus's masterwork in deceit and omission, the erasure of his very name ('my name is no-one' ... 'no one blinded me'). Unlike Homer's, Virgil's Ulysses 'does not forget who he is' when confronting such a terrible challenge ('nec [...] oblitus sui [...] discrimine tanto'; 3, 628–29) — how strange.

Even stranger, though, is the fact that Virgil's description of Polyphemus ('monstrum horrendum, informe, ingens'; 658: horrid, shapeless, enormous monster) reminds me of Baudelaire's Beauty ('monstre énorme, effrayant, ingénu'; 22: enormous, terrifying, ingenuous monster). It is the sound-embrace *ingens-ingénu* that does it, hijacking meaning, or hugging it away. *Nec oblitus*; poetry has memory. [Hello there, little agnition. We have been travelling in the same coach for a while, lovely to meet you finally.]

The last lines of the Virgilian episode of Achaemenides reveal it all (at least to me). After leaving the Cyclopes' island, the Trojans keep navigating the Mediterranean, and Achaemenides, whom they rescued, shows them some of the sites of his previous passage with Odysseus (i.e., the passages from the *Odyssey*):

> talia monstrabat relegens errata retrorsus
> litora Achaemenides, comes infelicis Ulixi.
> (*Aeneid* 3, 690–91)

> Such were the coasts pointed out by Achaemenides, comrade of the luckless Ulysses, as he retraced his former wanderings (translation by H. R. Fairclough, revised by G. P. Goold).

Yes!, I exult; this whole thing is really about reading. The shores formerly wandered ('errata [...] litora') that Achaemenides retraces ('relegens') and points out ('monstrabat') are also, and simultaneously, textual places on which one wanders and makes mistakes (the textual 'errata') that now one re-reads ('re-legere'), understands, and explains to others. In other words, Achaemenides is also a figure for the reader of the *Odyssey* (and perhaps the writer of the *Aeneid*) who returns to the text and re-reads, amends, explains, and makes changes. With Achaemenides, inside of the *Aeneid*, the reader of the *Odyssey* sees things in a different way, or simply in retrospection.

Homer's Odysseus and Dante's Ulisse are not destined, able, or willing to have retrospection. Hence: luckless, unhappy. They do not retrace their steps: one forever caught into the presentness of the moment and the feeble call of 'home', the other eternally tense and stretched towards an impossible future. It is so true that sometimes the obvious is just under your eyes ... Virgil *did* deserve something of Odysseus and his world: the art of re-reading, which is also the first, great, transformative rewriting.

Guess who has the 'last word' on Ulysses in the *Aeneid*? Diomedes! The Dantean plot thickens. Now head of a little kingdom in the south of Italy, he advises the Ausonian ambassadors against waging war on the Trojans, recalling all the misfortunes that befell the Greeks after the sack of Troy (11, 253–95). For Ulysses, predictably, he recalls the episode of Polyphemus. A tame and repentant Diomedes remembers Ulysses' near death at the hand of the Cyclopes. Or does he recall his most clever, 'modern' deed? Impossible to figure out; the Virgilian Diomedes' mention of Ulysses is impassive, empty of any emotion, telegraphic, adjective-less: 'Ulysses saw the Cyclops of Aetna' ('aetnaeos vidit Cyclopas Ulixes'; 11, 263).

The Virgilian Diomedes is clear: those stories are gone, the past is gone, he will not be summoned to battle, the old friends are dead. Doesn't it remind you of the beginning of an action movie, where 'they' try to recall from retirement the old, rugged, violent guy (cop, cowboy, soldier) who lives in a camper van somewhere in the wild and drinks cheap alcohol at 10am out of dirty cups fished from the scummy sink — for one last mission, they claim, and he initially says no? 'I don't wanna know shit about Troy'; 'I ain't fighting Aeneas again.' Luckily, this is a mournful and sophisticated ancient epic, so the hero remains in his dusty trailer, instead of showing up at the commando unit the next morning, sober and ready to sizzle a thousand figurines with a flame thrower. Diomedes takes leave from us with beautiful, profoundly pacifist lines: 'Ne vero, ne me ad tales inpellite pugnas: | nec mihi cum Teucris ullum post eruta bellum | Pergama, nec veterum memini laetorve malorum' (Do not, do not urge me to such battles! I have no war with Teucer's race since Troy's towers fell, and I have no joyful memory of those ancient ills; *Aeneid*, 11, 278–80; translation by Fairclough and Goold). A broken hero, a fellow human being, who might understandably be portrayed in Dante's silent Diomedes.

The second puzzling silence in the *Comedy* has to do with the doctrinal and spiritual significance of Odysseus's journey.

Homer's story is ultimately a νόστος (nostos), a voyage of return. The *nostoi* were both a theme and a genre in archaic literature, mostly but not exclusively retelling the stories of the complex return of various heroes from Troy. As we shall see later in this book, Odysseus, a tramp as he may be, is equipped with nost-algia, the aching desire for return, and to Ithaca he returns, back to being a warrior and a farmer. Dante's Ulisse is not.

The *nostos* pattern, of which the *Odyssey* is the most famous result, is ultimately simple: it is a journey home, complicated by adventures and misadventures. A king comes home with his trophy wife, riches, and drugs (Menelaus). Another king kneels and kisses the shore of his land just to be slain by his unfaithful wife (Agamemnon). Sometimes one stops on the way and settles in a new place (Diomedes). [Now; only the Greeks with their posh short-sightedness could manage to make of the headfirst, aggressive figure of the colonizer a 'returning hero'.] Someone leaves a broken home and establishes a new one in a foreign land (Aeneas). One is exiled and never finds a new home (Dante). Another leaves home one morning in Dublin.

Journey (+) Home. Such is life, isn't it? For a believer, the journey might be that of the soul, and 'home' might be the afterlife: paradise, god, a supernatural spiritual place, the eternal chaos from which lives issue forth. Or, at a sublunary level home might be a country, a place. But mostly it is a state, isn't it? For many of us, living for different reasons in a state of radical homelessness, home is built, over and over again, with the fluid matter of the present moment.

Any day, any single afternoon is a *nostos* for me. I am known (and made fun of) for 'making home' literally everywhere I go. Placing my things around me as to signify 'I reside here at this moment'. Taking over tables in coffee shops, benches on promenades, corners in other people's rooms. It doesn't matter whether my dwelling universe issues forth from a suitcase or a handbag or just my pockets. Someone calls me chaotic. My Ithaca is nowhere yet everywhere I go.

My children's early years were marked by incessant travelling. We moved places, travelled for holidays and for medium-length stays in many different countries. We had many homes. Once my son kept on speaking of 'our home in Paris' — yes, mamma, don't you remember it? It had green curtains. I was puzzled. It turned out to be a hotel room. This is when I slowed down travelling, but not the spirit of it.

My childhood, instead, was rather stationary, although marked by a strange, almost metaphysical, sense of rootlessness. As a child, I had a ritual before going to sleep. I would raise the cover over my head and imagine I was in a spaceship, and I (of course!) was manning the control console. From there, I could launch some kind of beams (but of a material kind, they looked like fluid or viscous filaments that opened up in large unbursting soap bubbles) that would reach and enclose all my dear people. They were, in order: my sister, her boyfriend (subject to change), my mother, my father, my grandmother, and my cat. I would make the actual gesture of toggling the lever switches and pronounce their names aloud, in a sort of lullaby string (alecarlomammapapinonnatigi), and they would be engulfed in my bubbles and connected with me. Only then could I fall asleep; my bed somewhat more rooted than Odysseus's yet suspended between the fifth floor of an anonymous apartment building in Milano and the immense night sky. I know what you are thinking: Freud goes to Ithaca. [I do have a shrink. She is called Penelope now that I think of it.]

I had not thought of this ritual for many years, until a couple of nights ago, when I caught myself in an instant of pure elation, the kind of moment where you clench your fist in an air punch and laugh from your throat and hope nobody sees you. The reason? My children had just come home. Big Ulysses from an afternoon playing football with his mates, and little Ulysses from a playdate that lasted a bit too long for my anxious taste. As soon as she passed the door, I was inundated with an absurd, irrepressible, wild happiness. Ithaca is populated again! Today's *Odyssey* is over.

I am a traveller who loves arrivals. I love Ithaca. I love how arrival renews the habitual, fans an ancient flame, blends experience into memory. Like Odysseus, unlike Ulisse. As a matter of fact, one of the aspects of Dante's story that the nostalgic in me finds most peculiar and thrilling is that, in crafting his Ulisse, Dante does not fall for the *nostos*, for the theme and narrative of return that was so easily spiritualized into the image of the soul going back to the supernal world, or 'god'.

Already in antiquity the question arose whether Homer was a philosopher, whether there was a moral message to his fanciful stories (with Plato notably denying this in the tenth book of his *Republic*, with a determination that sounds, at times, like sorrowful adieu). In the Neoplatonic tradition of antiquity and the early middle ages, however, Odysseus's travels were readily interpreted as the return of the soul to its spiritual origins, one of the most quoted examples being a passage in Plotinus's *Enneads* — that amazing zipper between classical antiquity and early Christianity — where we read of Odysseus's journey to Ithaca as the return of the soul to eternity: away from the lures of the world (the adventures), back to where it belongs.

Now, you may or may not want a taste of Neoplatonic writing (overstated by the rather passionate translation of an Irish nationalist): skip to the next page if not inclined. [Giovanni Boccaccio issued the same warning for the racy passages in his *Decameron* — so mind you: you might be missing something intellectually kinky.]

> But what must we do? How lies the path? How come to vision of the inaccessible Beauty, dwelling as if in consecrated precincts, apart from the common ways where all may see, even the profane?
>
> He that has the strength, let him arise and withdraw into himself, foregoing all that is known by the eyes, turning away for ever from the material beauty that once made his joy. When he perceives those shapes of grace that show in body, let him not pursue: he must know them for copies,

vestiges, shadows, and hasten away towards That they tell of. For if anyone follow what is like a beautiful shape playing over water — is there not a myth telling in symbol of such a dupe, how he sank into the depths of the current and was swept away to nothingness? So too, one that is held by material beauty and will not break free shall be precipitated, not in body but in Soul, down to the dark depths loathed of the Intellective-Being, where, blind even in the Lower-World, he shall have commerce only with shadows, there as here.

'Let us flee then to the beloved Fatherland': this is the soundest counsel. But what is this flight? How are we to gain the open sea? For Odysseus is surely a parable to us when he commands the flight from the sorceries of Circe or Calypso — not content to linger for all the pleasure offered to his eyes and all the delight of sense filling his days.

The Fatherland to us is There whence we have come, and There is The Father.

What then is our course, what the manner of our flight? This is not a journey for the feet; the feet bring us only from land to land; nor need you think of coach or ship to carry you away; all this order of things you must set aside and refuse to see: you must close the eyes and call instead upon another vision which is to be waked within you, a vision, the birth-right of all, which few turn to use (Plotinus, *Enneads* 1, VI, 8; translation by Stephen MacKenna and B. S. Page).

The language is abstruse, but the message is clear: Odysseus is an image of the soul coming back to the supernal spheres where it belongs, his navigation looking more and more like a flight. The Neoplatonic tradition minutely allegorized in this way several details from the *Odyssey*. In one Eustathius of Thessalonica (twelfth century), poor Calypso is read as her name, the Hider, the Enveloper; hence: the body, imprisoning and weighing down Ulysses-soul. From this to seeing the *nostos* as the return of the soul to God after its journey in embodiment and experience is a very short step. Some Christian interpreters (on the cuckoo spectrum) even equate Odysseus tied to the mast in the sirens' episode to Christ on the cross.

Augustine frequently uses the image of sea travel to signify the journey to god. It is ok, he says, to travel. Nay, it is necessary! But woe unto him (slash her?) who enjoys that which should be only used (= the journey, the adventures), for he (she? most likely she is automatically safe and bored at home) shall forsake the delight of that which is to be enjoyed only by (the universalizing subject that translates as) all: T(capital)he F(capital)ather. Sorry my language went all Neoplatonic-cum-glossator; you might want to listen to Augustine himself. His version of Ulysses is rather legit, his Latin a pleasure to read and to translate.

> Frui est enim amore inhaerere alicui rei propter seipsam. Uti autem, quod in usum venerit ad id quod amas obtinendum referre, si tamen amandum est. Nam usus inlicitus abusus potius vel abusio nominandus est. Quomodo ergo, si essemus peregrini, qui beate vivere nisi in patria non possemus, eaque peregrinatione utique miseri et miseriam finire cupientes, in patriam redire vellemus, opus esset vel terrestribus vel marinis vehiculis quibus utendum esset ut ad patriam, qua fruendum erat, pervenire valeremus; quod si amoenitates itineris et ipsa gestatio vehiculorum nos delectaret, conversi ad fruendum his quibus uti debuimus, nollemus cito viam finire et perversa suavitate implicati alienaremur a patria, cuius suavitas faceret beatos, sic in huius mortalitatis vita peregrinantes a Domino, si redire in patria volumus, ubi beati esse possimus, utendum est hoc mundo, non fruendum, ut invisibilia Dei per ea, quae facta sunt, intellecta conspiciantur, hoc est, ut de corporalibus temporalibusque rebus aeterna et spiritalia capiamus (*De doctrina christiana* 1, 4).

To enjoy something is to hold fast to it in love for its own sake. To use something is to apply whatever it may be to the purpose of obtaining what you love — if indeed it is something that ought to be loved. (The improper use of something should be termed abuse.) Suppose we were travelers who could live happily only in our homeland, and because our absence made us unhappy we wished to put an end to our misery and return there: we would need transport by land or sea which we could use to travel to our homeland, the object of our enjoyment. But if we were fascinated by the delights of the journey and the actual traveling, we would be perversely enjoying things that we should be using; and we would be reluctant to finish our journey quickly, being ensnared in the wrong kind of pleasure and estranged from the homeland whose pleasures could make us happy. So in this mortal life we are like travelers away from our Lord: if we wish to return to the homeland where we can be happy we must use this world, not enjoy it, in order to discern the invisible attributes of God, which are understood through what has been made or, in other words, to derive eternal and spiritual value from corporeal and temporal things (translation by R. H. Green).

The step to the religious allegory is short, but it is a step that Dante does not take with his Ulisse. In defiance of all 'sources' and previous interpretations, he makes his Ulisse a resilient, resistant, even morose image of something that the poet didn't even quite grasp himself, of a human being to come, and planted it in the middle of his Christian poem.

As much as I like the image of Dante peeking ahead in the inscrutable future, though, as much as I believe in the power of literature to foresee things that logic and science and ethics appreciate only much later, his version of Ulysses might actually look so new and unseen not because Dante is looking forwards, but because he looks back to a classical and secular image of the journey of Ulysses as the adventure of the mind (which, in turn, becomes modern in the rear-view mirror of the 'Renaissance').

For some Latin readers, Ulysses is the image of the intellectual adventurer, either enjoying or threatened by the journey of experience. Such is Cicero's Ulysses, intent at listening to the sweet lure of knowledge in the song of the sirens (*De finibus* 5, XVIII, 48–49). Similarly, Horace's Ulysses (*Epistles* 1, II, 17–30) is the champion of virtue and knowledge — 'quid virtus et quid sapientia possit, | utile proposuit nobis exemplar Ulixen' (of the power of worth and wisdom he [Homer] has set before us an instructive pattern in Ulysses; 17–18; translation by H. R. Fairclough) — an ordinary hero who is able to resist the lures of the world (the sirens' song, Circe's potion) and, therefore, to shine and distinguish himself from the spiritless ones, those who are mere ciphers in a faceless crowd, Circe's pigs, Penelope's suitors, fashionistas at Alcinous's court. And such is the interpretation of Seneca (who was already annoyed at how scholars harassed the *Odyssey* with interpretation): whether navigating in the Mediterranean pool or, more likely, in the big blue unknown, his hero is tossed and turned in the everyday adventure of anxiety and worry, complete with quotidian sirens and bloodthirsty Cyclops; his home, presumably the 'Ithaca' that only philosophy can afford (*Epistles* 88, 6–8).

Another possible take is that Dante's rendition focuses on one potentiality of the ancient story of Ulysses: that of 'textual adventure'. The adventure of language, writing, and reading was depicted since antiquity as a navigation in perilous waters, with shipwrecks and fortuitous landings; a sort of a winged navigation, indeed, feathered and penned. We shall see later in this little book that Dante makes a great use of this theme, and naturalizes his Ulisse in the dimension of writing-as-navigation.

Or perhaps it is the adventure that attracts Dante. Period. The journey of the human spirit into madness, into its own sickly fantasies, the nightmares of writing-and-being, of writing-as-being; whereby the discipline of writing, or 'art', keeps it a journey and prevents it from becoming a descent into psychosis. This is Ovid, of course, a writer who is present like no one else in Dante's closet, his perennial ghost source.

Book 14 of the *Metamorphoses* is an overwhelming tour de force in storytelling, in which Ovid mixes and expeditiously rewrites the *Odyssey* and the *Aeneid*, with touches of his own mad epic of shape-changing. He morphs one poem into the other, creating an epic monster that then is backwashed into the very poem that has produced it. It is astounding to read. It is alive.

The plot of this extraordinary creature is better enjoyed all in one breath, as a sort of long telegram gone awry. Or bumpy Sparknotes. Some kind of *bacchanalia* of reading. [Parentheses and brackets are the punctuator in me.]

It begins with the gobbling sea monster, Scylla, not yet paired into the swallowing duo, but rather a lovely naked nymph sitting alone in a solitary crevice. Glaucus, the former fisherman turned androgynous sea-god, falls in love with her and tells her the story of his metamorphosis. Not interested, she leaves (end of book 13). Glaucus goes to Circe for help. Here featured as a nymphomaniac, Circe tries to seduce him – he says no – she turns Scylla into the monster we know from the *Odyssey*, i.e., the torso of a woman planted on six dog-like beasts who devour sailors. Description of metamorphosis. Glaucus cries and [understandably] flees the scene. 'Scylla remained and, as soon as she could, she took revenge on Circe by robbing Ulysses of his companions' (*Metamorphoses* 14, 70–71; my hurried translation here and throughout this section). She would have gladly done the same later with Aeneas's Trojans, but she had already been turned into a rock (14, 72–74) [fastening of *Odyssey* and *Aeneid* in the rocky body of an unfortunate nymph]. In what follows (14, 75–157) Ovid grafts the *Aeneid* onto his own work, but he uses that part of the Virglian epic (books 1–6) that was already based on the *Odyssey*. Readers are dragged into a bewitched acceleration through the plot of the fourth (Carthage, Dido) and fifth (Mediterranean cruise-cum-funerary-rites) books of the *Aeneid*. Expansion on *Aeneid* book 6 (Virgil's own *nekyia*), with a further diversion on the transformation of the Sibyl, once a beautiful virgin loved by Apollo. Next, Aeneas 'arrived in the place that did not have the name of his nurse yet' (14, 157), the city of Gaeta that Aeneas later named as such after his nurse. [This is, incidentally, Dante's beginning of the episode of Ulisse: 'When I departed from Circe, who had detained me more than a year there near Gaeta, before Aeneas had so named it' (*Inferno* 26, 90–93).]

In this very as-of-now nameless place we find another Ithacan: Macareus, a freshly invented 'companion of long-suffering Ulysses', currently stranded in not-yet-Gaeta. Ulysses is enigmatically called 'experiens' (14, 159): experienced, long-suffering, patient, expert? [Remember Virgil's unhappy ('infelix') Ulysses? The Ovidian adjective may also give another hue to Dante's desire for 'esperienza' (experience).] We would love to linger on this, but a further surprise follows: guess who recognizes him? Achaemenides! [yes! him, the re-reader from the *Aeneid*]. A bewildered exchange of questions between the two former companions of unhappy/long-suffering Ulysses [one invented by Virgil and the other by Ovid] follows: (Macareus) 'what the fuck are you doing with them Trojans?' (Achaemenides) 'No, mate, I ask the questions now. The fuck are *you* doing here?' [or something of this kind]. An emboldened Achaemenides now retells for the nth-time the story of the Cyclops (14, 167–222), this time merging Virgil's and Homer's accounts. Gore galore. It is now Macareus's turn (14, 223–441). He picks up where they left Achaemenides [with the Greek boat leaving the Cyclopes' island] and retells the rest of the *Odyssey*: in order; Eolus's bag of winds, Lestrygonians, Circe (again, but less lewd and more witchy), with [no surprise] a long expansion on the metamorphosis of men into pigs. Ulysses overcomes and seduces Circe. One year is spent at her court. One year, the time for Ovid to have one of Circe's maids tell Macareus the long story of the marriage of King Picus and the nymph Canens [= she who sings, a sort of female Orpheus, who moves rocks and tames animals with her song]. The incorrigible Circe sees Picus, falls in love with him, snatches him, is rejected by him. 'Sed amans! Et lesa! Et femina!' (14, 385) — But she is in love! And hurt! And a woman! Go Circe! Badly pissed off, she turns him into a woodpecker and his companions into all sorts of wildly diverse monsters. 'Nobody kept their shape' ('nulli sua mansit imago'; 14, 415): this line is some kind of suicide by metamorphosis of Ovid's writing, at once triumphal and nihilist. Desperate Canens melts into song and tears.

We finally left Circe's island, says Macareus, and you know what? I could not take this shit anymore. I quit [I sympathize with you Macareus]. Aeneas calls Gaeta Gaeta (14, 441–44). Furious fast forward into the second half of the *Aeneid* (the half that is patterned after the *Iliad*, where the Trojans fight the Latins; 14, 445–580), with expansion on ... no you can't guess this ... Diomedes [yes! yes! I know that the few of you I have not yet lost are jolting with me now] ... Diomedes, and the Ovidian invention of the story of his attempted *nostos* and how he ended up in Latium, and how some of his companions were changed into birds by angry Venus [press pause for a minute: we have a fake Greek *nostos* implanted into the *Iliad*'s part of the *Aeneid* with some metamorphosis, of course: starts sounding and looking like the human centipede]. Breaking marks, the text is slowing down. Yet another metamorphosis, less frantic though; it sounds like a lull, a murmur of waves, the distant sound of the sea. Angry Venus morphs more things — this time, she turns the Trojan boats into beautiful sea nymphs to subtract them from the enemy fire — the mellowest metamorphosis of all, with wood softening into body, sterns into faces, oars into ... no, not wings unfortunately! [literature does not respond every time you knock] ... oars into fingers and legs for swimming, ropes into hair. The Naiads: splendid, kind creatures, yet still cruel enough to rejoice at the destruction of Ulysses' ship, and at the petrification of Alcinous's vessel [aka the liquidation of the *Odyssey*, where this story had been told in book 13, 149–87]. End of the *Aeneid* within the *Metamorphoses*. Hand brake, apotheosis of Aeneas (14, 581–609). *Stop! Arrête! Halt! Basta!* The beginning of Roman history ensues.

And we do really stop here, to notice that if Ovid's *Aeneid* ends with an apotheosis, Ovid's *Odyssey* ends with a whimper, with a character who [understandably] says NO:

> Talia multa mihi longum narrata per annum
> visaque sunt. resides et desuetudine tardi
> rursus inire fretum, rursus dare vela iubemur,
> ancipitesque vias et iter Titania vastum
> dixerat et saevi restare pericula ponti:
> pertimui, fateor, nactusque hoc litus adhaesi.
> Finierat Macareus.
> (*Metamorphoses* 14, 435–41)

'During that long year [the year they stayed at Circe's] I was told many things and many I witnessed. Now turned sedentary and slow [Dante: 'I and my companions were old and slow' ('vecchi e tardi'; *Inferno* 26, 106)], we are ordered to go to sea again, to spread our sails. Circe told us that our ways would be dubious, the journey long, and that the cruel sea still had dangers in store for us. Ok, I admit it: I got scared and, as soon as we got to this place, I stuck with it.' Macareus concluded (my translation).

'Finierat Macareus': here ends the story of Macareus. The anti-Ulysses, the non-character, or the super-character? Bartleby the scrivener. Leopold Bloom. *Nec plus ultra*. Here I stay. Try writing *my* story. I am the backwash of story. The Hercules' pillars of narration. The un-narrable character; the common human being.‡

---

‡ Loss of character is, incidentally, Plato's prophecy for Ulysses. In book 10 (614–21) of the *Republic*, after his slow and enamoured character assassination of Homer, Socrates famously proposes the story of his own epic hero, Er, who is allowed to bring back to the world news of life after death. (Er is a pre-Dante.) This is not 'one of the tales which Odysseus tells the hero Alcinous', Socrates hurries to preface, this is some kind of heroic-philosophical story. It is about the otherworld, an awkward, strangely modern, inconsequential otherworld. This is, surely, the revenge of Homer: Plato may be a great philosopher, but he does not know how to stitch together a story. At a certain point the souls encounter the figure of the Interpreter, who lays in front of them the 'possible lives' in which they might want to reincarnate. 'There was not, however, any definite character to them, because the soul, when choosing a new life, must of necessity become different' [so *this* is how intertextuality works]. Unlike the vain and impulsive Orpheus, who chooses to become a swan just to shun the women who killed him ('hating to be born of a woman because they had been his murderers'), and other heroes from the Trojan war, who [understandably] decide to take the shape of an animal, so disgusted they are by human nature, Odysseus, the last to come on stage, makes a peculiar choice. Odysseus too is fed up, but in a clever, more modern way: 'There came also the soul of Odysseus having yet to make a choice, and his lot happened to be the last of them all. Now the recollection of former tolls had disenchanted him of ambition, and he went about for a considerable

My story of intertextuality also ends here. Bits and pieces of Dante's Ulisse lie in the texts of many ancient authors, like polished pieces of glass in the shallow sea. In Cicero, an exciting interpretation of the siren as the lure of knowledge (see chapter 6), in Horace, the value of virtue and wisdom, in Seneca, the intuition that Ulysses probably did not navigate the quiet Mediterranean, but he went out 'in the high open sea', into the unknown ('extra notum nobis orbem'). And in Ovid, the naming of Gaeta, the old companions, and the mad liquidation of epic. There are more fragments in other texts that I do not mention here, and surely in those that I do not know.

Even my super-line, the one that I asked my readers to stop and wonder at, the very power and beauty of poetry, can be 'sourced' somewhere:

de' remi facemmo ali al folle volo

we made our oars wings in a mad flight

has a touch of the winged oars in the unread Homer. There is Ovid, of course, whose sirens (of course) navigate the sea on the oars of the wings ('super fluctus alarum insistere remis'; *Metamorphoses* 6, 558). [Now, neither you nor I have the bandwidth for another metamorphosis — but I hope to return to Ovid's sirens, so strange, and compassionate, and so girly.] Also a bit of Virgil who, at the beginning of the sixth book of the *Aeneid*, tells the story of Daedalus and Icarus, and mentions the 'remigium alarum' (6, 19), the oars of the wings (which today is still a concept in entomology — I think it signifies those little veins in the wings of the insects). There is more, I am sure.

---

time in search of the life of a private man who had no cares; he had some difficulty in finding this, which was lying about and had been neglected by everybody else; and when he saw it, he said that he would have done the same had his lot been first instead of last, and that he was delighted to have it' (translation by Benjamin Jowett).

What is left to Dante is a touch of folly ('folle volo'), but by now you know where to find it: it is the folly inherent in every act of reading, in every act of writing.

Back now to 'my' incarnation, then, one facet of the *polytropos* that becomes a turning point in the story of this character, a cluster that, in turn, unleashes a whole set of elements that become integral to the story itself. Several are the radical novelties of Dante's Ulysses:

- well; hell.
- the fact that Ulisse is disembodied. We see not the hero, but the flame engulfing him. What in the medieval context might be a punishment (for his false advice, for his burning desire for knowledge) is, in a modern fashion, his 'spirit'.
- the firmness of his 'I': the deed and the story are one (modernity in a nutshell).
- the cancellation of the return.
- the mad flight and the trespassing into the unknown.
- the reasons for it: to gain experience, and to pursue virtue and knowledge.

3. To Pursue Virtue and Knowledge

Does this still ring true? Is this still a fair portrayal of what it is to be human?

In today's expanded world such a question is either obsolete or so full of complication and controversy that it is futile to even attempt it.

Dante, you will remember, is ambiguous about this point, re-spinning this classical and medieval refrain first in his philosophical work, *The Banquet*, and then within the enclosure of hell, wrapped up inside Ulisse's 'small oration'. I can never quite decide whether hell × the-oration-pronounced-therewithin (yes, therewithin) is a product of negatives, hence a positive, or not.

'Fatti non foste a viver come bruti, | ma per seguir virtute e canoscenza' (you were not made to live as brutes, but to pursue virtue and knowledge; *Inferno* 26, 119–20) is the culmination of Ulisse's little speech to his sailors, and it is hard to quibble with it. Two large words that make sense together. 'C-a-noscenza'; I am sure there is a perfectly good linguistic reason whereby Dante (or a scribe, for that matter) uses this particular form of the word for knowledge instead of the more frequent 'c-o-noscenza': whatever the reason is, 'c-a-noscenza' is, to me at least but I hope I am not alone in this, an open, generous, fun, sunny word; something like knaawledge — something you cannot pronounce without a smile. 'Virtute', instead, a sumptuous and rigid Latinism (the more Italian form would be the truncated 'virtù'), is a tricky one, isn't it? Originally a male thing (of the 'vir', human being with dick), it becomes an abstract, feminine concept for all that is morally good on earth and in the heavens. The middle ages have seven virtues, four 'cardinal' deriving from classical philosophy (prudence, justice, temperance, and fortitude) and three 'theological' (faith, hope, and charity). They are often personified and become, therefore, authoritative women (i.e., female with dick).

Now, grungy 'canoscenza' and uptight 'virtute' may be a fashion mismatch, but they are comfortable together in Dante's line. They form a tenet with which it is difficult to both disagree and agree: that the ultimate goal of the human being is to pursue knowledge in an honest way, with the aim of the common good.

That to be human is to 1) differ from animals because 2) a more noble pursuit (than filling one's belly and emptying one's bowels or, in some cases, genitals) is available to us, an activity that 3) is of an intellectual nature and involves an equal measure of morality (virtue) and, roughly speaking, philo-sophy (as the love of wisdom, of knowledge, of research), still rang true, a little less than two centuries after Dante, to a scholar prodigy who did not get to change the world because he died too young. Or because the world cannot be changed by scholars.

In 1486, when he was only twenty-three, and taking himself very seriously as all young people do, Giovanni Pico della Mirandola wrote nine hundred philosophical theses, which were immediately deemed unorthodox by the Church, and shortly after he produced a preface to them, the *Oratio de homini dignitate* (*Oration on the dignity of the human being* — it is a little gimmicky but we do need to translate the Latin 'homo' as human being. We must. We cannot be forgetful and let 'man' slip. It is a little gesture that, I believe, does change minds).

It is no bedtime reading. Of a strange length (long essay, short book), and of an even stranger language and style, the crystal clear yet somewhat adamantine humanistic Latin, to read it properly one needs a myriad of footnotes. Yet to me it reads the same as the journey of Ulisse, a mad, daring, and generous flight into the unknown, taken by one of those few travellers of the mind who fearlessly bridge the gap between their desk and the beyond.

Pico constantly invokes sources in his *Oration* — Hebrew, Arab, Greek, and Christian — and in doing so he achieves not only an extraordinary (for his times) cultural syncretism, but a stunning (for his times) dialogue between cultures, and a subtle smoothing of faiths, creeds, and philosophies. It is as if the *Oration*'s heavy cultural load were intended not to sink the objections of others, but to produce a cultural relativism that, like a current, keeps its imagination of the human being as pursuer of virtue and knowledge afloat. In perpetual flight: this boat has wings.

Right at the beginning of this strange text, you will find an oration within the oration; god's speech to the newly created human being.

Igitur hominem accepit, indiscretae opus imaginis, atque in mundi positum meditullio sic est alloquutus: 'Nec certam sedem, nec propriam faciem, nec munus ullum peculiare tibi dedimus, o Adam, ut quam sedem, quam faciem, quae munera tute optaveris, ea, pro voto, pro tua sententia, habeas et possideas. Definita caeteris natura intra praescriptas a nobis leges cohercetur. Tu, nullis angustiis cohercitus, pro tuo arbitrio, in cuius manu te posui, tibi illam prefinies. Medium te mundi posui, ut circumspiceres inde comodius quicquid est in mundo. Nec te celestem neque terrenum, neque mortalem neque immortalem fecimus, ut, tui ipsius quasi arbitrarius honorariusque plastes et fictor, in quam malueris tute formam effingas. Poteris in inferiora, quae sunt bruta degenerare; poteris in superiora quae sunt divina, ex tui animi sententia regenerari' (*de hominis dignitate*, 18–23).

He therefore took *the human being*, this creature of indeterminate image, set *them* in the middle of the world, and said to *them*: 'We have given you, Adam, no fixed seat or form of your own, no talent peculiar to you alone. This we have done so whatever seat, whatever form, whatever talent you might judge desirable, these same might you have and possess according to your desire and judgement. Once defined, the nature of all other beings is constrained within the laws We have prescribed for them. But you, constrained by no limits, may determine your nature for yourself, according to your own free will, in whose hands We have placed you. We have set you at the centre of the world so that from there you may more easily gaze upon whatever it contains. We have made you neither of heaven nor of earth, neither mortal nor immortal, so that you may, as the free and extraordinary shaper of yourself, fashion yourself in whatever form you prefer. It will be in your power to degenerate into the lower forms of life, which are brutish. Alternatively, you shall have the power, in accordance with the judgement of your soul, to be reborn into higher orders, those that are divine' (translation from the edition by Francesco Borghesi, Massimo Riva, and Michael Papio) [from now on, asterisks signal my changes to translations, mostly having to do with the switch from 'man' to 'human being'. Here, the slight frisson between 'human being' and 'Adam' is meant to induce reflections on 'original gender'].

With no fixed abode; un-dowried and un-gifted; self-made; go-getter; no limits; 360-degree vision; in-betweenness; self-fashioning; degenerability and regeneration: yes! We recognize this: it is the script of the modern human being.

'Who would not marvel at our chameleon?' ('Quis hunc nostrum chamaeleonta non admiretur?'; 31). 'We all would!', we exclaim; we do feel some kind of solidarity with this description. It is exciting to think of ourselves in these terms, individually or collectively. 'We will marvel!', we would exclaim, were it not for a shadow, a ghost-shaped, dream-like shade that says 'no'. Plainly, unforbiddingly, even affectionately, this shade objects to the positive, forward-looking, progress-oriented vision of the human being.

This phantasm has many shapes and faces, like dreams. In my own poetic *nekyia*, I find it in the words of the Greek poet Pindar: my favourite ever, and never quite grasped, definition of the human being.

> ἐπάμεροι· τί δέ τις; τί δ' οὔ τις; σκιᾶς ὄναρ
> ἄνθρωπος
> (*Pythian* 8, 95–96)

> Creatures of a day! What is someone? What is no one? A dream of a shadow is *the human being [for god's sake!]* (translation by William H. Race).

It is not always needed, or helpful, to notice the passing shade, though.

The rest of the *Oration* implies that we must not degenerate but regenerate. That regeneration is a thing of the spirit, it is a pursuit of virtue and knowledge, like the quest of Ulisse in Dante. You won't be surprised that the tracks of Ulysses (Homer's and Dante's) are all over the *Oration* — Calypso, poor Calypso, now blinding human beings with fanciful mirages and turning them into brutes (wasn't it Circe? I wonder; 38), a winged soul (131), the 'oarlike stroke' (the Virgilian *remigium*) of wings and feet that swiftly abducts the soul away from this world (109), and a beautiful book never written:

> Homerus [...] ut omnes alias sapientias, ita hanc quoque sub sui Ulixis erroribus dissimulasse in poetica nostra theologia aliquando probabimus (*de hominis dignitate*, 224).

> Homer [...] likewise concealed this wisdom, just as he concealed all the others, beneath the wanderings of his Ulysses, as I shall eventually prove in my *Poetic Theology*.

I wonder what Pico's *Poetic Theology* might have looked like — maybe yet another mass of scholarship, becoming dusty and obsolete on the shelves of libraries, then going into the 'rare prints' department, then someone deciding not to digitize it, and whoosh, gone, back into the ethereal space of the books that never existed. Maybe the text that forever changed the idea of divinity. Either way, it is gone, vanished in the niche of erudition, in the young scholar's premature death, in the obstinate ticking of the clock of lost time.

The remark on Homer in the *Oration* comes in the context of Pico's defence of his last theses. These were concerned with magic, which he treats both as the apogee of human knowledge and the nature of true scholarship; an intellectual endeavour that dares, that flies and travels into the realm of the unknown to grasp the secrets of the universe. Ultimately, Pico says, this is what scholars of all doctrines and creeds — Greek (Pythagorean, Orphic), Eastern (Chaldean, Zoroastrian), Jewish, Muslim, and Christian alike — are seeking together.

Is Dante's Ulysses a scholar, a philosopher, a magus, I wonder? There is such an interpretation. Some believe that Ulisse in the *Comedy* is a sort of mirror for a 'Ulyssean' philosophical phase in Dante's work — daring and failed because it is rooted in logic and rationality (and, for some, even in heterodoxy), rather than faith. His *Banquet*, as we have seen, begins indeed with a bold 'Ulyssean' statement: 'Sì come dice lo Filosofo nel principio della Prima Filosofia, tutti li uomini naturalmente desiderano di sapere' (As the Philosopher says at the beginning of the First Philosophy, all *human f** beings, please!* by nature desire to know; *Convivio* 1, I, 1), and goes on to tangle itself into stating that if god is unknowable to the human beings, then it lies outside of the arc of the earthly desire for knowledge (*Convivio* 3, xv, 9–10).

The *Banquet* is a sorry little book, written in (very) unattractive prose, with long winding arguments that never quite land anywhere, a textual 'shipwreck', sinking towards the end of an impossibly long fourth treatise; to the relief of the reader, I must add: the original plan was in fifteen books. Its saving grace? The fact that the cues for the philosophical arguments are not philosophical or theological materials, but his own lyric poems, mostly talking about love (at least in the shape that has been handed down to us). That is, Dante establishes a vital nexus between love (of the poetic kind) and knowledge, between eros (of two lovers) and wisdom, between desire (both sensual and spiritual) and learning, between sex and text (actually, this last one is my wishful addition).

Such an unhinged and unorthodox philosophical phase would be portrayed, according to some, in the *Comedy*'s Ulisse in a somewhat apologetic, 'shipwrecky' mode. I do not believe in palinode, literary and otherwise, but I am not sure whether this is a limit or a limitation of mine. Minus the palinode, though, I like the Ulisse-scholar interpretation, and I like the way Pico della Mirandola is that kind of Ulysses, unapologetically back from hell.

Reading it today, the *Oration* has many weak spots, more or less apparent to the differently perceiving and wonderfully varied embodied minds who read it. It is universalizing and generalizing, and it has no sense whatsoever of the issues that matter to us today: gender, race, class, diversity in general. Its syncretism ends up being pretty Christian. It has no sense of politics, it is a piece of old, 'bookshelf' philosophy (if you are lucky enough to still have a bookshelf, that is, with a space for philosophy in it). Yet, its learning still moves me. The burning desire for knowledge. Its staunch idealism. Its naïf pacifism. I still read the discourse of god, and think it applies to me. On a good day, that is. Too bad he doesn't have a sense of humour — but that's because he was young.

Pico della Mirandola died young, in November 1494, still fighting the papal condemnation of his theses. Most likely poisoned. Only two months earlier, his friend (and perhaps occasional lover) Angelo Poliziano — a great humanist, a scholar of Latin and Greek, and an accomplished poet in both ancient languages and in Italian — died, most likely poisoned. Only two years before, in April, Lorenzo de Medici, patron of both and one of the few real poet-politicians who ever existed, died in Florence. In August of the same year, Columbus set sail. A world died and another was born. Renaissance, initially meaning the rebirth of ancient figural art, and the flourishing of the humanities came to mean the birth of the modern monster, enormous and ingenuous: firearms, nationalism, conquest, capitalism, colonialism. But also science, progress, revolution, evolution. Daily flights to the unknown.

As he was dying in the throes of arsenic poisoning, Pico could not imagine the world to come. His amazing scholarly flight is ultimately a backflip in the past. He could not foresee the new worlds across the Ocean and the bold and brazen greed that would soon send waves of people through Hercules' pillars; the end of the geopolitical supremacy of the Mediterranean and of Italy's political freedom. That mercenary armies would soon invade the peninsula, and that a simple soldier could now kill a *condottiere* by shooting an arquebus from afar. In his naïve attempt at reconciling faiths and creeds, in his mild, obedient rebellion against the Church, he could not have foreseen the Reformation, or thousands of *Landsknechts* sacking Rome in 1527.

There is always a third oration in my mind alongside Pico's to his fellow scholars and god's to Adam. Mine [not normally suffering of delusions of grandeur]. To a group of about fifty students some twenty years ago in Montreal. In comparison, it is truly an 'orazion picciola', a small oration, in all possible senses of minuteness. It was September 11. A Tuesday, around 11 am. Like every Tuesday and Thursday, I was about to teach my undergraduate 'Italian Renaissance' class. After a couple of introductory meetings, we were due to read, you guessed it ... the jewel in the crown of Humanism, the Manifesto of the Renaissance, Pico's *Oration*. I sat there for a bit in silence, even when the class had gathered, and there was no residual noise of steps and packsacks and notebooks and chatter. Considering whether it was wiser to just cancel the class. I said: 'Something has happened this morning, of which we do not know the causes or consequences. We are scared. We do not understand what is going on. A bit like those people witnessing the sack of Rome in 1527, as we saw in our historical introduction last week. It is in times like this that what we are — young, academic, humanists — matters most. In times like this, we embrace what we do. Reading and learning — with love, with passion, philologically, philosophically, critically, with erudition, with patience — is a profoundly pacifist act. Only in reading and learning will we find shelter against intolerance of all kinds, and solace against all fears. Let us do it together; let us make it more meaningful than ever today. Let us now open our course packs to the first of our Renaissance texts: the Manifesto of the Renaissance, Giovanni Pico della Mirandola's formidable *Oration on the dignity of man*' [back then I was less finicky with gender].

Two years later, a dear friend died in the Iraqi war. He was a journalist embedded with the US troops. A 'friendly' missile hit the barrack where he was staying with a group of destitute, unaware young soldiers, whose stories he was trying to collect and reveal. The next day, I was teaching the 'Early Italian Poetry' class. In a rather sombre and colloquial tone I told my students about my friend's somewhat rambunctious search for justice in various parts of the world and of his end, and recited some lines of Petrarch to commemorate him. They capture the moment of the death of his beloved Laura, they talk about snow and peacefulness. The opposite of what my friend's death must have been in the fiery Iraqi desert, among the noise of the grenades. Still …

> Pallida no, ma più che neve bianca
> che senza venti in un bel colle fiocchi,
> parea posar come persona stanca.
> Quasi un dolce dormir ne' suo' belli occhi,
> sendo lo spirto già da lei diviso,
> era quel che morir chiaman gli sciocchi:
> Morte bella parea nel suo bel viso.
> (Petrarch, *Triumphus mortis* I, 166–72)

> No, not pale. White. Whiter than the snow that
> falls gently in a windless day on a pretty hill. It
> looked like she was resting. Like when one is tired.
> You could almost sense a sweet sleep in her beautiful eyes, now that her soul had left her self. The
> fools call this moment death: Death looked beautiful in her beautiful face (my translation).

There is no sense of history, no high-sounding rhetoric, no generalizing in these lines. Just a young lover dying. No reason, but a rhyme. The death-defying power of poetry.

A year ago, another dear friend died. One of Covid's many senseless collateral losses, excess deaths they call them. I just cancelled the class. Not because I no longer believe literature and being a humanist have meaning in moments of crisis. Or that to pursue knowledge critically is to pursue virtue (whatever that is). Or that poetry can give more than comfort, it kindles fictional lives from death. Or that my friends — one a daring traveller, the other an uncompromising scholar — are not somewhere in some form attending to their quests and searches. But because I no longer can do so without crying. At his funeral I read the canto of Ulisse, though. The stained-glass windows of the chapel featured a boat, gently rolling through gentle waves, it seemed, in the uncertain light of mid-May.

Poems have tears. It is for us to cry them.

Now, to pursue virtue and knowledge. Does that still ring true? Well, it did, still, to someone, somehow, in the midst of history's most tragic storm. In Primo Levi's chillingly beautiful reading of *Inferno* 26 in his *Se questo è un uomo* (*If This is a Man*, 1947), the most profound and harrowing of Shoah writings. In one of the central chapters, entitled *Il canto di Ulisse*, Levi describes how he tried to teach Italian through Dante to a fellow inmate at Auschwitz, Jean, the 'Pikolo', the young factotum. This little lecture, set against the bleak background of the Lager, against the cacophony of orders barked in different languages, against the cold, the fatigue, the hunger, the despair, is a masterpiece of literature, and yet it is also literature defying itself. It represents, simultaneously, the impossibility of translating, the limits of comprehension, the utter dead-end of making oneself understood, and their opposites.

It is full of omissions, stuttering, and memory voids … It is interspersed with steps, voices, needs, and languages that do not translate and do not compute. The lacunae and the intromissions are there to underline the realism (I use this term without irony or doubt in this instance only) of the scene, as well as the radical frailty of memory; that of the reader-speaker (Levi), that of the reader-reader (us), and that of history.

In the Jewish Museum in Berlin, designed by Daniel Libeskind, there are 'memory voids': unused, useless (?), illogical, awkward, vertical areas. The museumgoer is brought to walk to their edges, and suddenly comes to reckon with the inexpressible, irrepresentable, unwritten, un-exhibitable. It is a very strange feeling: reckoning, and yet not knowing. Here, you will see, one such memory void gapes just after the Dantean 'Quando' (When), and we will all fall into a strange vertigo.

The chapter begins in a cistern that Levi is scrubbing with some other prisoners. In comes Jean, the kind and well-liked factotum, announcing that Primo will help him to carry the heavy load of today's ration, thus gaining them a precious hour-long walk in the bright summer day.

Two figures are carrying a large pot on two poles. People are passing by.

It begins with a lacuna

…

As in Odysseus's *nekyia*, we need to drink from this empty pit and cross the threshold between the page and the story, to place ourselves in some kind of liminal place and listen. We need to read these few pages all in one shot. We need to read them together, as if we were in the same room. The only Ithaca possible; the space where we are reading. Listen to how the voice, now mine, now yours, becomes the voice of the ancient narrator, with its stumblings, hesitations, and exultations. The narrator's voice turns into Dante's voice, and Dante's becomes Ulisse's. Ulisse's voice, in turn, is our voice.

> … Il canto di Ulisse. Chissà come e perché mi è venuto in mente: ma non abbiamo tempo di scegliere, quest'ora già non è più un'ora. Se Jean è intelligente capirà. Capirà: oggi mi sento da tanto.
> … Chi è Dante. Che cosa è la Commedia. Quale sensazione curiosa di novità si prova, se si cerca di spiegare in breve che cosa è la Divina Commedia. Come è distribuito l'Inferno, cosa è il contrappasso. Virgilio è la Ragione, Beatrice è la Teologia.
> Jean è attentissimo, ed io comincio, lento e accurato:
>
>> Lo maggior corno della fiamma antica
>> Cominciò a crollarsi mormorando,
>> Pur come quella cui vento affatica.
>> Indi, la cima in qua e in là menando
>> Come fosse la lingua che parlasse
>> Mise fuori la voce, e disse: Quando …

Qui mi fermo e cerco di tradurre. Disastroso: povero Dante e povero francese! Tuttavia l'esperienza pare prometta bene: Jean ammira la bizzarra similitudine della lingua, e mi suggerisce il termine appropriato per rendere 'antica'.

E dopo 'Quando'? Il nulla. Un buco nella memoria. 'Prima che sí Enea la nominasse.' Altro buco. Viene a galla qualche frammento non utilizzabile: '... la piéta Del vecchio padre, né 'l debito amore Che doveva Penelope far lieta...' sarà poi esatto?

...Ma misi me per l'alto mare aperto.

Di questo sì, di questo sono sicuro, sono in grado di spiegare a Pikolo, di distinguere perché 'misi me' non è 'je me mis', è molto più forte e più audace, è un vincolo infranto, è scagliare se stessi al di là di una barriera, noi conosciamo bene questo impulso. L'alto mare aperto: Pikolo ha viaggiato per mare e sa cosa vuol dire, è quando l'orizzonte si chiude su se stesso, libero diritto e semplice, e non c'è ormai che odore di mare: dolci cose ferocemente lontane.

Siamo arrivati al Kraftwerk, dove lavora il Kommando dei posacavi. Ci dev'essere l'ingegner Levi. Eccolo, si vede solo la testa fuori della trincea. Mi fa un cenno colla mano, è un uomo in gamba, non l'ho mai visto giù di morale, non parla mai di mangiare.

'Mare aperto.' 'Mare aperto.' So che rima con 'diserto' : '... quella compagna Picciola, dalla qual non fui diserto', ma non rammento più se viene prima o dopo. E anche il viaggio, il temerario viaggio al di là delle colonne d'Ercole, che tristezza, sono costretto a raccontarlo in prosa: un sacrilegio. Non ho salvato che un verso, ma vale la pena di fermarcisi:

... Acciò che l'uom più oltre non si metta.

'Si metta': dovevo venire in Lager per accorgermi che è la stessa espressione di prima, 'e misi me'. Ma non ne faccio parte a Jean, non sono sicuro che sia una osservazione importante. Quante altre cose ci sarebbero da dire, e il sole è già alto, mezzogiorno è vicino. Ho fretta, una fretta furibonda.

Ecco, attento Pikolo, apri gli orecchi e la mente, ho bisogno che tu capisca:

> Considerate la vostra semenza:
> Fatti non foste a viver come bruti,
> Ma per seguir virtute e conoscenza.

Come se anch'io lo sentissi per la prima volta: come uno squillo di tromba, come la voce di Dio. Per un momento, ho dimenticato chi sono e dove sono.

Pikolo mi prega di ripetere. Come è buono Pikolo, si è accorto che mi sta facendo del bene. O forse è qualcosa di più: forse, nonostante la traduzione scialba e il commento pedestre e frettoloso, ha ricevuto il messaggio, ha sentito che lo riguarda, che riguarda tutti gli uomini in travaglio, e noi in specie; e che riguarda noi due, che osiamo ragionare di queste cose con le stanghe della zuppa sulle spalle.

> Li miei compagni fec'io sì acuti ...

... e mi sforzo, ma invano, di spiegare quante cose vuol dire questo 'acuti'. Qui ancora una lacuna, questa volta irreparabile. '... Lo lume era di sotto della luna' o qualcosa di simile; ma prima? ... Nessuna idea, 'keine Ahnung' come si dice qui. Che Pikolo mi scusi, ho dimenticato almeno quattro terzine.

— Ça ne fait rien, vas-y tout de même.

> ... Quando mi apparve una montagna, bruna
> Per la distanza, e parvemi alta tanto
> Che mai veduta non ne avevo alcuna.

Sí, sí, 'alta tanto', non 'molto alta', proposizione consecutiva. E le montagne, quando si vedono di lontano ... le montagne ... oh Pikolo, Pikolo, di' qualcosa, parla, non lasciarmi pensare alle mie montagne, che comparivano nel bruno della sera quando tornavo in treno da Milano a Torino!

Basta, bisogna proseguire, queste sono cose che si pensano ma non si dicono. Pikolo attende e mi guarda.

Darei la zuppa di oggi per saper saldare 'non ne avevo alcuna' col finale. Mi sforzo di ricostruire per mezzo delle rime, chiudo gli occhi, mi mordo le dita: ma non serve, il resto è silenzio. Mi danzano per il capo altri versi: '... la terra lagrimosa diede vento ...' no, è un'altra cosa. È tardi, è tardi, siamo arrivati alla cucina, bisogna concludere:

> Tre volte il fe' girar con tutte l'acque,
> Alla quarta levar la poppa in suso
> E la prora ire in giù, come altrui piacque...

Trattengo Pikolo, è assolutamente necessario e urgente che ascolti, che comprenda questo 'come altrui piacque', prima che sia troppo tardi, domani lui o io possiamo essere morti, o non vederci mai più, devo dirgli, spiegargli del Medioevo, del così umano e necessario e pure inaspettato anacronismo, e altro ancora, qualcosa di gigantesco che io stesso ho visto ora soltanto, nell'intuizione di un attimo, forse il perché del nostro destino, del nostro essere oggi qui ...

Siamo ormai nella fila per la zuppa, in mezzo alla folla sordida e sbrindellata dei porta-zuppa degli altri Kommandos. I nuovi giunti ci si accalcano alle spalle. — Kraut und Rüben? — Kraut und Rüben — . Si annunzia ufficialmente che oggi la zuppa è di cavoli e rape: — Choux et nevets. — Káposzta és répak.

> Infin che 'l mar fu sopra noi richiuso.

... The canto of Ulysses. Who knows how or why it comes into my mind. But we have no time to change, this hour is already less than an hour. If Jean is intelligent he will understand. He *will* understand — today I feel capable of so much.

... Who is Dante? What is the Comedy? That curious sensation of novelty which one feels if one tries to explain briefly what is the Divine Comedy. How the Inferno is divided up, what are its punishments. Virgil is Reason, Beatrice is Theology.

Jean pays great attention, and I begin slowly and accurately:

> Then of that age-old fire the loftier horn
> Began to mutter and move, as a wavering flame
> Wrestles against the wind and is over-worn;
> And, like a speaking tongue vibrant to frame
> Language, the tip of it flickering to and fro
> Threw out a voice and answered: 'When I came …'

Here I stop and try to translate. Disastrous — poor Dante and poor French! All the same, the experience seems to promise well: Jean admires the bizarre simile of the tongue and suggests the appropriate word to translate 'age-old'.

And after 'When I came?' Nothing. A hole in my memory. 'Before Aeneas ever named it so.' Another hole. A fragment floats into my mind, not relevant: '… nor piety To my old father, not the wedded love That should have comforted Penelope…', is it correct?

> … So on the open sea I set forth.

Of this I am certain, I am sure, I can explain it to Pikolo, I can point out why 'I set forth' is not '*je me mis*', it is much stronger and more audacious, it is a chain which has been broken, it is throwing oneself on the other side of a barrier, we know the impulse well. The open sea: Pikolo has travelled by sea, and knows what it means: it is when the horizon closes in on itself, free, straight ahead and simple, and there is nothing but the smell of the sea; sweet things, ferociously far away.

We have arrived at Kraftwerk, where the cable-laying Kommando works. Engineer Levi must be here. Here he is, one can only see his head above the trench. He waves to me, he is a brave man, I have never seen his morale low, he never speaks of eating.

'Open sea', 'open sea', I know it rhymes with 'left me': '… and that small band of comrades that had never left me', but I cannot remember if it comes before or after. And the journey as well, the foolhardy journey beyond the Pillars of Hercules, how sad, I have to tell it in prose — a sacrilege. I have only rescued two lines, but they are worth stopping for:

> … that none should prove so hardy
> To venture the uncharted distances…

'to venture': I had to come to the Lager to realize that it is the same expression as before: 'I set forth.' But I say nothing to Jean, I am not sure that it is an important observation. How many things there are to say, and the sun is already high, midday is near. I am in a hurry, a terrible hurry.

Here, listen Pikolo, open your ears and your mind, you have to understand, for my sake:

> Think of your breed; for brutish ignorance
> Your mettle was not made; you were made men,
> To follow after knowledge and excellence.

As if I also was hearing it for the first time: like the blast of a trumpet, like the voice of God. For a moment I forget who I am and where I am.

Pikolo begs me to repeat it. How good Pikolo is, he is aware that it is doing me good. Or perhaps it is something more: perhaps, despite the wan translation and the pedestrian, rushed commentary, he has received the message, he has felt that it has to do with him, that it has to do with all *human beings* who toil, and with us in particular; and that it has to do with us two, who dare to reason of these things with the poles for the soup on our shoulders.

> My little speech made every one so keen...

... and I try, but in vain, to explain how many things this 'keen' means. There is another lacuna here, this time irreparable. '... the light kindles and grows Beneath the moon' or something like it; but before it? ... Not an idea, *'keine Ahnung'* as they say here. Forgive me, Pikolo, I have forgotten at least four triplets.

'Ça ne fait rien, vas-y tout de même.'

> ... When at last hove up a mountain, grey
> With distance, and so lofty and so steep,
> I never had seen the like on any day.

Yes, yes, 'so lofty and so steep', not 'very steep', a consecutive proposition. And the mountains when one sees them in the distance ... the mountains ... oh, Pikolo, Pikolo, say something, speak, do not let me think of my mountains which used to show up against the dusk of evening as I returned by train from Milan to Turin!

Enough, one must go on, these are things that one thinks but does not say. Pikolo waits and looks at me.

I would give today's soup to know how to connect 'the like on any day' to the last lines. I try to reconstruct it through the rhymes, I close my eyes, I bite my fingers — but it is no use, the rest is silence. Other verses dance in my head: '… The sodden ground belched wind…', no, it is something else. It is late, it is late, we have reached the kitchen, I must finish:

> And three times round she went in roaring smother
> With all the waters; at the fourth the poop
> Rose, and the prow went down, as pleased Another.

I keep Pikolo back, it is vitally necessary and urgent that he listen, that he understand this 'as pleased Another' before it is too late; tomorrow he or I might be dead, or we might never see each other again, I must tell him, I must explain to him about the Middle Ages, about the so human and so necessary and yet unexpected anachronism, but still more, something gigantic that I myself have only just seen, in a flash of intuition, perhaps the reason for our fate, for our being here today…

We are now in the soup queue, among the sordid, ragged crowd of soup-carriers from other Kommandos. Those just arrived press against our backs. '*Kraut und Rüben? Kraut und Rüben.*' The official announcement is made that the soup today is of cabbages and turnips: '*Choux et navets. Káposzta és répak.*'

> And over our heads the hollow seas closed up.

(translation by Stuart Woolf)

It has not eluded you that these powerful pages peak at two points. If you have read the passage with the interior voice of the narrator, your voice likely broke twice.

The first time, your voice became perhaps a little declamatory, in a self-conscious sort of way as if you were an actor on stage, at the moment when the 'voice of god' itself storms in — not like Pico's paternalistic speech, though, more as a trumpet blast. This is when the narrator, you have surely noticed, recalls the lines on 'virtue and knowledge'. The context provides a new meaning to them. It is as if I heard them for the first time, Levi says (it is the same for us, those who are reading together now, isn't it?); they apply, he says, to all human beings in travail, to those who from the depth of unthinkable hardships still dare to exercise the non-brutish part of themselves: virtue and knowledge. It is a tremendous statement. I would not fully believe it, were it not coming from Levi, otherwise the most sober of writers, not one to give into the flattery of rhetoric.

The second time your voice broke, in a more intimate way perhaps, is when Dante's ominous dusky mountain becomes dusk itself and the mountains of Levi's youth appear in the distance. The memory is too painful, though. Say something, Pikolo! Don't let me think about the mountains. Pikolo is silent. The lacuna is widening.

I know those mountains well. My mother — a few years younger than Levi — grew up near the same mountains. They were a sporty lot, my mum and her friends: hiking, swimming in crispy cold lakes, skiing on rudimentary runs in winter, and then climbing back with sealskins. Italian youths, some of them Jews like Levi, skipping through life until those mountains became the main site of partisan war, raids, and atrocities.

A passionate and implacable hiker, throughout the summer my mother would drag the family in long and unreasonably spartan walks. I have memories of blisters, fatigue, the random alpine flower, and the exhilarating tickle that comes from drinking from a mountain stream. It was not uncommon in those days to stop at a farmhouse in the mountains for lunch and share whatever the family living there were eating for just a little money.

Once, an old woman hosted us. Dressed in black, with heavy tights and black slippers, a washed-out black apron, and a grey kerchief on her head, she had two vertical wrinkles next to her mouth, and impossibly small eyes. She spoke quietly, in the coarse dialect of the area. After lunch — polenta and ragout; I still have the sweet taste of maize and the acrid sting of game in some corner of my mouth, I still see the florid yellow mass on my plate with a ringlet of smoke, I still smell it. After lunch, she became restless and insisted that she needed to show us something. She brought us to the yard and pointed to the place where her son, aged eighteen, had been killed by the Nazis as a suspected partisan. Here. They shot him. Nothing else I know of that young man. His age, the grief of his mother, and the corner of the forever sunny barnyard where he was killed.

Lo, I said something.

Levi's last moment of intuition — about destiny, about the Lager. About god, perhaps? — is washed away by the liquid reality of the dirty, Babelic soup that he and Jean are about to fetch. Like Dante's Ulisse, Levi is about to get somewhere, but is interrupted by the violent wave of the now.

Very much like the original canto of *Inferno*, our response to Levi's 'canto' is forever buried under 'the sea that closes over us'. In the monumental silence of Levi's suicide almost forty years later. Is the reading of Dante a form of consolation or desolation? Does it tear apart the oppressive plot of Auschwitz or is it part of it? Does a poem, can a poem ever restore, or does it merely register?

'Infin che 'l mar fu sovra noi richiuso.'

Like Dante, Levi is a core author of the curriculum I currently teach. Neatly (I think), *If This is a Man* is the first text we teach all students in their first year, and Dante's *Comedy* the last in their final year. It is hard to describe how extraordinary, how dramatic it is to meet bright young minds, mostly clean slates insofar as literature is concerned and with a vague but often ardent sense of the history of the twentieth century, over a book like Levi's. A text that defies genres; so calm, crisp, and clean it is as it recounts unfathomable horrors; so honest in the appraisal of human vice and virtue; so beautifully written in a language that, at times, sounds terse as matter, and yet it is meek, unassuming. A text so profoundly human.

The 'Dantean echoes' and the chapter on Ulysses are perhaps the most difficult bits to explain to freshers, as Dante is for them a very vague sort-of-Christian, dark-agey type of poet. But I do not mind. I believe in the *longue durée* of our job as teachers: I cannot wait to see them again four years later, after they have studied Dante seriously, and to bring back Levi, like some kind of *coup de théâtre*, in the last lecture on *Inferno*.

Year in, year out, an issue becomes more and more burning. Memory is fading, survivors are dying. Soon there will be no more eyewitnesses of the Shoah. Things have changed even in the ten years during which I have taught this particular curriculum. I find myself in a room with students for whom the Shoah is history — not a burning stain on their very moral makeup, like it was for us, people of the past century, irrespective of our provenance. Victims, and perpetrators, of the Shoah were of the generations of my grandparents, and even of my parents. Some of the dead and survivors were younger than my father and mother. I, born some twenty-five years after the end of the war, carry still, like many of my generation, a mark, an unspoken and little understood fear deriving from that past, a quiet astonishment, a frail moral imperative, and some vague but inescapable responsibility towards it.

In first-year seminars, the students are asked to give short presentations on various aspects of the author and the text we are reading. We often begin, predictably, with the easy, often sadly wikipedish, presentation on 'life-and-works'. Not so long ago, a student began the usual rigmarole

[With one part of the brain, I listen and make sure that dates and data compute, with the other, I mentally scroll the shopping list. So now you know: my other form of solace is the online supermarket. Plutarch, and Ocado. And Revery. An oddly sitting triad, I must say. (The revery alone makes do.)]

'Primo Levi was born in such-and-such year, graduated from that high school, studied chemistry at the renowned university of dot-dot-dot. In October doubledigit-doubledigit, Levi joined the partisan resistance in the Alps, and shortly after he was arrested, and, upon declaring himself a Jew, was first brought to an internment camp in Italy and then …, then to … I don't quite know how to pronounce this … Ausc…pitz?'

Something had rung me out of my lull. Unguarded, I had a fit of rage, instantly repressed and substituted by the remorse of having felt angry at an unknowing young thing. The two forces cancelled each other into a nonchalant aside

… Au·schwits … please go on …

A sacrilege. A curse: that's what I had just heard. Someone forgive them, for they know not what they are doing.

I am still angry (and still feel guilty). Angry that the sky did not come tumbling down; that nobody was disturbed but me, not even the Jewish student in the seminar; that it was a trifle about foreign pronunciation, like, say, how do you pronounce Leipzig, or Beckenbauer. That I could not walk out in silence and leave the group to wonder why I did that (these days, it would not be deemed acceptable pedagogy. I might be suspended from my job, a committee would be created, and then a subcommittee, and then the sub-committee [with hyphen] of the subcommittee to investigate my actions). That I could not quietly say: 'Let's call it a lesson. See you on the other side of history.' Hear me out — I am not angry at the student, or at 'young people' or at 'current times'. I myself surely mispronounce Auschwitz; I mispronounce everything. But Auschwitz is not a word for me, not even a place. Auschwitz is a sound that raises the hair on my skin, it is a brand of fire into my 'human' soul, it is something that I contemplate in a haze of fear, and that forever casts a shade of trauma, doubt, and estrangement in all my thought processes. Like small black birds caught in a mad, senseless flight, other words dive and disappear into it

καλός καὶ ἀγαθός, democracy, *virtus*, *pietas*, *culpa*, canoscenza, redemption, *cogito*, monad, progress, capital, psyche

What I had witnessed then, in a quiet autumn day in Oxford, the light already dimming into the mid-afternoon, a gentle, not unpleasant drizzle glistening in the arch of the window, was that word losing all its dimension, and becoming print on paper.

The wave of history closing over us.

Do you want to hear my coup in the last lecture on *Inferno*?

The last day of term. Usually a bleak winter day, say 3 or 5 December, with an air of Christmas though; mince pies will be served for the admin staff in this very stuffy room sometime this afternoon, non-denominational decorations hanging and not yet dangling. In the last lecture of the term, we look at the bottom of hell, 'il fondo'.

Dante-poet (remember him?) feels the need for a new proem to account for the enormity to come:

> S'ïo avessi le rime aspre e chiocce,
> come si converrebbe al tristo buco
> sovra 'l qual pontan tutte l'altre rocce,
> io premerei di mio concetto il suco
> più pienamente; ma perch'io non l'abbo,
> non sanza tema a dicer mi conduco;
> ché non è impresa da pigliare a gabbo
> discriver fondo a tutto l'universo,
> né da lingua che chiami mamma o babbo.
> Ma quelle donne aiutino il mio verso
> ch'aiutaro Anfïone a chiuder Tebe,
> sì che dal fatto il dir non sia diverso.
> (*Inferno* 32, 1–12)

> If I had harsh and grating rhymes, as would befit the dismal hole on which all the other rocks converge and weigh, I would press out more fully the juice of my conception; but since I do not have them, it is not without fear that I bring myself to speak; for to describe the bottom of the whole universe is not an enterprise to be taken up in sport, nor for a tongue that cries mamma and daddy. But may those ladies aid my verse who aided Amphion to wall in Thebes, so that the telling may not be diverse from the fact.

There is some horrible solemnity in Cocytus, the bottom of hell, a majestic four-zonal realm made of ice, because the sin punished there, treason (in modern terms: hate), freezes the human heart. Ineffability turns into despair, fear conquers language, the Muses, once benign divinities, are now invoked as those who razed Thebes to the ground (remember Thebes?). A new poetry, rough and hoarse, must describe 'il fondo', a depth that the poet needs to contemplate with no other tool than his young, messy, vulnerable mother tongue, the 'language that cries mummy and daddy'. Incidentally, the same thing will happen on the stage of the vision of god, where the poet feels like 'an infant who still bathes his tongue at the breast' (fante | che bagni ancor la lingua alla mammella; *Paradiso* 33, 107–08).

The poet finds, however, harsh and grating rhymes within his inept yet potent maternal language: the whole canto 32 of *Inferno* is a virtuoso exploit of metrics and poetics, with a clash of rasping rhymes (-icchi, -ogna, -accia, -isto, -etti, -olli, -ecchi, -azzi, -ezzo, -una), biting comic language, and images that read like hallucinations. Listen to a couple of examples.

Witness the infernal glacier, more desolate than the desolate north, a perfect realm of ice, whose very silence encircles an ominous creak, and the vertigo of a mountain falling on your head. Perfect stasis and mayhem side by side, articulated by the ugly, aggressive rhyme '-icchi'.

> Non fece al corso suo sì grosso velo
> di verno la Danoia in Osterlicchi,
> né Tanaï là sotto 'l freddo cielo,
> com'era quivi; che se Tambernicchi
> vi fosse sù caduto, o Pietrapana,
> non avria pur da l'orlo fatto cricchi.
> (*Inferno* 32, 25–30)

> Never did the Danube in Austria, nor the far-off Don under its cold sky, make in winter such thick a veil for their current as there was here: for had Tambernic fallen on it, or Pietrapana [= had two mountains fallen on it], it would not have given a creak even at the edge.

The damned are stuck and frozen in this icy wasteland; the only sound, the shrieking of their teeth: -agna, -ogna, -accia.

> E come a gracidar si sta la rana
> col muso fuor de l'acqua, quando sogna
> di spigolar sovente la villana,

> livide, insin là dove appar vergogna
> eran l'ombre dolenti ne la ghiaccia,
> mettendo i denti in nota di cicogna.
> (*Inferno* 32, 31–36)

> And as the frog lies to croak with muzzle out of the water, when the peasant girl dreams often of her gleaning so, livid up there where the hue of shame appears, were the doleful shades within the ice, setting their teeth to the note of the stork.

Don't let yourself be fooled by the bucolic touch of 'the little peasant girl' — it is the translator who just could not take it in. This is an image of bleak poverty, and even exploitation: a poor peasant woman who is having dreams about collecting from the field the leftovers from the harvest, perhaps her family's only source of livelihood. This was a backbreaking and unrewarding job, done mostly by women and girls until not so long ago. I don't think she dreams: she has nightmares. In this image, there is also a striking conflation of the peak of summer (the season of the harvest and of creaking frogs) and the eternal otherworldly winter. Why is that? Why am I thinking of a winter frog? Nightmares are a-seasonal, it seems.

The revolting faces of the damned are of a creepy colour: 'cagnazzo'; a rare, and violent, adjective that retains something of a rabid dog ('cane') and describes the nuance of a livid shade, somewhere between green, blue, purple, reddish, and black (murray and morello are approximations). The rhyme is unforgiving: -azzi; -ezzo; -azzi.

> Poscia vid'io mille visi cagnazzi
> fatti per freddo; onde mi vien riprezzo,
> e verrà sempre, de' gelati guazzi.
> (*Inferno* 32, 70–72)

> After that I saw a thousand faces made purple by the cold, whence a shuddering comes over me, and always will, at frozen fords.

The surface of the iced lake smooth as glass; the damned, still full of hate, rebuke the traveller: 'perché cotanto in noi ti specchi?' (Why do you gaze so much on us?; *Inferno* 32, 54. Again, the translator folds, and I don't blame him: 'specchio' is a mirror; and 'specchiarsi' means to look in the mirror of something). Why do you mirror yourself in us? Why do I see myself in the mirror of you? The answer is necessarily shattered, mangled, cried out in the ruthless, desperate sound of rhyme: -ecchi; -(i)ùe; -ina, -ombra; -ina; -ù; -oni; -azzi; -ezzo; -(a)una; -este; -etta; -ui; -etta; -ora; -ota ... -omi; -occa; -onta; ... -uca; ... -ecca; ... -angi ... 'se quella con ch'io parlo non si secca' (if that [tongue] with which I speak does not dry up): this is the final line of canto 32 (139).

In this utter desolation we hear by far the most horrible story of hell and beyond. The Pisan Count Ugolino della Gheradesca, gnawing the skull of his enemy, the archbishop Ruggieri, tells how he and his children and grandchildren were locked up by Ruggieri in a tower and then left to starve. How the boys were trying to comfort him, while he was petrified inside, unable to talk. How they even offered themselves as food to him. How he saw them falling one by one, and how, made blind and feeble by consumption, he groped over them crying out their names, and how, eventually, 'fasting overcame grief' ('più che il dolor potè 'l digiuno'; 32, 75) ... you know how the story goes: the legend of Ugolino eating his children has circulated since the middle ages. While I speak, I have in the background this picture, given to me by a student in the first ever Dante class I taught. The detail of Ugolino's wrung, knotty, gnarled foot in Jean-Baptiste Carpeaux's *Ugolino and his Sons* (*c.* 1865), now at the Metropolitan Museum in New York (Figure 1).

This is, and is not, about eating his children, I explain. It is about the unspeakable — call it cannibalism, or Eu-

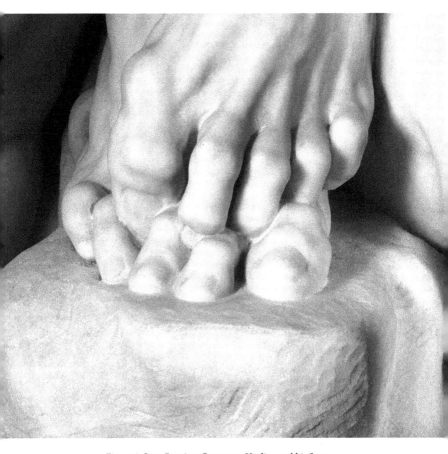

Figure 1. Jean-Baptiste Carpeaux, *Ugolino and his Sons* (detail).

charist, call it what you want. Dante shows us that the ineffable (Eucharist, 'eat my flesh') was once unspeakable (cannibalism). Already a lot to chew on.

The unspeakable, incidentally, is tucked away, indeed 'lost in translation'. At the outset of Ugolino's speech there is a fairly visible quote from Virgil's *Aeneid*. Ugolino begins:

'Tu vuo' ch'io rinovelli | disperato dolor' (you want me to renew a desperate pain; *Inferno* 33, 4–5; my translation). Asked to tell the story of the fall of Troy, Aeneas begins: 'infandum [...] iubes renovare dolorem' (you ask me to renew an unspeakable pain; *Aeneid* 2, 3; my translation). Eliminating the *infandum* (that which cannot be talked about, the inenarrable, even the unthinkable), Dante emphasizes its annihilating powers. He says: here, reader, you will witness something more unspeakable than the unspeakable. The taboo. You will be alone with it.

But now — let us close the books, let us leave behind Cocytus and the shell of hell. Let us step back into the space of this lecture room, into this winter, bleak and yet not unconceivable, the motors of the tourist buses on St Giles sputtering some unpleasant noise, the grating rhymes of our everyday life. Let us look at each other, mirror into each other's eyes.

Feeling for a moment as charismatic, screwed up, and punchy as Coleman Silk, I venture into a sweeping tirade. (I am, in reality, a very sober mother of two in her fifties; with a soft voice, very little human stain, I am proud to say, zero *physique du role*, and not the caustic type.)

What is the real unspeakable, then? Well, it is really unspeakable, isn't it? It is the sum of things that makes up hate, which leads to the killing of innocent children (everyday-today-now) and to the despair that petrifies a father and makes him hate and hate and hate. The unspeakable is us, the troubling nature of the human being. The great modernity of Dante, what makes us read the *Inferno* over and over again, is the profound intuition that sets Dante apart from any other medieval writer: that real hell is not the infernal ditch, monsters and demons, sin and punishment. Hell is us. As we read, we fell in love with the beautiful, and often fragile, creatures that populate Dante's *Inferno*. We looked at ourselves in the mirror of their passions, their obsessions, their addictions — to love, friendship, fame, competition, politics, desire, greed, deception, envy, and hate. Other characters we liked less, they kept us on our toes, but still we mirrored ourselves in them. Others, we disliked, but with the repulsion that sometimes we feel towards our fellow humans.

Remember Primo Levi from your first year? Remember the chapter on the arrival in the Lager. Can anybody recall the title of that chapter? It was called, dantesquely, 'Sul fondo' (On the Bottom) ...

> Quando abbiamo finito, ciascuno è rimasto nel suo angolo, e non abbiamo osato levare gli occhi l'uno sull'altro. Non c'è ove *specchiarsi*, ma il nostro aspetto ci sta dinanzi, riflesso *in cento visi lividi*, in cento *pupazzi* miserabili e sordidi [...].
>
> Allora per la prima volta ci siamo accorti che la nostra lingua manca di parole per esprimere questa offesa, la demolizione di un uomo. In un attimo, con intuizione quasi profetica, la realtà ci si è rivelata: siamo arrivati sul fondo (emphasis mine).

> When we finish, everyone remains in his own corner and we do not dare lift our eyes to look at one another. There is nowhere to look in a mirror, but our appearance stands in front of us, reflected in a hundred livid faces, in a hundred miserable and sordid puppets [...].
>
> Then for the first time we became aware that our language lacks words to express this offence, the demolition of a *human being*. In a moment, with almost prophetic intuition, the reality was revealed to us: we have reached the bottom.

There is no mirror in the antechamber of the Lager, but there is mirroring ('why do you mirror yourself in us?') of a hundred faces ('cento visi'; they were a thousand, 'mille visi' in Dante), 'livid', like Dante's damned infixed in the ice. They are 'pup-AZZI' (puppets): the most stunning stint of poetic memory, recalling the harsh rime '-azzi' and the thousand faces made purple by the cold ('mille visi cagnazzi').

I am sure you do remember what Levi said about language: it was one of the first-year essay titles, often recurring in exams, so we made sure we had all the good quotes at hand. I often asked you to memorize this one. [Yep ... at Oxford, students still handwrite their closed-book exams, so we do actually instruct them to memorize quotes. It is half institutional pretentiousness and half institutional ineptitude, but if it fosters one poetic memory in a thousand years, I will still abide by it.]*

> Noi diciamo 'fame', diciamo 'stanchezza', 'paura', e 'dolore', diciamo 'inverno', e sono altre cose. Sono parole libere, create e usate da uomini liberi che vivevano, godendo e soffrendo, nelle loro case. Se i Lager fossero durati più a lungo, *un nuovo aspro linguaggio* sarebbe nato (emphasis mine).

> We say 'hunger', we say 'tiredness', 'fear', 'pain', we say 'winter' and they are different things. They are free words, created and used by free *people* who lived in comfort and suffering in their homes. If the Lagers had lasted longer a new, harsh language would have been born.

You see where Dante's 'harsh ('aspre') and grating rhymes' are heading. Actually, you see where they come from.

Remember the poem that serves as an epigraph to Levi's book? In our first year we wondered about it — it

---

*   As I give the last touches to the manuscript (funny we still call it this), I hear that most likely the pandemic has liquidated the closed-book, handwritten exam. A sigh of relief: goodbye illegible handwriting and ludicrous memory blunders; welcome cut and paste. A sigh of sadness at the bulldozer of normalization tearing down the niche of strangeness.

is the only time when Levi's tone is accusatory. You may not remember the image of the frog in there. It describes a woman crouching in the winter cold. But now, as you read, you see that it is a spectre from Dante's Cocytus. In Levi's poetic memory, the woman and the frog collapse onto each other and are placed in the cold winter of the Lager. So, it *was* a nightmare. A Kafkaesque one, for that matter. Dante's 'little peasant girl' was actually dreaming of being turned into a frog and feeling cold, and cold, and colder.

> Voi che vivete sicuri
> Nelle vostre tiepide case,
> Voi che trovate tornando a sera
> Il cibo caldo e visi amici:
>> Considerate se questo è un uomo
>> Che lavora nel fango
>> Che non conosce pace
>> Che lotta per mezzo pane
>> Che muore per un sì o per un no.
>> Considerate se questa è una donna,
>> Senza capelli e senza nome
>> Senza più forza di ricordare
>> Vuoti gli occhi e freddo il grembo
>> Come una rana d'inverno.
> Meditate che questo è stato:
> Vi comando queste parole.
> Scolpitele nel vostro cuore
> Stando in casa e andando per via,
> Coricandovi alzandovi;
> Ripetetele ai vostri figli.
>> O vi si sfaccia la casa,
>> La malattia vi impedisca,
>> I vostri nati torcano il viso da voi.

> You who live safe
> In your warm houses,
> You who find, returning in the evening,
> Hot food and friendly faces:
>> Consider if this is a man
>> Who works in the mud

> Who does not know peace
> Who fights for a scrap of bread
> Who dies for a yes or a no.
> Consider if this is a woman,
> Without hair and without name
> With no more strength to remember,
> Her eyes empty and her womb cold
> Like a frog in winter.
> Meditate that this came about
> I commend these words to you.
> Carve them in your hearts
> At home, in the street,
> Going to bed, rising;
> Repeat them to your children,
> > Or may your house fall apart,
> > May illness impede you,
> > May your children turn their faces from you.

We love survivors, don't we? Until they point the finger at us. We love poetic memories, until they dig like ice axes in our frozen hearts.

Having managed to chill the young things for a moment, I add, sadistically … With this, I wish you a merry Christmas, then … enjoy the holidays. Let us call it a term, see you on the other side of the vac.

Silence then falls momentarily in the lecture room and engulfs us all, even the buses on St Giles, even the next class humming outside. We look at each other, confused, anxious, suspended, inquisitive. That fraction of time — thirty seconds, perhaps before the noise of a chair pushed back or the ruffle of paper being stuffed in the packsack announces officially that the lecture is over — is a teacher's best reward. It answers the question 'why do we mirror into each other?', or even 'what is it to be human?'.

4. '... And Maybe Sometime'

If Dante were writing today, I am pretty sure that he would fit somewhere in his story Lawrence Oates's last words before he stepped barefoot outside of his tent to meet his death in the Antarctic blizzard.

'I am just going outside' ... if we can strip it — and I do appreciate it is hard — of layer after layer of veneer of gentleman-ness, educated-ness, stiffupperlip-ness, soldiering-on-ness, memorable-ness, and reported-ness (not to mention the class, colonial, and masculine sense of superiority that might be churned all over such -nesses [now this is an upper-class white man talkin'!]), Oates's last words strike us as pure madman-ness. Or, rather, the point where bodily exhaustion, in this case hypothermia, becomes some sort of mysticism. These words are rhetoric defying itself. The long journey of Ulisse's speech comes to an end a few metres outside a tent in Antarctica, where a small company of young men, having failed their goal of reaching the South Pole, exhausted, bitten by frostbite, devoured by hunger, were sputtering the last gags of their unwillingly anti-heroic story and writing unintentional poetry.*

'I am shitting my pants' — this is what the common person would probably say.

Navigators, explorers, cosmonauts, they are all wrapped up in the myth and rhetoric of Ulysses, which derives from a strange combination of the Homeric and the Dantean: modern Ulysseses do not repudiate Ithaca, but they are also attracted to the unknown. *Ex halòs*: they may or may not die out there; they may, or may not, come back.

Starting with Columbus's voyage, several enterprises of exploration by sea, land, and even space have been troped with aspects of the story of a navigation turned flight turned plunge. And here is my own (I, as the antihero par excellence) mean little smirk at heroes: when I learned that cosmonauts need to wear nappies in space. But look at it another way, this tells us that there is a proper, heroic way of shitting one's pants.

Bruno Nardi, a great Italian scholar of the early twentieth century, concluded his essay aptly entitled 'The Tragedy of Ulysses' ('La tragedia di Ulisse', 1937) with the grand statement that Dante had 'discovered the discoverer' — and by means of words alone, I would add. However, such a discoverer is a wishful, even pathetic figure, a bit like Plato's philosopher king.

---

* One Ulysses from the literary tradition does indeed die in Antarctica. Kazantzakis's Odysseus, the protagonist of the mastodontic rewriting-continuation of the *Odyssey* in 33.333 verses, eventually fulfils Tiresias's prophecy, lacrosse stick and all, as well as Dante's journey in the southern hemisphere, and dies both away and near the sea, on an iceberg. Here too we read a defeat of rhetoric and story, but of a very different kind. Kazantzakis's Odysseus dissolves (under the pressure of too many words, I think).

Dante's philosopher-discoverer is powered by a simple yet potent rhetoric: ardour, experience, the world, vice and virtue, brutes vs humans, virtue and knowledge, flight and navigation, a touch of folly. Some of these words are revolving doors: enter 'ardore' (burning desire), exit 'ardimento' (daring, courage, with a slight aggressive tinge), enter 'vice-and-virtue', exit 'sin-and-salvation', enter 'brutes vs humans', exit 'them vs us'. Virtue might be taken for privilege (the entitlement that the old *vir* had over the moral ground), knowledge as knowing better. Sputtering and crackling, the modern machine begins to whir.

Before coming to a halt outside that tent in Antarctica, and to shipwrecks more tragic than the blizzard that killed those young men, the Ulyssean rhetoric journeys and journeys, coils and uncoils for centuries over sea and land. It marches and marches, it measures, opens, destroys, and builds. It explores, invents, discovers, progresses, achieves; it marches and marches, one millimetre ahead of every expedition, of every experiment, like an invisible, insolent little banner. It casts a shade, but we refuse to see it. We refuse to accept that the discoverer is a tragic figure.

Here enters the other word from Ulysses' speech — 'esperienza', experience: to do it and see it for yourself. To know first-hand. To have been there. To put to a test, to experiment, to get one's hands dirty. *Ex-perior*: '*to try, to prove, to test'*, recites the dictionary going quasi-Tennysonian. [I wish the dictionary form ended with a resounding *and not to yield* but it closes with a rather sharp and just a tad unmetrical '*to endure*'.] Similar but not cognate to *per-ire* (to get lost, to lose oneself, to disappear, to die), this verb carries the mark of trespassing and a speck of death. To be experienced and to perish is the same thing in some corner of the self and of the world. To live experientially one's life is 'a race to death' ('correre alla morte';

Purgatorio 33, 54), as Dante puts it somewhere else in his poem.

Ulisse, remember, mentioned 'esperienza' twice, and now that we think of it, in a rather contradictory way. First, to explain why he did not want to go or stay back home: 'they' (island, father, son, wife) were not enough to quench the ardour he had to become expert of the world and of human vice and worth ('del mondo esperto | e de li vizi umani e del valore'; *Inferno* 26, 98–99). Places and people, geography and ethics; this ancient tourist, we thought, is somewhat familiar to us. The second time experience is mentioned within the 'small oration', however, the stakes are higher. Now Ulysses seeks the ultimate place and no people; an extreme, a-moral, metaphysical geography: the experience of the other side of the sun, the unpopulated world ('non vogliate negar l'esperïenza, | di retro al sol, del mondo sanza gente'; 116–17). 'Do not deny the experience': double negation is our hero's favourite rhetorical tool. Ulisse affirms himself by saying no to the rest, by opposing objections.

THE REBORN

Come the Renaissance (with that absurd name), and Ulisse's profound nihilism is gone. The shell of hell is gone, gone is the vortex at the edge of the world, gone the ontological solitude. Adieu stillness, silence, immensity; suddenly there is a whole circus past Hercules' pillars. The basics of Dante's Ulysses — leaving the familiar behind, voyage, exploration, a vast unknown area, Eden, and folly — interlace in often predictable, and sometimes risible ways in the future stories. Come the Renaissance, and the story of Ulisse is turned into a strange reality, while the spiritual gravity of Dante's character is lost. His loss is lost. In its stead, a violence called glory finds place in the narrative. As we read it from the point of view of the modern era, we realize how profoundly pacifist the story of Dante's Ulysses is. He is not at war either with people or with nature. Not even with the divinity, whose angry retaliation he accepts rather stoically if with a hint of scorn ('com'altrui piacque', as pleased someone else, he says of the vortex sinking his ship [if only Dante had heard of 'and may be sometime' ...]). There is no conquering, penetrating, taming; no reward, no celebration, no triumph waiting for them back at home or, worse, in heaven.

Throughout the so-called modern era, as the dark mountain in the lonely hemisphere becomes a sequence of lands that actually exist, as expedition after expedition 'discovers' them, and the cartographer's millimetres press upon the sailor's nautical leagues, one after the other after the other, leaders and their small crew set sail towards mad enterprises, becoming new Ulisses, breaking open boundaries, upholding noble ideals and giving short inspired speeches (or so their chroniclers say), some dying, others finding new worlds that are beautiful, plentiful, and dangerous (the comparison is often with a young 'exotic' female), coming back with full loads of goods. We know the story; we are all children and victims of that mad flight.

The story of exploration and discovery becomes citational. A narrative of forwardness, daring, and breaking boundaries is pounded and pounded and pounded like a hammer, until you believe it is true. Snippets, and fragments, and splinters of Ulysses inhabit it, like glass shards under our nails. The involuntary Mediterranean tourist, the sombre philosopher-voyager become the Explorer and are thrown into a story of conquest called discovery, of greed called civilization, of a disaster called glory. A story that is also unavoidable. Our history.

I know I know I know ... there is a saving grace in iteration. Identity comes with alterity, originality with forgery. There are small differences and cracks, there is parody, there is resistance, there are ways of retelling the same story backwards, inside out, from bottom to top and top to bottom, in another genre, with another tone, in someone else's voice, but it does remain the same story, and oftentimes it does become reactionary. Take Camões for instance, the proper poet-discoverer. What do we make of the colonial *Odyssey*, complete with pagan and Christian deities? It is not unproblematic to handle the variety and brutality of the *Lusíads*, the tale of Portuguese expansion in the sixteenth century, and to reconcile the curiosity of an Odysseus-like poet with the destructive and self-destructive drive of the empire he represents.

Or witness this other mutation of the old tale. In one of the editions of Abraham Ortelius's *Theatrum Orbis Terrarum* (Theatre of the World; first printed in Antwerp in 1570), one of Magellan's ships, the Victoria, crops up just past the Tropic of Capricorn (Figure 2).

Victoria says: 'I was the first to go around the world with winged courses, led by you, o Magellan, through the new strait. I circled the world, and rightly I am called Victoria: my sails are wings; my prize (or: reward), the glory; my battle, the sea.' (Prima ego velivolis ambivi cursibus Orbem, | Magellane novo te duce ducta freto. | Ambivi, meritoque vocor Victoria: sunt mî | Vela, alæ; precium, gloria; pugna, mare.)

Although rather uncomplicated, this compound of words and image can be read as part of the Renaissance fascination with the making of meaning. The sails are wings, an image as trite as it is intuitive, and yet in it we catch still a relic, I believe, of Dante's oars as wings in the mad flight (so much more beautiful, now that we can pause and think

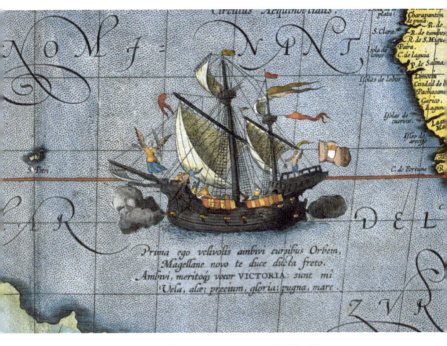

Figure 2. Ortelius, *Descriptio Maris Pacifici* (detail).

of it). The new strait through which Victoria flies implies the old (Gibraltar). Magellan is a barely disguised new Ulisse. (Again, Dante's light touch is soothing. His Ulysses is no commander, no leader, no *dux*.) Here the winged sails support the flight of ambition (the Latin verb *ambire* meaning both 'to go round', hence 'circumnavigate', and 'to strive', 'aspire'). They are paired with the winged woman — 'victory' being traditionally represented as such. The battle of? against? the sea is rather visibly inscribed by the two cannons firing from the back and from the front into the sea itself. So this is actually aggressive. But then we get to the most elusive point of all:

Precium, gloria
my reward is glory

Now, glory was not a name that Dante's Ulisse would employ. For only this once, I am thankful to the Christian background in which Dante's story is written for reserving glory to god and the blessed, and using it sparingly for other earthly matters, often more for literary and artistic endeavours than for military ones. Ulisse and his men are out not in the pursuit of glory, but of 'virtue and knowledge' — it is for themselves, not for others. [Hold on, though, we will find some glorious sailors later.]

What is mundane glory to begin with? Success, I guess, is the modern translation of it. Success and fame. There is no glory if it is not sanctioned by other people. The strangest thing happens when I click on the word 'glory' (on the virtual page, that is) to find synonyms [I do that sometimes, you have already noticed it; like when you found 'haphazard' instead of 'random' and thought: c'mon, Elena, you can do better than that]. Well, this time even I am baffled: splendor-praise-grandeur-splendour[*sic*]-triumph is the short screen, and the long list … the long list is a perverse embroidery of 'magnificence', 'brilliance', 'exaltation', 'credit', 'stardom', 'laurels (dictionary form)' [as if dictionaries were the lamest thing you can possibly consult], 'glorification', 'resplendence', 'aura', 'nimbus', and 'gloriole' [which I had to look up yet again]. A rhetoric of light (well that one has to do with Christians and the radiant status of the saints and god), sparkles, and aggression runs through the longlist, and yet it does not explain what glory is, and how we tell ourselves the tale of glory. A heavily gilt mirror, 'glory' always reflects meaning away.

What dazzles me in the glorious Renaissance tale of exploration and conquest is the strange way in which history and story prop each other up. How the age of conquest is also the age of utopia, how knowing more creates more fiction rather than more rationality. Ahead of the banner of glory there flies the little bird of the absurd. Thus, the no longer great unknown keeps on being punctuated by anecdotes, legends, and wonders; by dangers, irrational places, and nonsensical people. Some absurdity is Homeric — monsters, giants, strange sea-creatures — but some of it is Dantean, or Christian (Danteo-Christian, how is that?). Eden, which Dante placed at the top of the ominous mountain of Purgatory, still looms large in the early travels.

Journey after journey, the homeless, stateless, languageless Cristoforo Colombo, Cristóbal Colón, Cristopher Columbus became more and more despotic and delusional. While convulsively looking for a trade route to the East, he was blabbering about discovering Eden. He became convinced that he was a prophet, the bearer of Christ, as his first name indicated, or the winged drive of the soul, as his last name implied. [Now, the feminine *columba* does refer to the dove to which the soul is often compared, but *columbus*, let us be frank, is a common pigeon. As much as I loathe pigeons — an endemic presence in my hometown, Milano — I also think they are the sole antidote to monumentalism of all kinds. A statue is never safe, never immune from irony and dissent, never martial, or virile, or assertive as long as there is a pigeon around ... pigeons, I think, and, perhaps, the routine reading of Aristophanes' *Birds* are enough to defy the stone-carved assertion of glory.]

Speaking of birds, even the worldly and sharp-witted Antonio Pigafetta, the chronicler of Magellan's voyage, supernumerary sailor of the Victoria, and one of the few survivors of that rather disastrous expedition, did not blink when he was presented with the skins of two 'birds of paradise', a species, he was told, coming from Eden itself — so soft and feathery they were, so elegant, just ever so slightly unnatural. They had no wings, according to Pigafetta, only feathers, whereas in other versions of the legend this popular bird had no feet and was, therefore, in perennial flight: like the angels, or the soul. It didn't bother him or other travellers and naturalists of the time that these birds were never seen alive. Maybe it is the fate of imagination, to take flight from carcasses.

It doesn't take much to make Eden, does it? It is a sensible, palpable, tasteable place. It is something we have seen before somewhere, sometimes (the proliferation of some+ having to do with indetermination, not my lousy writing). Perhaps a lovely spring day. [Today. 16/03/2021.] Eden is of this earth, on this earth, it is just a distance away from a semi-known land, it is even mappable. Medieval and early modern maps placed it variously in South Asia, Africa, Antarctica, or in the Atlantic, either on steep mountains or on islands. How did they know of its existence? Rivers flow from it, we are told in the book of Genesis, and they are firmly of this earth (Euphrates, Tigris, Nile, and Ganges were all said to originate in Eden). Eden (and all its cognate versions of a golden age, an impendent paradise, or a morally and geographically magical place) always means good weather, a satisfied digestive system, and time for play. Eden is very mild. A very simple ex-perience, with the inevitable shard of death. Feelin' good was easy, Lord.

Take for instance the Fortunate Isles that many geographers and historians since antiquity identified with the Canaries or other Atlantic islands. My hyper-rational Plutarch knows, and knows not, that earthly paradise is just a myth, but he is happy to embrace it. Plutarch relaxes in the description of two islands past the Strait of Gibraltar — he rarely does.

> Here he fell in with some sailors who had recently come back from the Atlantic Islands. These are two in number, separated by a very narrow strait; they are ten thousand furlongs distant from Africa, and are called the Islands of the Blest. They enjoy moderate rains at long intervals, and winds which for the most part are soft and precipitate dews, so that the islands not only have a rich soil which is excellent for plowing and planting, but also produce a natural fruit that is plentiful and wholesome enough to feed, without toil or trouble, a leisured folk. Moreover, an air that is salubrious, owing to the climate and the moderate changes in the seasons, prevails on the islands. For the north and east winds which blow out from our part of the world plunge into fathomless space, and, owing to the distance, dissipate themselves and lose their power before they reach the islands; while the south and west winds that envelope the islands from the sea sometimes bring in their train soft and intermittent showers, but for the most part cool them with moist breezes and gently nourish the soil. Therefore a firm belief has made its way, even to the Barbarians, that here is the Elysian Field and the abode of the blessed, of which Homer sang (*Life of Sertorius*, 8; translation by Bernadotte Perrin).

The 'he' in the story is Sertorius (*c.* 123–72 BCE), a Roman general ruling southern Spain during the troubled times of the civil war between Marius and Sulla. In a sort of Roman twist to Dante's Ulisse, Sertorius is, at one point, forced to cross Gibraltar by battling winds. This is when he hears about the Fortunate Isles. Plutarch imagines Sertorius's unspoken desire (see why I love him?):

> When Sertorius heard this tale, he was seized with an amazing desire to dwell in the islands and live in quiet, freed from tyranny and wars that would never end (*Sertorius*, 9).

I also want to go, says the writer between the lines. And me too. With you, Plutarch: where I feel no boredom, I forget all my troubles, I do not dread poverty, and I am not terrified by death.

What is Eden after all, if not the impossible match of innocence and abundance? Atlantis, Cocagne, Utopia; places where moralists can dream of a good society, and starving peasants of rivers of milk and mountains of cheese, and where these can be, illogically, the same thing.

The modern tragedy arises, I guess, when Eden is placed on the same maps that are used for travel, expansion, and trade: when you call it the Eden of another. Like the River of Gold in central Africa that was said to originate in Eden and was relentlessly pursued by travellers; or El Dorado, the golden king or kingdom in the heart of South America, the absurd goal of many early modern expeditions.

'Quid non mortalia pectora cogis, | auri sacra fames?' (O sacred hunger of gold, there is nothing you would not push a human heart to do; *Aeneid* 3, 56–57 [my attempt: the translation of these elegant lines is impossible, unless you find the verbal timbre of indignation]). Greed is hunger, the ancients thought, but of a fearful, nefarious, 'sacred' kind. Similarly, at the outset of Dante's *Hell*, greed, the worst challenge to the moral life, is represented as a scrawny she-wolf, 'laden with every craving' ('di tutte brame [...] carca'; *Inferno* 1, 49–50), who 'after feeding is hungrier than before' ('dopo il pasto ha più fame che pria'; 1, 99).

'Stay hungry!', the modern prophet demands.

'A boire! A boire! A boire!' (A drink!) exclaims the newborn giant Gargantua, Rabelais's comic impression of the new Renaissance self. The modern man [intended] is born thirsty, hungry, their un-sacred appetite never satisfied. They are affected by gigantism, megalomania, and enormous urges. Gargantua's son Pantagruel, bulimic and curious like his father, travels by land and sea through all utopias, religious, political, and otherwise, just to bring back the imperative 'trinch!' (*Gargantua*, chapter 7 and *Pantagruel*, book 5, chapter 44).

It is dizzying to think that Pico's *Oration* and *Gargantua* and *Pantagruel* were written some forty years apart. In between, the gaping, all-devouring new anthropocentric horizon, always at a distance, always within reach. Still, a profound love of learning binds the two works, with the difference that Rabelais had the philosophical intuition that the dignity of the human being was not a lofty and complicated thing — it is laughter, the sole explanation of what it is to be human ('rire est le propre de l'homme'; *Aux lecteurs*, 10).

THE REVENANT

Our solitary hero and his abstract, metaphysical navigation, however, make a rather spectral comeback on the other side of the Renaissance. As land upon land becomes known, as river after sea is navigated and turned into a route of commerce and travel, the 'unknown' becomes transcendent and ominous: an aggressive, tremendous force from beyond nature or from inside the human being that sinks boats and enterprises. Madness and hallucinations abound; utopia becomes dystopia; the Cocagne a wasteland; monsters are tucked away at the margins, in the abysses of the sea, in the soul-sucking grip of the great north or the icy south, in the thick of the jungle.

The margins ... One of the mysteries of my discipline, medieval studies, are the monsters in the margins of the manuscript page. Ludicrous, smirking, vulgar, often obscene creatures; un-related, unaccounted for, un-glossed. Yet glossing. They are not curiosities, they are not doodles — as Michael Camille, a famous art historian, demonstrated — but their relation to text and page, story and blankness is still mysterious. Likewise, the page of modern history is cut and lined by marginal monsters that laugh and scream at us. Calling them fictions does not help.

Later stories tell the tale of sailors who, often after a life well spent in the cogs of the modern machine (commerce, service, war), see some version of a terrifying divinity in the vortexes of the sea. The Ancient Mariner, Moby Dick, the Kraken. Captain Nemo: no-one, of course. There are one-(crazy)-man exploits, ragged small crews, small orations, straits and untravelled waters, sea monsters and angry 'an-others' lurking in the margins. Kurtz: blank maps, a heart of darkness along the river, and a disfiguring wound in the fold of the psyche. The Horror. We will all go mad! scream the artists of the nineteenth century as their peers destroy, pillage, and subjugate. We did all go mad; millions of lives lost in the abyss of greed-as-glory, the obscure heart of the twentieth century.

If I am allowed to lean history on story again (I am allowed, I am allowing myself), I will briefly pause on one nineteenth-century venture, whose mysterious end seems to be more gothic than any of the stories I have just mentioned.

Another icy wasteland, the Arctic this time, hides the secret of the Franklin expedition. I guess polar expeditions are the closest we get, in modern times, to the quasi-metaphysical journey of Dante's Ulisse in the 'world without people'. Immense loneliness, abstract landscape, creaking silence, blinding suns, and enduring night. In this setting, horrible and solemn like Dante's Cocytus, an imperial Ulysses meets Ugolino. It begins in 1845 with two ships, the *Erebus* and the *Terror*. Why, I wonder, would someone in their sane mind board a ship with that name? Erebus is the scariest of all terrifying ancient divinities, a darkness so unformed and unfathomable that it becomes a name for the underworld itself. Erebus, child of Chaos, incestuous sibling of Night, the sticky terror parent to us all. Listen to Hesiod:

> ἤτοι μὲν πρώτιστα Χάος γένετ'· αὐτὰρ ἔπειτα
> Γαῖ' εὐρύστερνος, πάντων ἕδος ἀσφαλὲς αἰεὶ
> ἀθανάτων οἳ ἔχουσι κάρη νιφόεντος Ὀλύμπου
> Τάρταρά τ' ἠερόεντα μυχῷ χθονὸς εὐρυοδείης,
> ἠδ' Ἔρος, ὃς κάλλιστος ἐν ἀθανάτοισι θεοῖσι,
> λυσιμελής, πάντων τε θεῶν πάντων τ' ἀνθρώπων
> δάμναται ἐν στήθεσσι νόον καὶ ἐπίφρονα βουλήν.
> ἐκ Χάεος δ' Ἔρεβός τε μέλαινά τε Νὺξ ἐγένοντο·
> Νυκτὸς δ' αὖτ' Αἰθήρ τε καὶ Ἡμέρη ἐξεγένοντο,
> οὓς τέκε κυσαμένη Ἐρέβει φιλότητι μιγεῖσα.
> (*Theogonia*, 116–25)

> In truth, first of all Chasm came to be, and then broad-breasted Earth, the ever immovable seat of all the immortals who possess snowy Olympus' peak and murky Tartarus in the depths of the broad-pathed earth, and Eros, who is the most beautiful among the immortal gods, the limb-melter — he overpowers the mind and the thoughtful counsel of all the gods and of all human beings in their breasts. From Chasm, Erebos and black Night came to be; and then Aether and Day came forth from Night, who conceived and bore them after mingling in love with Erebos (translation by Glenn W. Most).

When Odysseus cuts the sheep's throat open and collects the blood in the pit, 'there gathered from out of Erebus the ghosts of those that are dead, brides, and unwed youths, and toil-worn old men, and frisking girls with hearts still new to sorrow, and many, too, that had been wounded with bronze-tipped spears, men slain in battle, wearing their blood-stained armor' (*Odyssey* 11, 36; translation by A. T. Murray and George E. Dimock). Erebus is a word that crosses literature like a chilling tremor, a hair-raising accent. *Erebus* is *Terror*; yet off they sailed in search of the Northwest Passage.

In this story, there is a sentimental portrait of a Victorian lady waiting at home, although a faint crease in her smile reveals more volition than expected, and the curling spirals of smoke in the wood-panelled rooms of the British Admiralty; a wealth of sideburns; wine decanters and monkeys brought on board (see? the absurd is always one word ahead); and badly tinned canned food that later might have given some of the crew lead poisoning. Scurvy is sitting ghostly on the mast, grinning with decayed teeth and bloody gums. Anthropophagy hiding in the hull, sucking discreetly on a tibia. There is the immense blinding whiteness in which *Erebus* and *Terror* are stranded and a long, desperate march on ice. A lifeboat dragged ashore and on ground for a long time, containing useless goods (silken handkerchiefs, scented soaps, the absurd). Other expeditions looking for the lost ones; friendly Inuits reporting bits of news and returning reused objects, their versions of the story not trusted by search teams. Radars, sonars, autopsies, and hypotheses. And, to this day, no clear picture of how these men died.

Now that Erebus is conquering again the icy wasteland, and melting glaciers spin out frozen remains of explorers, now that the top of the Himalayas is full, I read, of hikers' shit and their rubbish, I have an entry for your reading list — Mordecai Richler's splendid rewriting of the Franklin story in *Solomon Gursky Was Here* (1989). One thread of the story follows Ephraim Gursky, a Jew whose family came to England from Russia on foot, as he becomes the sole survivor of the Franklin expedition and the founder of an Inuit-Jewish cult as well as of a rampant dynasty of tycoons. You can't stop reading, while epic falls to pieces all around you. Although hardly making the ecocriticism syllabus, it is an omnivorous, desecrating, diasporic, northern *Quixote* that buries forever the epic of exploration under glaciers of irony.

THE TRESPASSING

Dante's Ulisse is aware that he must not cross Gibraltar, that 'narrow outlet where Hercules set up his markers [or: placed the sign of limit], that *human beings* should not pass beyond' ('quella foce stretta | dov'Ercule segnò li suoi riguardi | acciò che l'uom più oltre non si metta'; *Inferno* 26, 107–09). His story is one of borders, limits, and trespassing.

The culture of the time of Dante was very ambivalent towards all such concepts, and some of them were not even engrained in it. National borders, for instance, did not exist, either on maps, in the way today we envision those thin black lines, or in the cultural imagination; yet cities and castles were heavily walled and regularly defended. Cultivated lands were painstakingly marked and bitterly argued upon, yet 'space' was a rather undifferentiated concept. Fortresses abounded, religious identities were great divides, whereas vernacular languages travelled quite freely along their paths, under the cover of the pan-European Latin. The concept of frontier was as enormous as it was vague — beyond it; the magic, the horror, the barbarians, Gog and Magog, lions and monsters, and the great blue unknown. The 'iron gates', said to be built by Alexander the Great to contain the 'barbarians' from the East, are the opposite of Hercules' pillars. 'No entrance' one gate says in the east; 'no exit' a pillar answers in the west. And please stand clear of the closing door, we are told with a suave voice by the modern monster. By all means; mind the gaps: you might fall into them and never be found again. [The Barbarians were allophones, incidentally. Bar-bar; this is how their language sounded to the Greeks. They probably did not read those signs.]

Boundaries and confinements were strict, and yet transgression was viewed as the nature of the human being. The story of Genesis is one of boundaries trespassed — adamant, naïve, and yet foundational — and it is not the only one. Disobedience, sometimes multiple, is the core of many ancient cultures; it seems to dwell at the heart and origin of what we call the human being. I wonder if these stories are traces of some kind of genetics; if disobedience is the cultural name for variation, the motor of evolution.

These days, I am quite fond of a fairly new science, 'genetic archaeology' — although I fear that in a couple of centuries it will look to posterity like eighteenth-century mesmerism appears to us. The scion of carbon dating, this science examines the DNA of ancient plants, animals, and humans to spin sometimes trenchant data on who we are. I feel this approach is rather rudimentary with respect to the sophistication, ambivalence, and subtlety that can be gathered from millennia of human culture, but revolutions are not gala dinners (said the one who put intellectuals to work the fields). As mesmerism shared some concerns with psychoanalysis, so maybe a new science will soon revolutionize our concept of what it is to be human.

I wonder if one day we will find out that the human being, the fast-evolving animal, is just an artful trespasser in the sphere of genetics; that what religions call free will is merely some chemical disobedience, which is both our curse and power.

Either way, the divinity is never happy about disobedience. He-She-They (as both plural and, hopefully, trans) punish the trespassers as a parent would do, taking privileges away (such as immortality, giant stature, common language, and all-you-can eat free buffet), or act like a faceless state, condemning the culprits to, well, 'life' (embodiment, hurting, labouring, ageing, dying). But also to being excited or frustrated (desiring, missing, longing, exercising, savouring).

If variation is disobedience, is evolution the punishment, I wonder?

'What is your favourite animal?'

When the oracular voices of little children ask me that question, I often become pensive. After the predictable cat and the inevitable dolphin (the only reason I mention it is because it is tattooed on my best friend's shoulder, but my questioners need not know), there is my really favourite animal. The Dodo.

Dodo ineptus: 'first they exterminated it, and then they called it inept', a friend of mine remarked in front of the stuffed model of the 'Oxford Dodo' at the Natural History Museum. Relaxed inhabitant of some Eden-like islands, Mauritius, the dodo was a kind of fat turkey, with rather clumsy wings and sloppy habits, like laying eggs on the ground. The legend of the dodo celebrates it as a special case in the story of evolution. It became rapidly extinct in the course of fifty years or so during the seventeenth century. When Portuguese and Dutch boats brought rats, pigs, and humans, it didn't bother to run, hide, or elevate its nest. It didn't adapt. It just let go.

Although surely modern biology has a good explanation for how this happened and normalizes the dodo into an overarching story of evolution and extinction (just don't call it providence), for environmental romantics like me, the dodo remains an exception. Exceptions do not confirm the rule. Exceptions defy the rule. That's why the dodo is my favourite animal — so ironic, so intelligent. Lazy and fatalist; I imagine it like Oblomov, looking with a warm and sad smile onto its own world disintegrating, at the future it did not want to live in.

Children also delight in asking impossible questions, such as 'would you rather be in a pool with sharks or in a room with lions?' To which I reply with my own oracular interrogation: 'would you rather be the last dodo or the trillionth cockroach?'

Dante is certainly ambivalent about the idea of trespassing and disobedience. Apart from Ulisse, he depicts a rather defiant portrait of the two delinquent forbearers. For instance, he consistently pairs Eve, the most maligned woman of all times, with Mary, she who 'undoes' Eve's sin, as a common medieval boustrophedon holds: AVE (hail) is the reverse of EVA (Eve). Mary and Eve are sitting together in Dante's heaven (*Paradiso* 32, 4–6). The whole point of Christianity is precisely this — there is no Mary without Eve, no Christ without Adam. No Christianity: hence the two trespassers are both loathed and needed. If, on the one hand, they lost for the whole humankind the joys of a truly hedonistic, and epidural, paradise on earth — nudity, fecundity, perennial springtime, youth, and no pain in childbirth — on the other, they have activated 'humanity' (as a composite of virtue, vice, and choice) and allowed a perennially locked-in divinity to unfold, to articulate, to enter into dialogue, to write itself in the narrative, to make itself flesh. *Felix culpa*; original sin is, on balance, a fortunate event. [Or so medieval preachers say. As for myself, I could have stayed in Mauritius with my dodo pet and my unashamed body for a while longer.]

Dante mentions Eve at the scene of her coup, in the earthly paradise that he imagines visiting on the top of purgatory, as an empowered woman; brave, independent, and rebellious. He seems almost to praise 'Eve's daring, that, there where earth and heaven were obedient, a woman, alone and but then formed, did not bear to remain under any veil' ('l'ardimento d'Eva, | che là dove ubidia la terra e 'l cielo, | femmina, sola e pur testé formata, | non sofferse di star sotto alcun velo'; *Purgatorio* 29, 24–27). Of course, he then says that she should have stayed under the veil (of ignorance, of the power of men over women, of chastity and modesty, as the main interpretations go), but with words that sound more like admiration than stigma.

In paradise, we encounter no less than the first man himself; Adam, the great transgressor, whom Dante celebrates rather triumphally and whose desire he importantly shapes in the same way as he does Ulisse's transgressive ardour. Adam's desire for the forbidden fruit is defined as the trespassing of a set limit ('il trapassar del *segno*'; going beyond the mark; *Paradiso* 26, 117), and recalls Ulysses' transgression of the geographical boundaries, the marked signs of the known world, posited by Hercules on the coasts of Spain and Africa ('*segnò* li suoi riguardi'; *Inferno* 26, 108; emphases mine). The trespassing of both Ulisse and Adam is impelled by their desire for the forbidden unknown.

The eschatology and the grandiosity of the story of Dante's Ulysses, the fact that he almost gets to access the mountain of purgatory and Eden, the abstractness, the literary elitism, the philosophical content, and the parallel with Adam: these all seem to be clues to a symbolic reading of this story of trespassing.

On my desktop there is always a folder named 'ideas'. I am one of those simple souls ('bless us') who are always full of ideas. Naïve, impracticable, foolish, haughty ideas. Inside an old computer that I can no longer turn on there must be, under that heading, a file with the title 'Ulysses/baptism of desire', and very little written in it. For a very short time I entertained the idea that I would convince my illustrious fellow Dante scholars that in the episode of Ulisse, Dante had inscribed an instance (and perhaps a criticism? Scholars like this kind of oscillation) of the so-called 'baptism of desire'.

Now, you might be happy to know that there are three ways to inceptive salvation for a Christian: first, the customary water; second, blood, when an unbaptized person goes through martyrdom for the faith and is automatically welcomed into it (bit gory, but a sure thing); and third, desire — if you really really really want it (and god agrees), you get it (dubious, but worth a try if you are not into blood, or water). With my back covered by authoritative authorities such as Augustine (*On Baptism Against the Donatists* 4, 22) and Aquinas (*Summa Theologica* III, 68.2), I thought I could prove a positive religious intention in the way Dante shapes his Ulisse (no longer interested in this), an optimistic reading of the modernity that Ulisse foreshadows (no longer sure about this), as well as the productive, powerful, all-driving, all-conquering, mad impetus of desire (in which I still faintly believe).

Ulisse almost got there by means of human desire alone. He gets to see the earthly paradise in the distance, for god's sake [no inflection or irony intended]. He almost manages to climb the lonely mount that Adam had left, and to re-establish us, the cheeky, cunning, curious, inadequate human beings, to the place that our foreparents had made deserted by reason of *hybris*. He was about to discover it, for god's (accented) sake! Desire *is* the human superpower. We are beautiful creatures of desire and language, I once believed. The repetitious 'almost' that mars Ulisse's achievements is nagging me, though. What went wrong? Not quite sure (and here my little idea sinks with Ulisse's boat next to the mountain). Perhaps (retrospective thought) he was too cocky too soon: 'Noi ci allegrammo' (we rejoiced; *Inferno* 26, 136). I guess if you are about to be granted the baptism of desire you should be a little more serious, humbler. What a drag.

It doesn't quite work, as you plainly see, but it is a charming little idea now shaking and throbbing frailly somewhere in the cold black hole where old computer data is stored. I cannot access it any longer, but if someone can, please pull the plug. Pull the plug on the happy arrogance of youth, on assumptions, presumptions, grand beliefs, and the ardent longing for the universe to make sense, for things to be whole. Journeys without anchorage are dead. Long live desire.

The academic re-emerges from the shipwreck of her little idea with another intuition. [Them academics! Always with another angle. They should try working in the fields.] If the baptism of desire hypothesis brings the symbolic reading of Ulisse to an untenable position, let us turn back to the sea, then, and consider what kind of geographic background a contemporary of Dante could apply to the navigation of Ulisse. In our reading we saw a Mediterranean cruise turn into a mad flight beyond the pillars of Hercules. This meant different things to different people. A monk sitting in the refectory of the Hereford Cathedral shortly after 1300 would be familiar with an image of the world like it is presented in Figure 3. A merchant or a navigator, also around 1300, would recognize the drawing in Figure 4.

Figure 3. The Hereford Mappa Mundi, *c.* 1300.

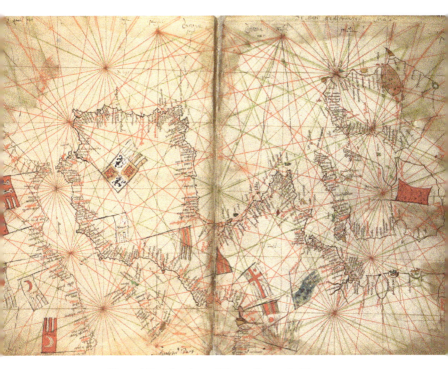

Figure 4. Portolan chart of Western Europe, by Pietro Vesconte, *c.* 1310.

These are two completely different and yet concomitant views of the world. In the Hereford map, Hercules' pillars are placed at the bottom sinkhole of the world, at the exact opposite of a rather anthropomorphic god. If you let yourself down such a drain, you will be forever sucked outside of the known or imagined world. The portolan chart requires but a slight, if painful, twist of the neck for you to inhabit a representation of Western Europe that overall resembles the one we are used to: Gibraltar no longer a plughole in the lowest parts of the world, but a strait, as we know it today, and the British isles only necessitating

Figure 5. T-O map.

a little flight of imagination to be identified, as opposed to the rotten-muffin-like mass squeezed on the left side of Hereford map.

With all its complexity and squiggles and doodles, the Hereford map actually holds to a funny metaphor; it is a T-O map, meaning *Orbis Terrarum*, or world, in reverse. This arrangement is often schematized in a much more abstract fashion (Figure 5). This diagram, diversely perpetuated in the middle ages, has an east-west orientation. In it, the T is the Mediterranean sea, dividing the three continents, and the O the 'Mare Oceanum', the big blue unknown. We can fathom Ulisse sliding inexorably in the sinkhole of the

Hereford map, or more metaphysically disappearing like a little radar dot from the T-O diagram.

The portolan chart in turn reminds us that in antiquity and the middle ages merchants and navigators were travelling the west coast of Europe, that they had crossed Gibraltar before, and searched the sea around it both north and south. It reminds us of the many unrecorded navigations or excursions in unknown lands, of cultural encounters that were never registered, or left lighter, and possibly gentler, traces than the grand Renaissance travels.

The fact that we are more familiar with the portolan than with the T-O should not prevent us from reflecting on the strangeness, one may say the absurdity, of mapping; of geometry unleashed on life. The oddity of geo-graphy; the writing about the land, of the land, on the land, The Scripture of the Land.

Is Dante's Ulisse Adam or a merchant? Was Dante thinking of a T-O or a portolan? Is the great unknown sea map or metaphor? Are we doing geography and economics or metaphysics? These distinctions might be somewhat vitiated. A merchant called Adam, perhaps, going in search of God-knows-what, yet something that could be computed, monetized, and yet called knowledge and virtue: this is perhaps what the discoverer is.

MARCO? MAARCO??

A merchant of this kind exists in Dante's times, but Dante is strangely silent about the account of the travels in the Far East of his quasi-contemporary Marco Polo.

Accountable and accounting merchant turned ambassador and curious traveller meets failed romancier in a Genoese jail in 1298. Merchant's handbook meets adventure fiction in a Franco-Italian patois; it is both exciting and explosive. The journey of its title says it all: The Description of the World (*Le Devisement du monde*), The Book of the Wonders of the World (*Le Livre des merveilles du monde*; *De mirabilibus mundi*), The Book of the Gran Khan (*Li Livres du Graunt Caam*), only relatively recently branded as *The Travels of Marco Polo*. In Italian it is known as *Il Milione*: although scholars vouch that it comes from the nickname of the Polo family (*Emilione*), to me it sounds too endearingly like 'The Million Bucks Book'.

The worldly merchant travels, sees, annotates, measures, listens, and hears about. On his page, observation and legend sit gracefully together. Polo follows an earthly, merchant ethos of 'virtue and knowledge', questions the meaning of divinity, embraces wonder with a graceful understatement, calls the rhinos 'unicorns' but is unfazed by their alleged symbolic meaning (they are ugly beasts — he notes — not the cute, maiden-friendly, Christ-like creatures we claim they are). He returns home. It is no surprise to us that Polo's return to Venice was compared to that of Odysseus to Ithaca.

Although wide open to the accusation of today's Orientalism, for its own times Polo's account is actually rather open-minded. 'When you depart from *** riding towards Levant for seven days, you arrive to the land of ***. There are Muslims, idolaters (Buddhists), and Nestorian Christians. They are artisans and merchants. They weave rich brocades with gold threads, and handsome silk fabrics. There are many cities and castles and oxen large like elephants that produce very fine wool. The people there are short, dark, and beautiful (or tall, fair, and ugly, or a combination of such adjectives)': this would be an average paragraph in Polo's account. In other words: people, religions, landscapes, and product are placed on the same plane, with very little moral judgement. Diversity is curiosity; merchant's realism (not mercantile greed) is the gold standard. It is a hugely invigorating and carefree reading, once you get accustomed to its rolling pace, a bit like a horse gait. [Your bottom hurts when you get off, though.] The reasons why Dante did not engage with the million bucks book — he only mentions in passing 'Tartar embroidery', which is clearly not enough of a clue — are mysterious. Dante does not do Orientalism, is the short answer. Or he is a moralist. You choose.

A flimsy precedent of Ulisse has been found, however, in the mercantile epos of the late thirteenth century. In 1291, two brothers, Ugolino and Vadino Vivaldi, armed two ships and departed rather grandiosely from their hometown of Genoa, then one of the most dynamic naval powers in the world. They crossed Gibraltar and disappeared. The most trusted document on the expedition is found in the annals of Jacopo Doria, writing only four years after:

> Eodem quippe anno Thedisius Aurie, Ugolinus de Vivaldo et eius frater, cum quibusdam aliis civibus Janue, ceperunt facere quoddam viagium, quod aliquis usque tunc facere minime attemptavit. Nam armaverunt optime duas galeas, et victualibus, aqua et aliis necessariis infra eis impositis, miserunt eas de mense Madii de versus Strictum Septe ut per mare Oceanum irent ad partes Indie, mercimonia inde deferentes. In quibus iverunt dicti duo fratres de Vivaldo personaliter, et duo fratres Minores. Quod quidem mirabile fuit non solum videntibus, sed etiam audientibus. Et postquam locum qui dicitur Gozora transierunt, aliqua certa nova non habuimus de eis. Dominus autem eos custodiat, et sanos et incolumes reducat ad propria.

In that same year, Tedisio Doria, Ugolino Vivaldi, and his brother, with some other citizens of Genoa, embarked on a journey that nobody had attempted before. They richly armed two galleys, and having stocked them with food, water, and all other necessary things, they set sail in the month of May towards the strait of Ceuta, in order to go through the Ocean towards the Indies, with the intention of bringing back from there useful goods to trade. The two Vivaldi brothers went on the galleys in person, and with them two Minor Friars. This enterprise was truly wondrous for both those who witnessed it and those who heard about it. And after they passed a place called Gozora, we no longer had reliable news of them. May god preserve them, and bring them back home safe and sound (my, very literal, translation).

This source can be prodded and questioned in many ways. A list of questions and a sketch of the answers may look like this:

- Where? The journey never travelled before; Ceuta and the 'deep open sea': these are both features of our Ulisse. The Indies; Gozora: was their intention to circumnavigate Africa or to attempt the Atlantic passage? Most historians today believe the former hypothesis; and I, of course, love the latter (I also love, but with a hint of boredom, 'the former' … 'the latter' type of construction: it is the first pseudo-scholarly expression I learned in English).

- Where is Gozora? The coast of Morocco, the west coast of Africa, perhaps the Canaries, are some of the hypotheses.

- Who? 'Optime' and 'personaliter': it is rather striking that the galleys were armed and serviced with unusual richness by a group of Genoese magnates, and the fact that two of the shipowners were on board emphasizes the grandiosity of this journey.

- Why? Merchandise and Franciscan Friars: was the intention mercantile or evangelical? Historians readily notice that the fall of Acre, which also took place in 1291, meant that a very profitable Genoese commercial route towards the East was closed, so this might be a mercantile endeavour. The role of the Franciscan Friars is less discussed. Were they on board to care for the souls of the sailors or to conquer new ones?

- History or story? They are already blurred in the annals: there is wonder ('mirabile'), witness ('videntibus'), and hearing about ('audientibus'); the same wonder, indeed, takes hold of the eyewitnesses and of the posthumous 'readers'. This, for us, also generates the question of Dante's position: is the Vivaldi expedition a 'source' for Dante's Ulysses, or is Dante's Ulysses dictating the way we look at the Vivaldi brothers?

- And may they come back home ... the final optative brings us all to the docks of the medieval port, to pace it with parents, and spouses, and friends, and children, hoping to see the sails on the horizon, dreading another day without news.

A handful of contemporary documents add a couple of details: the ships' names might (or might not) have been *Allegranza* (Happiness) and *Sant'Antonio* (Saint Anthony). The former (see?) has a double, if tenuous, delicacy to it: the fact that the northernmost island of the Canaries is actually called Alegranza, and ... remember the joy of Ulisse's crew? ... 'noi ci *allegrammo*' (*Inferno* 26, 136, emphasis mine): may this be a trace of the Vivaldi expedition, one scholar has wondered? Historians cringe, while I rejoice.

Later on, the story of the Vivaldi brothers fades into legend, as the annals already implied. The anonymous *Libro del conoscimiento de todos los reinos* (The Book of Knowledge of All Kingdoms), for some time believed to be the record of a real journey in the known world travelled in 1305 and written shortly after, and now deemed the fiction of an imaginary journey written in the second half of the fourteenth century, has one of the brothers Vivaldi stranded in modern-day Sudan, and his son Sorleone (or Sor Leone: Mr Leone, Mr Lion) in Ethiopia or Somalia looking for him, but being dissuaded to travel to Sudan by the local leader, who fears Sorleone might lose his life (chapter 82). Apparently Ugolino did have a son named Sorleo, who was also a merchant and a navigator and might understandably have gone in search for his father. But we could also be reading about the Fantastic Adventure of Mr Lion in the Big Scorching Desert. In another passage we hear that in the city of Graciona in Ethiopia there are 'the Genoese men that escaped the galley that broke up in Amenuan, they never knew what happened to the other galley that escaped' ('los ginoveses que escaparon de la galea que se quebró en Amenuan, et de la otra galea que escapó nunca sopieron qué se fizo'; chapter 80). Between and around the two semi-realistic statements there are luxuriant descriptions of earthly paradise ('dantesquely' placed on high, unpopulated mountains) and of the River of Gold, a true 'cash-flow' originating in the Antarctic pole that the author declares he saw in his travels.

There is some kind of strange pleasure in reading the *Book of Knowledge*. You feel like a Lilliputian, hurried and breathless, rushing on tiptoes on a large globe. Almost every ten lines or so a new section begins with 'I departed ...', or 'I left ...', ('Parti' ... 'Sali'). Life is a continuous take-off for the author of the *Libro del conoscimiento*, an endless self-inflicted fleeing from one place to other, spurred by a strange mix of curiosity and haste, even though for both him and us it is simply following our fingertips on a map. Even coming back is a departure. This is how the book ends: 'e dende vin me para Sevilla donde sali primera mente' (and from there I came to Sevilla, from where I first left; chapter 120).

The last early modern source on the Vivaldi are the journals and letters written around the middle of the fifteenth century by one Antonino or Antoniotto Usodimare, my favourite name ever for an adventurer. Little Tony Used to the Sea — this is how his name sounds — says that he met a descendant of the survivors of the Vivaldi expedition in Guinea, and that he heard its 'definitive' story, one boat beached in a shallow, the other landed in Ethiopia and its crew captured by adepts of Prester John.

Prester John is like the hardback cover for many medieval and early modern stories. In the wise, Christian ruler of an Eden-like kingdom in the heart of Africa or of Asia, by some identified as a descendant of the Magi, by others as the Wandering Jew, alterity and identity are so minutely calibrated that many stories of exploration and discovery are not afraid or ashamed to dive into and come to an end in this strangest of fictions. In the thirteenth century, while many were taking seriously the absurd forgery of an alleged letter by Prester John to the European emperors, calling them to unite against the Muslims and to liberate Jerusalem as well as rehashing the fabulous riches of his kingdom, Polo, with his casual worldliness, makes Prester John yet another Asian king at war with Genghis Khan, good and bad and real like any other ruler.

TO PURSUE MONEY AND GOLD?

Besides the tenuous clue around the Vivaldi brothers, there is another indication, perhaps, that Dante was considering a mercantile heritage for his Ulisse. His doomed discoverer may be found not in literature or on maps, but in the busy workshops of his burgeoning city. Dante might be grappling here with his troubled and non-linear reflection on the worth of 'expansion' in productive, financial, and political terms — an ongoing process in his hometown and many city-states in the Italian peninsula. He might be trying to come to terms, in other words, with the 'capitalist' in the 'discoverer'.

At the very beginning of the canto, the image of Florence spreading her rapacious wings over land and sea condenses into one negative droplet the elements of the main episode: wings, sea, ambition, and expansion.

> Godi, Fiorenza, poi che se' sì grande
> che per mare e per terra batti l'ali,
> e per lo 'nferno tuo nome si spande!
> (*Inferno* 26, 1–3)

> Rejoice, O Florence, since you are so great that over sea and land you beat your wings, and your name is spread through Hell!

As opposed to the staged ambiguity of the rest of the canto, this image is entirely negative; 'battere' (or, today, 'sbattere') 'le ali' (to beat one's wings, to flap, flutter) describes an agitated and graceless flight; 'spandere' (to spread) speaks of an expansion that takes place only in hell. Such a rapacious image of mercantile Florence is a constant throughout the poem and reflects Dante's ambivalent position towards his beloved and behated hometown.

A simplification of the typical understanding of Dante's politics that you would read in textbooks may sound like this: Dante was a Guelph, and the Guelphs upheld the independence of city-states, papal politics, lower-aristocracy claims (Dante came from one such family), and some aspects of mercantile initiative against the universalizing prerogatives and reign of a (rather vacant) Emperor and an often violent and politically entitled high aristocracy (the Ghibellines). The actual chessboard of local politics at the time was much more complex, though, with Guelph and Ghibelline distinctions blurred by local interest, neighbourhood brawls, and interfamilial jealousies. When he was still active in Florentine politics, in the 1290s until his exile in 1302, Dante belonged to the White Guelphs, who, together with their antagonists, the (guess?) Black Guelphs, were a specifically Florentine faction of the Guelph party. After the exile due to the Black Guelphs' alliance with a quite interventionist pope, Boniface VIII, Dante's position became somewhat eschatological and made him veer towards more 'Ghibelline' ideas — the vision of an all-powerful, impartial, and enlightened emperor who, having received his investiture from the pope, is able to rule 'the world' wisely and justly, as he writes in his late political work, the *De monarchia* (On the monarchy). Plainly: it seems to me that Dante is a loser at realpolitik and a naïve political thinker.

Dante's position towards Florence's economic expansion is ambiguous to such an extent that it can be stretched between a quasi-visionary condemnation of the dangers of proto-capitalism and a blunt reactionary stance. In *Inferno* 16, for instance, Dante-traveller meets three of his fellow citizens, who ask him about the state of their city, in particular whether the slippery values of 'cortesia' (courtesy) and 'valore' (valour) still dwell in it or not (16, 64–72). Dante's reply is bitter:

> La gente nuova e i sùbiti guadagni
> orgoglio e dismisura han generata,
> Fiorenza, in te, sì che tu già ten piagni.
> (*Inferno* 16, 73–75)

> The new people and the sudden gains have engendered pride and excess in you, O Florence, so that you already weep for it!

'The new people' are new in two ways. They come from outside Florence, from the *contado* (the countryside around the city that provided for its agricultural needs), and they are not part of the established elite. Their profits are large and sudden, and they are the cause of Florence's moral and political decline. [Not true, by the way: Florence's politics were troubled like those of any other *comune* in the early fourteenth century, but the city developed into a political and financial powerhouse thanks to its dynamic economy and in the next century it became the most influential city-state in Italy under the 'republican' leadership of the Medici, a family of bankers. But it takes Machiavelli, two centuries later, to reveal, with a grand and generous gesture, that politics is real, it favours dynamism and cynicism, it is a hard exercise, and it is separated from morality.]

Here Dante draws a quadrilateral of principles; the current 'pride' and 'excess' are the antitheses to two old, slightly hollow values, 'courtesy' and 'valour' ('cortesia e valor'; 16, 67). 'Dis-misura' — dis-measure — is the key here. It is a perversion of 'measure': to measure, count, quantify, estimate, size, amount, and even to trade, are not damnable per se, Dante seems to say, but their excesses are. The touchstone? Women, of course! Yesterday they were modest and plain, attending to husbands and children, and today they are all jewels, accessories, make-up, and loud fashion. In the olden times, 'there was no necklace, no coronal, no embroidered gowns, no girdle that was more to be looked at than the person' ('Non avea catenella, non corona, | non gonne contigiate, non cintura | che fosse a veder più che la persona'; *Paradiso* 15, 100–02). The speaker here is Cacciaguida, Dante's ultra-conservative ancestor, who compares old, 'sober and chaste' (15, 99) Florence, ruled by few and moderate families, with the new city that has attracted more and more people from outside, who now are 'made Florentine and are money changers and traders' ('fatto è fiorentino e cambia e merca'; 16, 61; my translation). Here we read a blood-chilling statement for us moderns, that 'the intermingling of people was ever the beginning of the harm of the city' ('Sempre la confusion de le persone | principio fu del mal de la cittade'; 16, 67–68). Chilling to those of us, that is, who believe in the energy of intermingling, who are incurably intermingled.

Newcomers, *nouveaux riches*, and female extravagance — how many times have we heard this spiel? And how many times will we? All the while, *vieux riches* are laughing, then and now, while enormous hypocrisies surrounding social mobility still haunt many of us.

In the broad socio-economic interpretation suggested by the beginning of the canto, then, the whole episode of Ulisse might be a condemnation of mercantile dynamism from a traditionalist point of view.

Even the sighting of mount Purgatory could be meaningful in the mercantile reading of the canto of Ulisse. Purgatory is the new otherworldly realm, its doctrine drafted at the Second Council of Lyons in 1274, only a few years before Dante wrote his poem. According to Jacques Le Goff (*The Birth of Purgatory*) there is a proto-capitalist culture at the basis of the invention of the 'third place'. Although this thesis has been nuanced over the years, it is true that a culture of pain and gain, calculations and advancements, down payments and rewards, ventures, deals, and negotiations underlies purgatory, as well as the complex accounting whereby the prayers and resources (and money) of the living help the dead in their otherworldly climbing. Dante, who has the privilege of being the first poet of purgatory, fills that vast white page with productivities, not necessarily social or financial (although there is a bit of that too, and lots of accounting of the years and months that one spends there). Dante's purgatory is the place for a poetic and textual productivity as well as the spiritual and redemptive one. Even pain is productive in Dante's purgatory, as my friend Manuele Gragnolati has demonstrated.

The *Purgatorio* is an intriguing piece, loaded with symbols and paraphernalia of salvation. It is also a funfair of reading, so many are the ways in which it can be interpreted. It is reactionary, even fanatical in its imperative to drop everything earthly, twist all desires and self-flagellate (literally) in order to cleanse oneself from sin. It also contradicts itself by being full of friends, and hugs, and love poetry, and lovers. It is the closest thing we have to an otherworldly jail (in it, you do time until you are free to ascend to heaven). It can be also read as a gigantic church, filled with visual examples of purification and redemption. [A student of mine said that it reminded her of a gym, but those were the nineties in New York City.] I wonder if it has something administrative (The Central Office of Salvation), financial (The World Bank of the Souls), or even industrial to it (the busy plant where the souls are made clean), like the textile workshops that were Florence's proto-capitalist pride, or the Venetian arsenal that Dante famously describes at the beginning of *Inferno* 21 (7–18), delightfully turning technical terms of manufacturing into the crackling of poetry.† Whether Dante's purgatory (and perhaps even the whole poem) has the energy (and potential alienation) of a production line. Whether stories (of salvation and otherwise) are self-sabotaging assembly lines.

Redeem ... doesn't it also mean to recover, repay, pay off, cash back? [It does; it was one of those annoying rhetorical questions — the Latin etymology plainly encompasses the prefix *re-* and the verb *emere*, to buy. *Redemptus* (redeemed) means no less than bought again, or back, or off in ancient times and in today's English.] Salvation is an otherworldly voucher, a posthumous promotional code, the busy merchants of Europe are starting to think. Only now the irony hits me that 'to pay' ('pagare', 'payer', 'pagar') derives from the Latin *pacare*, to pacify, and ultimately

---

† Another passage worth listening to, not only for its technical prowess, but also for the curious fact that it describes the place where broken ships are fixed. They are mended, we learn, with pitch. A pitch-black atmosphere dominates this and the following cantos (*Inferno* 21–23), known as a 'comedy within the *Comedy*', where Dante embraces the depths of comic style and language to face the sin of political corruption ('baratteria', barratry, the buying and selling of political positions) of which he was accused by the Black (like pitch) Guelphs at the time of his exile. Broken ships, political sell-out, enemies, and exile: Ulisse meets Machiavelli in Dante's disturbed political unconscious: 'Quale ne l'arzanà de' Viniziani | bolle l'inverno la tenace pece | a rimpalmare i legni lor non sani, | ché navicar non ponno — in quella vece | chi fa suo legno novo e chi ristoppa | le coste a quel che più vïaggi fece; | chi ribatte da proda e chi da poppa; | altri fa remi e altri volge sarte; | chi terzeruolo e artimon rintoppa —: | tal, non per foco ma per divin'arte, | bollia là giuso una pegola spessa, | che 'nviscava la ripa d'ogne parte' (As in the Arsenal of the Venetians, in winter, the sticky pitch for caulking their unsound vessels is boiling, because they cannot sail then, and instead, one builds his ship anew and another plugs the ribs of his that has made many a voyage, one hammers at the prow and another at the stern, this one makes oars, that one twists ropes, another patches jib and mainsail; so, not by fire but by divine art, a thick pitch was boiling there below, which overglued the bank on every side; *Inferno* 21, 7–18).

from *pax*, peace. The financial and the spiritual go oddly hand in hand.

Merchants of the time were no strangers to the calls of moral and spiritual values. Merchants' books recorded not only transactions and debts but also wishes for a pious afterlife through earthly dealings. They amassed treasures both earthly and spiritual, and measured salvation like a piece of cloth, one span at a time. Dante's 'good merchant' is a case in point. When getting old, the noble soul recalls all its good deeds — like a merchant nearing his port is pleased with all the money he has made and routes he has taken.

> E fa come lo buono mercatante, che, quando viene presso al suo porto, essamina lo suo procaccio e dice: 'Se io non fosse per cotal cammino passato, questo tesoro non avre' io, e non avrei di ch'io godesse nella mia cittade, alla quale io m'appresso'; e però benedice la via che ha fatta. (*Convivio* 4, XXVIII, 12)

> It [the soul] acts like the good merchant who, as he draws near to his port, examines his profits and says: If I had not made my journey along this road, I would not have this treasure, nor would I have anything in which to take delight in my city, to which I am drawing near; and so he blesses the way he has taken.

The greedy merchant, though, is cursed to never find peace, 'by failing to perceive that he desires to continue desiring by seeking to realize an infinite gain' ('e in questo errore cade l'avaro maladetto, e non s'acorge che desidera sé sempre desiderare, andando dietro al numero impossibile a giugnere'; *Convivio* 3, XV, 9). Desiring to desire, is this the curse of the modern human being? Is Ulisse's curse (the philosopher's, the merchant's, even the poet's) to try and go after the number that is impossible to reach?

Within the socio-economic reading, then, we might say that in having his Ulisse-merchant dimly approach the place of redemptive productivity, Dante might hint (whether consciously or unconsciously I don't know, and, as you probably have guessed, I don't care) at the tricky transition between an old, cautiously mercantile political ethos and the acceleration of this same politics in the hands of unscrupulous or too dynamic politicians, between 'good' (old) and 'greedy' (new) merchants. Ulisse, called to navigate again to pursue old, hollow values ('virtue' and 'knowledge'), and yet led astray by his own expansive energy and desire, comes to see, and to die in front of, the 'redemptive' place, the supernal Chamber of Commerce, built by merchants for merchants in their attempt to measure and mete the afterlife.

But when I turn to Ulisse, I am not convinced. I fail to reconcile the immense aperture of his mad flight with the constriction of hell. In the semi-public confessional of the lecture room — don't quote me on this, guys — I always wonder. When drawing the episode of Ulisse, is Dante

- a proto-humanist? forging, through a creative rewriting of the classics, the unforgettable figure of the modern human being that will be fulfilled only a couple of centuries later through the advancements in knowledge, explorations, technology; in one word, progress? Did he extract, that is, what was modern and even timeless in the classics, and in this ex-pression, through the visionary power of poetry, foresee the times to come? This kind of reading appealed to me when I was young, when 'to pursue virtue and knowledge' rang true, when progress meant only one thing, and when right and wrong were fully demarcated.

- Or is he being, poor Dante, what he was; not a 'medieval', which is our construct, but firmly a pre-modern, and condemning Ulisse and progress from the narrow standpoint of his Christian and Guelph beliefs? A backwards, or downward looking Dante. Easy for both those who celebrate the Christian, conservative Dante and those who loathe him. Safe. But how boring.

My kids (I do think of my students as my kids, with apologies to them for the unintended infantilization), my kids are smarter than this. They deserve better. This is when, prefacing it with a 'don't quote me on this, guys', I share with them my absurd hypothesis.

That a double foresight underlies Dante's Ulisse. Of progress and its discontents; of knowledge turning into greed; of technology yielding gunpowder; of exploration becoming exploitation, colonialism, ecological disaster. That poetry is visionary, but its vision turns sometimes into a nightmare that, in a truly psychopathic way, is more vivid and better than the dream. That Dante is super-modern. His discoverer has found the beauty and horror of 'us'.

Modernity, however, ignored Dante's warnings, hailing the discoverer as the best type of the human being. The rhetoric of glory and exploration, perversely (or perhaps only 'versutely') grown out of Homer's and Dante's characterization of Ulysses, variously mixed and matched with positivism and with a touch of romantic rhetoric, is very much around. 'To strive, to seek, to find, and not to yield' is not, it seems, the last whimper of an old, demented king, but the tattoo on the oiled bicep of a young adventurer. The hungry heart keeps piling life on life, death on death.

YESTERDAY AND TODAY

In 1970, a book claimed that there is some kind of 'Ulysses gene' in the (typically male) human being, which would push the human race to always out-discover itself. I would not normally mention *The Ulysses Factor: The Exploring Instinct in Man* if we did not need a bit of relief from the pressure of the tragic stories of exploration that are the stuff of this chapter, and if it had not been written just fifty years ago — in my lifetime, in our shared cultural environment. Someone must have taken this seriously at some point, seriously enough to publish it.

Weaving literature (mostly Homer and Tennyson) and modern, newspaper-style stories of feats of endurance, the book claims that the call to adventure is a proper human gene, a 'factor' indeed in human constitution, different from survival, or greed, or desire for knowledge. This is the seventies — when the age of earth discovery had just passed, and that of space discovery just begun — so the adventures celebrated therewithin (yes, therewithin!) are of the futile kind, like crossing the North Atlantic on a raft eating only sunflower seeds in the company of a single Siamese cat, and should a storm hit, they will fish me out anyway.

Throughout the book the author does not hide his belief that the Ulysses factor is a white, Western, upper-class, male, heterosexual thing. In current times, he says, it is manifested especially in 'people of British and French stock' [I kid you not]. There is, of course, the token 'Oriental Ulysses' [not kidding], and the chapter on 'Women', which I leave to your imagination.

There is even a list of qualities that the type-figure owns:

Courage

Selfishness

Practical competence

Physical strength

Powerful imagination

Ability to lead

Self-discipline

Endurance

Self-sufficiency

Cunning

Unscrupulousness

Strong sexual attraction [still not kidding]

'Sexual attraction' — we read shortly after — 'may be no more than a part of virility. The attraction of Ulysses' [the name is Bond?] 'is not crude, and certainly not coarse. He is intensely virile', [yes, yes you told us already five times; is there something you want to discuss with your doctor?] 'quick witted and ready with a compliment' [and to light up your smoke, but-there's-some-place-that-he'd-rather-be]. 'He is an exciting person, and not merely physically exciting. You can sense that he had a quick delightful smile, you want to talk to him, and you want him to talk to you.' [In a bar?] 'Women were strongly drawn to him, perhaps a little wanting to mother him', [isn't it what we always want to do?] 'as well as to sleep with him' [no, we didn't! well perhaps Circe, but she screwed him more than he screwed her]. 'He enjoyed women, but was ready enough to leave them' [poor Calypso always on the walk of shame] 'and sex does not seem to have been a powerful motive in his own life.' End of laughter. And beginning of concern when we think how much this 'type' and his bards are still around.

And today? As I write, billionaires and sci-fi actors are being shot into space. I have not read much about this *boutade*, but I have the impression that it is a somewhat grotesque impression of what is to come. Space travel is, of course, the new frontier, the new trespassing. But we will not see it.

As a child, gorging on adventure books, I remember experiencing a sense of slight nausea at the thought that there was nothing left to discover, no place where the human being had not been, which had not been mapped, centimetred, placed, paced. I also used to feel dizziness, almost vertigo, when studying astronomy and learning how unthinkably big the universe is. Very naive, I know, but taken together, I wonder whether that giddiness is not the compound reflux of an entire era, stuck between leaps. We call ourselves the 'postmoderns', but what will they call us? The pre-futures?

In 1990 (in my prime, if I may say so), a probe named Ulysses was sent towards the sun. I quote, emphasize, and gloss from the NASA website: 'The Ulysses spacecraft was designed as a five-year mission to study the *never-before-examined* ['do not deny the experience'] *north and south poles* of the Sun [Oates and Franklin in one machine]. Far *outliving* its planned mission lifetime by 13 years ['neither … nor … nor ': I have no desire for return says Dante's Ulysses] and *collecting treasure troves* [ouch. Polo!] of data on solar wind, interstellar dust and the three-dimensional character of solar radiation, Ulysses became one of the most prolific *contributors to knowledge* ['to follow (virtue and) knowledge'] of the solar activity cycle. The spacecraft also performed a number of technical *feats* [epic] including making an *unprecedented* gravity assist manoeuvre at Jupiter *to hurl itself out* [never travelled before! success! glory!] of the elliptic plane and into its solar polar orbit.'

I wonder, is this Ulysses also naturally sexy?

More seriously, I ask, are we back into Dante's great metaphysical unknown? In the abstract painting, in the immense silence, in the unthinkable solitude. Does interstellar dust glitter like hope or grime like grit? I wonder whether the tridimensionality of solar radiation and the epic thrust out of the elliptic plane are loud enough to silence more anguished questions: what is this boundless, lofty place I am in? what is this incommensurable loneliness; who am I? where does my short wandering, where does your immortal course tend to? [I am paraphrasing here another poet and a great nihilist, Giacomo Leopardi; a disabled philosopher who, in the early nineteenth century, saw through positivism with the keenest of rational and secular eyes].

When it hurled itself out of the traction of the angry, erupting god, did Ulysses dance and jest like the ancient hero ... 'I am no one! I am nothingness, you cannot catch me', or did it let go, torpidly obeying its momentum, like Dante's boat in front of the vortex?

Did it come back, I wonder? The front website calls the mission 'completed', and you have to dig a bit into the subsections and subfiles to find this story:

> After just over 17.5 years, the mission is approaching its end. The declining output from the Radio-isotope Thermoelectric Generator (RTG), which provides power for the craft and its payload, is unable to provide enough heat. This means that the

fuel for the thrusters will freeze. In mid-January 2008, the situation worsened when the main radio transmitter failed — its warmth kept the fuel from freezing.

To overcome these difficulties, ground controllers have been using a smaller transmitter to ensure that as much science as possible is returned from Ulysses in the last few weeks of its life.

The mission is expected to end by 1 July. Once it is clear that the fuel needed to keep the main antenna pointing towards Earth has started to freeze, ground controllers will put Ulysses into a stable configuration.

It will continue to orbit the Sun indefinitely.

It is heartbreaking, isn't it? This Ulysses too will not come home, forever trapped into its icy heart, in darkness. I am going outside, in the cold, in this unknown, incommensurable loneliness. There is something comforting in letting go, in foundering. And maybe sometime.

Incidentally. On the front page of NASA's Ulysses website, we are invited to 'explore other missions', according to the textual and commercial virtual hierarchy we are so accustomed to. I am mesmerized by some of their names: Mariner Six, Rosetta Orbiter, Sea Winds, Genesis, and ... Psyche. I feel that if I unlock this rebus correctly, I will get the key to a room where a hero dressed in latex and named Prester John will explain to me the meaning of humanity, past, present, and future.

Dante, however, manages even space exploration. In heaven, he describes two earth-bound gazes. It is a technical feat in itself, if you think of the time they were imagined. They do look like satellite views of the earth. The first time (*Paradiso* 22, 124–54), he places the traveller in the 'heaven of the fixed stars', where Beatrice, his guide, asks him to look at 'how much world' she 'has already set beneath his feet' (22, 128–29), and Dante spectacularly turns his gaze to contemplate the seven planets, and the earth, 'the little threshing floor which makes us so fierce' ('l'aiuola che ci fa tanto feroci'; 22, 151), while readers feel they are watching some kind of *mappa mundi* from above, with little humans on it, expanding, fighting, and pillaging.

The second time (*Paradiso* 27, 76–87), when the traveller is about to turn his gaze upwards and focus at last on things truly divine, he bids farewell to earthly matters by looking down one last time. He gazes at the south shore of the Mediterranean sea, west to east, from Hercules' pillars to Lebanon (the site of Phoenicia where the nymph Europa was abducted by Zeus in the form of a bull):

> sì ch'io vedea di là da Gade il varco
> folle d'Ulisse, e di qua presso il lito
> nel qual si fece Europa dolce carco.
> (*Paradiso* 27, 82–84)

> so that, on the one hand, beyond Cadiz, I saw
> the mad track of Ulysses, and on the other nearly
> to the shore where Europa made herself a sweet
> burden.

The earth itself now bears the mark of Ulysses' folly: the strait is now a 'varco', a door, an opening, but also a break, a rift, a scratch. The enjambment 'varco | folle' (literally: the passage | mad of Ulysses) tears poetic language apart rather than clasping it as this figure normally does. Try it: it has to do with accents, and with the clash of consonants and vowels.

On the other side, the vulgar violence of the divinity.

The wound of the earth; the rape of Europa. And ferociousness. Us.

5. It Was Sunset

> Era già l'ora che volge il disio
> ai navicanti e 'ntenerisce il core
> lo dì ch'han detto ai dolci amici addio;
>   e che lo novo peregrin d'amore
> punge, se ode squilla di lontano
> che paia il giorno pianger che si more
> (*Purgatorio* 8, 1–6)

> It was now the hour that turns back the longing
> of seafaring folk and melts their heart the day
> they have bidden sweet friends farewell, and that
> pierces the new pilgrim with love, if he hears from
> afar a bell that seems to mourn the dying day

It was sunset. Things happen at sunset. Or, rather, non-things do not happen at sunset, and this vacuum produces a prickling, piercing sentiment; the pain itself of places, people, events bygone and irretrievable. It is not our pain; it's theirs. *Sunt lacrimae rerum.*

    It is nostalgia, a modern coinage — from *nostos* (return) and *algia* (pain) — for a malady old as the human being: the painful desire to return to some place that no longer exists as it was. The hue of this word is pale blue, its association with the sea almost inevitable. Dante was right to pour some of his best poetry just to say 'It was sunset'.

In this image, Dante captures the mechanics of nostalgia, caught and stretched between two desires: an active, painful, punctual awareness in the sudden turning and piercing, and the passive, quasi-sadness in the softening of the heart and the mourning of the day. He suffuses it with the positive subtext of friendship, and the love that springs forth from the piercing. Nostalgia is a *nostos* that never closes the circle.

From afar ('di lontano'): only nostalgia is close to travellers. All the rest — friends, bell tower, land — is distant, remote, absent. It is incredibly sad and sometimes (but only occasionally) invigorating.

There are two sets of characters in this image, similar but different: the plural seafarers (all seafarers, seafarers in general) and their friends, and the single pilgrim.

I sometimes wonder if these sailors are Ulisse's crew. 'Seafarers' suggest consummate travellers, used to leaving and returning home. Their sea voyage implies the circular pattern of the *nostos*, the story of maritime journey and return. The sailors' desire is captured in the moment of its heading home — it is 'turned back' — yet the emphasis is on the day of the departure, the moment of farewells. But perhaps those farewells were rushed on both sides, and careless for a good reason; the sweet friends thought they would see the seafarers again, while the seafarers stared at them, then at the harbour, and then at the island becoming smaller and smaller, sighed with a mix of sadness and relief, and turned their gaze in front. It doesn't need to be catastrophic. They might see each other again. Older, changed. Homecoming. Inbound.

May I ask you, reader, to bring yourself to the port where you once waited for a boat to arrive? Isn't there always some kind of flutter, some aimless preparation, some unsteadiness? It needn't be a harbour — an airport, a train, or a bus station will do; the motor of a car pulling over, or the unmistakable sound of certain steps on the stairs. And may I leave you there, to savour the concept of 'waiting', and ponder changes on faces that you only know? Or to inhabit instead the other side of the door of time, and be the incoming traveller, still entertaining some kind of motion inside, even when you have set foot on land, even when you are sat on the sofa.

When I was young, there was a certainty to all my travels; that my father would be waiting for me at the station, or at the airport. He was kind of short but, waving his arms like a flat windmill, he managed to stand out in the crowd, no matter how big it was. With my myopia aggravated by travel, all I could see was a pair of waving hands and a large smile, and a commotion that piloted me through the crowd. Until the day he was no longer there. The doors of the arrivals hall at Linate airport in Milano still make the same noise when they slide open, some kind of vacuum-sucking sound, or that of a blunt slash. *Lacrimae rerum mearum.*

In the sunset image, Dante flanks the seafarers and their sweet friends with a singular pilgrim. Unlike the seafarers, the pilgrim is 'new' ('novo'); he has left home recently, for the first time perhaps, he is inexperienced, and the duration of his journey is unsure. In his sunset there is also the sound of the bell, which exacerbates the 'turning' into a proper piercing of the heart and adds a layer of uncertainty to this image. Where is the bell tower? In the town the pilgrim just left behind or ahead, in a village that he may reach tonight, so similar yet so different from the 'original' one? Or is this sound truly ahead, perhaps even in his head, the ghost tolling of the bell tower of the holy site, the awaited end of the journey? What inflames the pilgrim with pain could be the homeland that he has left behind, or the one that awaits him forward; his desire could equally be nostalgic or anticipatory, stretching between past and future in the sound of the present bell. Either way, the sound of 'this' bell has a nostalgic nuance; it laments the dying day, a day like no other, the ever fleeting, ever elusive, and yet only form of existence. The ever dying now.

The figure of the pilgrim, then, adds a new tone to nostalgia — it turns the time of travel into a temporality, and the place into a geography; it messes with space and time, turning the where into a when and then hanging both upside down. You can never measure at the same time the desire (momentum) and the location (position) of the nostalgic traveller. Nostalgia should be made into a law of physics, some kind of Heisenberg principle of the human spirit. Loss would be the unit of measure of this equation. I wonder what would emerge from looking at the universe as nostalgic.

Peregrinus: foreigner, stranger, and wayfarer; this Latin word comes to identify those many people who in the middle ages and beyond left home and travelled for religious reasons, for long months or sometimes years, to visit a holy site (be that Rome, Jerusalem, or Santiago) and gain some spiritual currency in return. Pilgrimage was a key social and spiritual practice in the Christian middle ages. The sole truly multicultural and multilingual phenomenon of the time, pilgrimage had refractions in the full range of medieval culture, from spirituality to geography, from economy to law, from literature to art, through architecture, with villages and towns, churches and markets, languages and cultures developing along pilgrimage roads, some of which are still routes of European travel today.

The practice of pilgrimage affects the understanding of concepts such as 'homeland' and 'foreignness', 'old' and 'new'. In the actual homeland, one is spiritually foreign, and thus needs to undertake the journey in order to seek the spiritual homeland, in which one is actually foreign. In the holy site, the pilgrim finds the new under the form of the fulfilment of an old, missing promise of the self; in returning to the homeland the old is rearticulated by renewal. 'Return' is not a straightforward matter in this narrative. At each moment, the place to go back to is both behind and ahead.

Modern tourism is sometimes said to be pilgrimage's scion, which broadly makes sense, including the bourgeoning of cheap commerce around the holy/beautiful site, the ecstatic glimpse/photo of a crucial object or landmark, and the 'I-was-there' token souvenir. Even the leisure that is part of pilgrimage, ancient and modern, even the sense of renewal that is key to tourism. There is something ill-fitting in this comparison, though, which I cannot quite pinpoint. Perhaps the absence of the ghost text of salvation, the the lack of free atonement and tokens for the afterlife, or simply the accelerated temporality of modern travel.

In my determinately secular and pathetically unspiritual life I have seen pilgrims only once. My father, the arrivals-hall windmill, although a man of science, was strangely superstitious and avoided holy places. They brought bad luck, he said. I guess it was his own mild revolt against what he felt was an oppressive, or hypocritical, presence of religion in his youth. As a consequence, I have only seen the Vatican through a school trip and went to Assisi only after his death. That is: my childhood and teens were deprived of Michelangelo and Giotto, admittedly a middle-class problem, but not without corollaries.

It was early morning in the airport of Bangalore, I was boarding a flight to the UK, and they were embarking for the Hajj, wearing the traditional white robes. I, the reluctant tourist whom life had brought briefly and precariously to the enormous Indian city, whose images, scents, and noises were still passing in my mind in a strangely silent, fast-forwarded film, clutching the poor relics of the I-was-there in my handbag (a silk dupatta, a small stone chariot, souvenir of Hampi, a carton of the much-coveted Mysore sandal soap), heading back to the established estrangement of my life in Britain, and they, the large community of a local minority, men, women, and children, leaving their own estranged establishment for the holy site. Attending the same routines at different gates, sketching the same gestures to fight the boredom of the long wait and perhaps anticipating the pang of fear and excitement of the flight, pacing with the same steps the airport halls, cramped airless spaces dressed up like a street fair, were we at peace with whatever we needed to make peace? About to have our gravity disconcerted by the in-human experience of flight whilst being subsumed in the most anodyne commercial experience — tea or coffee, chicken-or-vegetarian, pleaserinsethebasin — two flights side by side, leaving what looks on earth like a foamy wake in the big blue sky, we were perhaps an atom, an incarnation of Ulysses in his voyage of (no) return, or of the lonely pilgrim, our hearts soon to be pierced by the tolling bells. D-ling d-lling — you may now unfasten your seat belts. But please remain seated. Stay where you are. Be where you are.

Of that crowd of pilgrims, I only remember the children being children and one of the elders, tall, thin, and sinewy, with a grave yet witty smile. With two immaculate worn-out towels thrown around his body and his gnarled walking stick, he looked, strangely, like a John the Baptist figure.

Peregrini et hospites: pilgrims and strangers (or even: aliens and visitors, foreigners and homeless). So Paul describes humans in Hebrews 11. 13–15. Life on earth is a long journey, a spiritual pilgrimage towards a non-place (both home and holy land) that is found only in the afterlife: birth is the necessary departure from the soul's maker, and death, the longed-for return to 'it'. The notion of spiritual pilgrimage is intricately connected to but also different from the practice of pilgrimage: in it, home and holy land are the same and they are largely unknown; the experience of the new is at once the retrieval of the old. The story of the Exodus in the Bible, telling the wanderings of the Jews away from Egypt and towards the homeland, is the foundational narrative of this journey. In the narrative of biblical Exodus and its allegorical transposition of life as pilgrimage, the existence of a holy/home-land is certain, but its geographical and spiritual location is unclear. Errancy and travel are one. Exodus is a radical experience of foreignness and estrangement.

Strip it of the uncertain point of departure and arrival, and the journey is all that is left. Embodiment is all that is left. 'Five senses; an incurably abstract intellect; a haphazardly selective memory; a set of preconceptions and assumptions so numerous that I can never examine more than a minority of them' … goes a quote by J. C. Lewis. Blood, shit, and desire, I would add [long ago a friend of mine witnessed me declaring this to be the human triad]. A very vague sense of what is good and what is bad (sweet is good, bitter is bad: this is the infantile truth underlying all ethics, and all fruit salads); appetites and curiosities to follow a very poor, illegible, or blank map; sounds grafted onto each other to form words, a couple of metaphors, a set of embellishments, and two or three stories, always the same.

Exodus, the way out. The way out of. The way into, but only for some. Egypt and Israel. Captivity and freedom. An obdurate, waxen Pharaoh. Blood, bread, scourges, and wild chariot chases. Water and wilderness. Manna from heaven and Moses, the damaged hero. 'I am not good at this!' — he keeps saying — 'I am slow, and hesitant, I am a halting speaker.' The ultimate human being, the quintessential nostalgic, Moses is forever trapped in the all-consuming now. For him there is no going back to the homeland, just a sight of the never-occurring there-as-then. His people do return, though. I guess they are too busy, or too oblivious, to realize that homeland is a spatio-temporal mirage.

An incurably jealous god and his interminably unruly people: too bright, too curious, too ironic to withstand a rule for too long. Severe yet ever-crumbling writings on stone; the disintegrating shape of human behaviours. Obsessive, grinding repetitions — of names, and tribes, and herds, and laws, and detailed instructions, and materials, and measurements — which make the Bible both the most human and the most illegible book of all. And the profound, existential stillness of the desert. The scorching heat, the uncanny silence. The night is enormous and cold. Homelessness.

In our perennially reflected and refracted culture, exodus means everything and nothing. In my own native country, Italy, come the first of August when the summer vacation starts for most people, and the media start frantically speaking of 'exodus' (basically meaning long queues on seaside-bound highways). Come August 31st and it is the equally panic-stricken report of a 'counter-exodus'. It seems like it has to go back to tourism, sweaty and agitated people, and the smell of cheap sunscreen. This, I must add, was truer when I was a child, when everybody but us left the city in August. Arrivals-hall windmill and his stern wife never allowed vacation in August, and I ended up spending most of my childhood summers in an empty, claustrophobic, abandoned metropolis that, under the humid lashing of the leonine sun, had the metaphysical grit of a De Chirico painting. It was home, but in a feverish nightmare. Home you have the urge to run away from. I wonder whether my exodus-less childhood has made me the nomad that I am.

Figura. The story of Exodus is, in turn, the quintessential place for Christian exegesis — the pivot one may say, of the 'old' and the 'new' testament, the very binding of the two books into the Christian bible. At least on the surface, it looks like a watertight yet elastic story where everything hinges: historical and spiritual slavery, Moses and Christ, Passover and Easter, exile and return, sin and redemption, bread and body, down to the minutest detail. All elements in the 'old' story are said to prefigure the 'new'. The 'new', in turn, heeds the 'old'. This parallel yet overlapping form of interpretation is called 'figural', 'typological', or 'allegorical': there is no hard distinction between these terms. Crudely: figures and types are said to be 'truer', more 'historical', like Moses prefiguring Christ, and allegories more fictional, like the flight of a dove symbolizing the elevation of the human soul to god.

In my view, the positive aspect of figural/allegorical reading is the renewal and the creativity that goes with it. The negative is that it does not give the 'then' the same weight as the 'now'. Now is better! Figural reading proudly announces. It pushes forward. Details are jerked and twisted to produce general coherence. Texts are coerced into the consistency of meaning. The 'then' is just the manna of the bulimic 'now'.

Figures abound, therefore, in and around the Christian interpretation of the Bible: no word is left unturned, down to two little goats that are said to be figures of Christ's first and second coming. Waiting to be fulfilled, the *figurae* look, at times, like toy figurines, about to be set up by the rough and excited hand of a colossal child-player. Like childhood play, figural and allegorical reading is imaginative, tyrannical, and repetitive. In this game, figures are serious and sad like toy soldiers, allegories merry and queer like dress-ups. The Player is not orderly or methodical, though, they make do with what they have in their box, like when my three-year-old son used a plastic dinosaur, a violet *pachycephalosaurus* for that matter, to impersonate Mary Jane, Spiderman's girlfriend, in his bathtub play. The Player sent a storm, but the articulated plastic figure saved 'her' from drowning.

Some early church fathers, with a plethora of unbeatable late antique names (such as Athanasius, Methodius, Hippolytus) called it 'recapitulation', a way in which Christian history interprets itself in the unfolding, so that the beginning coincides with the end. Their spokesperson is a certain Irenaeus (2nd century CE), and their canvas yet another narrative of lapse and return that makes Adam the figure of Christ, and history a giant loop away from and towards god; incarnation the furthest point of the loop, and the beginning of the return. Reset this in Christian life, and birth is the Adamic moment, death the homecoming. Thus, history is like embodiment; its death, the day of Judgment. Or maybe an asteroid.*

---

* It is intriguing that recapitulation became in the nineteenth century a now discounted theory of evolution — the notion that 'the develop-

For all its universalizing pretence, *re-capitulare* is a humble word from the material act of writing — in antiquity and the middle ages *capitulum* is a chapter, a heading, an index, even a paragraph break. It is the minimal yet intriguing symbol that has survived even into today's virtual writing, that slim yet full reverse P (¶) that unties our thoughts on the page, in little clots of sentences, modest units of self-sufficiency. When we re-capitulate, we harvest the headings of our writing into some appearance of sense. We nudge, direct, even force our thoughts into 'meaning'. Or, perhaps, it is just a resistance against the blankness of the page ahead. [Sometimes, when I start a piece of writing, I begin by keying in a whole page of paragraph breaks. Only when I reach page 2 do I go back and begin my text. It scares solitude away. It integrates the beginning into a non-existent end. It moves the end away with each character I type.]

Figuralism, I guess, is not solely a Judaeo-Christian matter. Many cultures and religions are populated with before and afters, pre- and pro-phets, with the incessant re-reading, updating, and universalizing of the same story. It may be just the very material consequence of being stuck with old, incomprehensible texts, or perhaps this is how memory, the enormous, terrifying, ingenuous monster, works: shortening, selecting, making sense of things with new information, adapting to one's benefit, embellishing or disfiguring according to our needs. Thankfully, in both memory and in figural/allegorical reading there are some remote pockets where all that is not functional, all

---

ment of an organism from conception to maturity repeats the same sequence of stages as have occurred during the evolution of its species or race' (quick Oxford reference). I am not sure there is an echo of Irenaeus & Co. here, but the ideology is similar: a capacious text, variation, and return.

that fails to 'convert' into meaning is stored; pre-versions, per-versions, a-versions, sub- or super-versions. Traumas and dreams. All that which is not coming home. Or either, the stowaway.

If I were to rewrite the figural representation of Exodus, I would, perhaps, not deny the parallels between Moses and Christ, but would focus on how they are both flawed, unfulfilled, tragic heroes. Why me? says Moses. Why me? says Christ. I am halting, I am fragile. Quick! The night is short, says Moses. Pack unleavened bread, fasten your sandals, and gird your loins with belts. We have to run. We will always have to run, over land and seas, with our rituals impenetrable even to ourselves, holding this book, where I am said to write my own death, this book that will not allow my steps to disappear in the sand. Oh, I wish this quiet warm night in the garden of Gethsemane would last forever, says Christ. Don't go quite yet, sweet friends, we have time. If you would remember me, says Christ at Easter, if you would remember me truly when eating this bread, do not, do not remember only the concise and coherent story, but also its failures, the irreducible details, the dreams, the traumas. My shit and blood. Mine, and Moses', and that of all flawed idealists. And desire.

Peregrinus amoris. Desire brings you places. Desire and the journey are one for the 'pilgrim of love'. For Augustine, it is, quite literally, a physical force, one with an equation and a unit of measure.

> Corpus pondere suo nititur ad locum suum. Pondus non ad ima tantum est, sed ad locum suum. Ignis sursum tendit; deorsum lapis. Ponderibus suis aguntur, loca sua petunt. Oleum infra aquam fusum super aquam attollitur, aqua supra oleum fusa, infra oleum demergitur; ponderibus suis

aguntur, loca sua petunt. Minus ordinata inquieta sunt: ordinantur et quiescunt. Pondus meum amor meus; eo feror quocumque feror (*Confessions* 13, 9, 10).

I am almost tempted to leave this terse excerpt untranslated. There is something tetragonal about its shape and sound that makes it interpret itself while you read it, even in a foreign language. It is the kind of passage that squares the circle inside and reassures me of my shared humanity. The climax about the weight of love is like an invisible language dart that pulverizes my gravity and makes me feel weightless and carried by my love. Whatever that is, wherever it carries me.

But I am more tempted to translate it myself — I, an inept translator from and into any language. Here we go:

> Each body is striven [ungrammatical, but somehow true] by their weight to the place that is theirs. Pay attention, here: weight does not mean down, it means to the place that is yours. Fire tends upward, stone downwards. Submitting to their weights, they are seeking their place. If you pour oil in water, it will emerge; if you pour water in oil, it will de-merge. Submitting to their weights, they are seeking their place. Less ordinate things are restlessly desirous: once they find order their desire experiences stillness. My love is my weight; by it I am carried wherever I am carried.

Or maybe this is the real translation:

Weight = one's place
Weight ≠ down or up
The experiment of oil and water
place = repose
love = (weight + place) ÷ (rest + desire)
The unit of measure? me

The image of the sunset at the beginning of the eighth canto of *Purgatory* that opens this chapter is supremely pre-Augustinian, as it captures the indeterminate, sweet, nostalgic instant before the weight of love pushes you wherever you need to go: whether that is forward, back, down or up, in a circle or on a tangent only you know. The heart is weightless in this suspended moment, motionless the spirit.

Off we go now.

Desire brings you places in different ways. In the practice of pilgrimage, desire is a force; push, traction, attraction. Physical pilgrimage (and some version of tourism, for that matter) implies journey, destination, change and exchange, and return. Like pilgrimage, desire is movement, it is transit toward and from a longed-for object. The main narrative of pilgrimage (and of desire) is as straightforward as the displays in airports and stations: check in, gate, departure, return. And yet, shifting softly as an electronic display, or noisily as the old-style board with thin plastic letters (of which, let us face it, some of us have dreamt, at least once, to be the omniscient typesetter), subjects and objects, points of departures and arrivals, are unsteadied.

It is a game of both purpose and irresolution. In these journeys there are maps, schedules, fares, layovers, hostels, and places where we are, indeed, *hospites*. These are, in turn, spaces for encounter, storytelling, retrospection, wasted time, sweet friends, new and old; for bells tolling from nowhere, for pleasure, and for mourning.

A superstition that I like involves setting an extra place at the table for a mysterious guest: the place of Christ. This is the way I was told it works (I have not checked its veracity; never to verify is the mode of the superstitious): you set an extra place at the table, a plate, a glass with a drop of wine, cutlery, and a napkin in case a pilgrim, rugged and hungry, knocked at your door during a stormy night asking for shelter. That traveller, any traveller, might be Christ, or a genie (for the secular me), or a blessing in disguise (for the rational me). It is not about the pilgrim coming, though. It is about them not coming, and the empty place at the table. For me, it is about those who do not return: it is the place of longing, the place of loss. [I also kiss the stale bread goodbye before I throw it in the compost bin, but this might be more information about me than you want to hear.]

In the notion of spiritual pilgrimage, desire is more of a momentum. In the story of life as an uncertain wandering of the soul toward an undefined destination (god), there is more reliance on an instinctual kind of attraction. The ineluctable and necessarily digressive (because necessarily embodied) instinct that blindly guides the human soul back to its creator must become the deliberation and the map for the journey. In the search for the divinity (or, more secularly, for one supreme object or goal) desire concentrates, governs, and regulates itself. It is even a proof of existence for both the desiring subject and the desired object: 'I desire, therefore It exists', so goes the premodern *cogito*.

In this story there is more digression, ambiguity, and errancy than in a real journey (you can't plan life as a trip), but the moral is even stricter than that of an actual journey: the desiring self needs to recognize the roads, the carriers, the encounters either as useful (not pleasurable) things, or as errors. As we saw with Augustine and the Neoplatonic reading of the *Odyssey*, it is ok to travel, to stop somewhere, and be curious, but Ithaca must be always in sight — no lingering, no excitement, no enjoyment of the journey itself is allowed. The aporia of this Christian narrative is that it ends up pinning desire against pleasure. Desire recoils and sometimes creates monsters.

Dante inscribes the double story of the pilgrimage of desire in the fourth book of his *Banquet* (*Convivio* 4, XII, 14–19), with some rather telling twists. As soon as it starts the new and untravelled journey of our life, Dante explains, the soul aims to return to god and acts as a pilgrim who, travelling on an unknown road, thinks that each house he sees is the inn where he will rest. [It is refreshing that there is no holy land in sight in this story, just an inn where one can find shelter for the night. This pilgrim, although cast in a religious narrative, is 'just' a foreigner. This is Dante soon after the exile. He knows how painful, how scary it is to walk on unknown roads alone. He knows better than to blabber grand statements about Home.] Duly going from house to house, the pilgrim eventually gets to the inn. ['This country road dotted with farmsteads is pleasant' — we can imagine the foreigner's thoughts and conversations — 'but as much as I enjoy the scenery, I am a bit anxious about finding shelter for the night.' 'No sir, not here, the hostel is that way, another couple of hours. But if you want to sit with us, we always set an extra place at the table. After dinner, we often gather in the barn and listen to old stories of battle, journey, and love.' 'It is kind of you, good woman, but I cannot linger, I must be on my way.' 'The sunset is beautiful, it reminds me of my sweet friends back home, but it also tells that the day is about to die. I might get lost. It's getting cold. It may be some time.'] So too should behave the newly embodied soul, continues Dante, and walk the journey of life moving from one experience to the other until it reaches god. Being young, however, the soul cannot quite tell the small from the big objects of desire (the houses from the inn) and turns her attention to all. Dante's order of desire is properly funny: an apple, a little bird, fine clothes, a horse, a woman, riches, riches, and more riches [chocolate, a puppy dog, designer clothes, a car, a trophy spouse, riches, riches, and more riches]. This is not bad per se, says Dante, as long as you keep your eye on god, the ultimate object of desire ['eye on the prize', says the modern tale]. Otherwise, you will miss the direct road to the city [oh, sweet Dante: midway through the paragraph he forgets about pilgrimage, houses on the road, and the inn, and starts talking about a city. There is no way back to your city, you fool]. The good walker goes on the straight road, gets to the city, and rests; the bad walker takes the errant road, the one full of detours, keeps on walking, and gets more and more tired, hungrier and hungrier.

The narrative of the journey to the holy land or the supernal homeland, with all its twists, turns, and strangeness, brings into relief the all-conquering power of desire, its capacity to bridge distances, to embrace even the most distant objects, even those that are long gone, lost, dead. Desire is capacious and elastic. It writes and reads figurally. It makes sense of the most absurd and disparate things (because I want them …).

Like figural interpretation, however, desire has some traits that are difficult to sympathize with: it can become exclusive, authoritarian, even martial, especially when it is espoused with a hypertrophic willpower and a lack of finesse. It learns to identify as extraneous all desires that diverge from the ultimate goal, whatever that is. No need for the religious subtext here: the road of determination, with its ugly-sounding co-ordinates obsession and success, is paved with the tombstones of murdered desires, either too fragile or too unfamiliar to match the main goosestep.

Anchora. Desire is like an anchor, Augustine says, a magic one, for that matter: from afar it is thrown in the promised land and firmly pulls the Christian soul to its maker. There may be some bumps, but no shipwreck.

> Iam desiderio ibi sumus, iam spem in illam terram, quasi anchoram praemisimus, ne in isto mari turbati naufragemus. Quemadmodum ergo de navi quae in anchoris est, recte dicimus quod iam in terra sit; adhuc enim fluctuat, sed in terra quodammodo educta est contra ventos, et contra tempestates: sic contra tentationes huius peregrinationis nostrae, spes nostra fundata in illa civitate Ierusalem facit nos non abripi in saxa (*Enarrationes in Psalmos* 64, 3).
>
> We are already there through desire. Already we have dropped hope, like an anchor, in that land, so that, distressed, we do not sink in the storms. Of a ship that is anchored, we rightly say that it is already landed: even though it still tossed in the waves, it is somehow landed, notwithstanding winds and storms. In the same way, against the temptations of our journey, our hope is grounded in that city of Jerusalem that helps us avoid crashing against the rocks in the sea (my translation).

Anchorless Ulisse! However ardent, his desire did not moor him.

Anchors are strange, says the incompetent seawoman. They are like reverse fishhooks; a tiny boat trying to catch the big earth.

In my youth, I once dreamt of a symbol — it was half an anchor and half a lyre. [I usually do not dream symbols, I dream stories, and of the rubbish kind, usually. Incurably terrigenous, I have never dreamt of flying, which I hear from aerial people is one wondrous sensation.] Thus, attempting an allegorical interpretation of my dream, I established that the anchor and lyre was 'my' symbol — it was the closest I ever got to getting a tattoo. A nice version of me, that is; the one that you are happy to wear on your fleshy sleeve. But of what? Of my half determined and half ephemeral personality. Of my half landed and half suspended life story. Of my half grounded, half improvised mores. Of navigation and music, two talents that are utterly alien to me, but chillingly, and tenderly, my ex-husband's skills (was this a figure of my future or of my ex-husband? is the excruciating question). Of desire and poetry. Of life and writing, perhaps. Of nothing! A sardonic voice muffles my musings. Of the fish I ate the night before while listening to Bach's cello suites. A poorly understood music, a sea creature consumed in haste: they resisted figuralism. Indigested, un(re)cognized; they gave me dreams.

Peregrinatio pro amore dei. It is my favourite: the pilgrimage for the love of God that was said to be practiced in the Celtic and early Anglo-Saxon church, a curious midway between the actual and the theoretical aspects of pilgrimage. The pilgrim 'for the sake of God' strived to reconstruct the wandering pattern of the Jews by setting to travel without a destination, or by establishing a random destination that was not necessarily linked to a holy site, but that provided the experience of estrangement. At times this exercise was so radical as to suggest the pilgrim to board a little boat and to float away without direction. In modern life, this makes me think of those bathers who drift away from the beach on a float. Children or drunkards; they say god protects them.

Still, to embrace illogically the fullness of one's own desire, to eschew the need for a port of arrival and the tyranny of meaning, to embark upon error as the only viable path, might be the only way to do desire justice.

Ultimately, any desire is a pilgrimage, a journey of unequal return. The journey of desire is acceleration in slow motion. It is to be already there and not yet arrived. Under perfect conditions (such as those, for example, of Dante's paradise, but also, I believe, in many instances of earthly happiness), desire is at once stimulated and fulfilled, in an ever-burning present that knows neither frustration nor satiety. When desire is now, paradise is here.

Desire both establishes and bridges the distance between the here and there, the now and then. And at once, it calls the traveller back home. 'Pilgrim desire', in other words, is a desire that simultaneously calls backwards and forwards, that is both thrust and nostalgia, plunge and resurface. For some, it is an ever-piercing wound of the heart, for others, a tiny lesion that pulls but softly. It is the sunsets where we turn to look at our journeys and try to make sense of them within a coherent story. It is the irreducible detail that makes us the endlessly misshapen, hapless *figurae* of ourselves.

THE ANTI-ULISSE

Dante's Ulysses, although driven by the most ardent desire for travel, is not nostalgic, we know that. No-nay-never will the sweetness of home (father, wife, son) affect his journey. He feels nothing at sunset. Maybe just the pangs of hunger for dinner. To me, this is the only punishment that Dante metes out for him.

The beginning of *Purgatory* is a big anti-Ulyssean moment. Dante-traveller has reached in a rather fortuitous manner the 'mountain dark in the distance' (*Inferno* 26, 133–34) near which Ulisse's ship sank. Rather than going by sea, Dante and Virgil go all the way to the centre of the earth, and then climb over Lucifer's slimy, velvety body that is stuck there; first descending on his upper parts 'between the matted hair and the frozen crusts' ('tra il folto pelo e le gelate croste'; *Inferno* 34, 75), then performing some rather audacious acrobatics on the devil's own crotch, they then start ascending on his legs planted upside down in the southern hemisphere. I feel for Dante; there were times I was so terrified of flying that I would have done anything not to set foot on a plane, including climbing on the devil's pubic hair, as he does in this rather memorable scene that has reminded a student of mine of the fantasy of an anal birth.

After crossing a long and claustrophobic tunnel, Dante eventually emerges with his guide on the shores of Purgatory, and he understandably takes revenge on the one who thought he could go there by a simple boat ride. At the same time, he starts shaping his text as a grand textual navigation that goes hand in hand with the sobering acceptance of divine wings.

The first canto of *Purgatory* begins with a non-mad sea journey and the poet's talent lifting the sails in order to sing the second realm. More about this in the next chapter: for now, notice how Dante employs the same words he had used at the beginning of the canto of Ulisse: 'correre' (to run) and 'ingegno' (talent, genius) — here, however, his genius can run (sail, fly) unrestrained.

> Per correr miglior acque alza le vele
> omai la navicella del mio ingegno
> che lascia dietro a sé mar sì crudele
> (*Purgatorio* 1, 1–3)

> To course over better waters the little bark of my genius now hoists her sails, leaving behind her a sea so cruel.

Upon arrival to the shores of purgatory, a contrast is also established between 'experience' and 'inexperience'. 'Experience' — one of the main attributes of Ulisse, who wanted to gain experience of the world, and of human vice and worth ('del mondo esperto | e de li vizi umani e del valore'; *Inferno* 26, 98–99) — is here underplayed (or overplayed?). Here, we learn openly of Ulisse's 'mistake': his proleptic, projectile desire for experience, which pushed him 'out there' to almost reach the place of salvation, did not make him expert, or competent in returning. Only Dante-traveller is strolling the 'desert shore, that never saw *anyone* navigate its waters who afterwards had experience of return' ('lito diserto | che mai non vide navicar sue acque | omo, che di tornar sia poscia esperto'; *Purgatorio* 1, 130–32). Moreover, everyone is depicted as inexperienced in this foundational scene: Dante, Virgil, and the newly arrived souls are not 'experts' of the place, but, guess what?, they are 'pilgrims':

> [...] Voi credete
> forse che siamo esperti d'esto loco;
> ma noi siam peregrin come voi siete.
> (*Purgatorio* 2, 61–63)

> Perhaps you think we are acquainted with this place; but we are pilgrims, like yourselves.

True pilgrims of desire, their journey is one without a map; together with the purging souls, Dante and Virgil proceed to inhabit and explore the new realm like 'one who goes but knows not where *one* may come forth' ('com' om che va, né sa dove rïesca'; 2, 132).

Ulisse, then, puffed up with his desire for experience, was not able to secure the most necessary expertise of all: that of coming back. He was not able to entertain thoughts of return, to re-read, to think retrospectively, to rewrite and recapitulate his story. Ulisse is a non-nostalgic non-returner; the quintessential discoverer, it seems.

Unlike the protagonist's acrobatic cave climbing, the regular souls arrive to purgatory by boat. But this ferry is of a divine nature. It is, once again, a matter of navigation-cum-flight, as the ferry-angel pushes the boat with its wings. The same rhetoric of oars ('remi') and wings ('ali') that constructed the magic of Ulisse's mad flight is now reversed. The angel of god

> [...] sdegna li argomenti umani,
> sì che remo non vuol, né altro velo
> che l'ali sue, tra liti sì lontani.
> (*Purgatorio* 2, 31–33)

> [...] scorns all human instruments, and will have no oar, nor other sail than his own wings between such distant shores.

You won't be surprised to hear that the souls on the boat are singing in unison Psalm 113, *In exitu Israel de Aegypto*, on, well, Israel's exodus from Egypt (and all the good things that god did on that occasion), and that Dante on the shores of purgatory creatively tampers with the whole notion of Exodus and of its figural reading. With a perfectly executed shell game, or four-card monte, Dante brings together the freedom of the Jews from the Egyptian captivity, its standard interpretation as the liberation of the Christians from sin through the sacrifice of Christ, the otherworldly journey of himself-as-character (the journey of D-traveller in the afterlife, that is) in search for spiritual reformation, and the suicide (sin) of an old pagan (sin) republican enemy of Caesar (sin): Cato, a super-controversial figure that he places as the guardian of the second realm.

The setup of this flawless trick is simple. We (the readers) have just arrived to the shores of purgatory, ferried by Dante's textual boat. Expertly steered away from strangeness and incongruity by our cleverly ambiguous author and by the enthusiastic crew of his commentators, we barely noticed a gurgling vortex next to the island: 'no worries, folks, nothing to look at there, just show us your ticket and we will disembark soon. Check out that other boat instead, the fancy yacht, full of happy travellers singing their corporate hymn, *In exitu Israel de Aegypto*'. Timid like sheep, inexperienced, we start walking as those who go but know not where they may end up, comforted by the sweet light of the morning, the vevelty pale blue of a rare sapphire. [It is not sunset; we are safe from melancholic longings.] To our surprise, we are met by the screams and shouts of the beach's guardian, a crazy-looking old man. [We are scared and puzzled, but remember, it is just a trick.] While we are trying confusedly to figure out whether we know him from another story, he starts barking invectives at us: 'The hell are you doing here all dazed? You lazy bums [well, 'spiriti lenti', you laggard spirits; *Purgatorio* 2, 120]. Quick! This way. No lingering with sweet friends, old songs, and pagan bullshit, and, especially, no mentioning of my fucking ex-wife; we've got atonement to do. This is not a resort, for chrissake! This is sal-va-tion, a prison that will set you free. Stop looking back at the sea, we already told you: No-body sank there; it is just a natural whirlpool. This way, quick! Follow the signs that say *Return*'. [My rather free rendition of cantos 1 and 2 of *Purgatory*.]†

---

† The ex in question is Marcia, whom the historical Cato allegedly married twice, and who currently resides in Dante's hell among the pagan souls with Virgil. At the outset of this episode, Virgil addresses Cato in the name of Marcia, provoking his fury (canto 1: the pagan bullshit that I mention above is, indeed, Virgil's *captatio benevolentiae* to Cato, here described as mere flattery, or 'lusinghe', *Purgatorio* 1, 92 [Do read, if you wish, the shockingly comic punishment of the flatterers in *Inferno* 18]). Irascible Cato has another fit when Dante asks an old friend — the musician Casella, one of the souls who have just arrived in purgatory — to entertain him with the sweet sound of an old love song (canto 2).

 The fun anecdote is that in the *Banquet* Dante had interpreted in a figural way the story of Cato and Marcia getting together twice, as

A few words on Cato are needed, to better appreciate Dante's provocation here: he is known as Cato the Younger (95-46 BCE), to distinguish him from his equally austere great-grandfather; or as Cato Uticensis, a name that strangely turns suicide into an honour (Utica is the place where Cato killed himself, after allegedly reading Plato's *Phaedo* twice, a strange death scene told with horridly vibrant tones by my muse Plutarch in the *Life of Cato the Younger*, 67-70). During the civil war that saw the end of the Roman Republic, Cato was the true enemy of Caesar, at least in my rather schematic and heroic appreciation of this time of history. Much more than bloated Pompey, he is the proper symbol of Roman vir-tue and high morality: loyal, tough, incorruptible, stern, sober, sporting a lean musculature, and yes, a little dreary were it not for the lucky fact that his bard is the most dysfunctional epic poet ever — Lucan, the cantor of *bella plus quam civilia*, of 'more than civil' wars. His *Pharsalia*, of which, I fear, I am the only surviving fan, tetanizes the epic poem with an internal poison; it is some kind of autoimmune reaction of the genre. While banning divinity and marvel from the epic (no nymphs, or

---

the narrative, now well known to you, of the return of the soul to god (*Convivio* 4, XXVIII, 13-19). On the shores of Purgatory, Dante rejects such an interpretation, curtly saves Cato and damns Marcia, and denies the weight of the past (classical, literary, sentimental, and otherwise). Sly readers like me, however, catch him red-handed, when he has his brutal Cato pausing for one vowel too long on the name of his ex. When rebuffing Virgil's address in the name of Marcia, Cato gives a plain and rational explanation for it: he loved Marcia, he says, as long as that was 'correct', and now that he has moved into a new narrative, he no longer does (easy, no?). He starts his speech by mentioning her name: 'Marzïa piacque tanto a li occhi miei' he says (*Purgatorio* 1, 85); I used to love Mar-z-ii-a so much. Oh, he lingers on her name. Oh, does he still love her. Ii-it still hurts. Readers who hold that people are in Dante's *Hell* for a reason will deny this hint of nostalgia and say that the syllable stretch is just a metrical necessity. I say life is a poem, where every syllable counts. (Augustine agrees).

Cyclopes here, or infuriated gods), the *Pharsalia* projects horror and misadventure on human history: the enemy, the monstrous, the unforgiving divinity are us — a dishevelled and paranoid Cato seems to pronounce from a very real, historical stance that looks in every minute detail like hell. Dante, an attentive reader of Lucan, knows this very well [or maybe he knows now that I told him].

To place Cato as the guardian of his Purgatory: now this is what I call the creativity, and the radical openness of figural writing. It is no longer Moses and Christ, Jews and Christian, earthly and spiritual freedom. It is Moses, and Christ, and me, and Cato — all lined up in a verse that blasts like a bullet:

> libertà va cercando, ch'è sì cara
> (*Purgatorio* 1, 71)
>
> He [Dante, says Virgil to Cato] goes seeking freedom, which is so precious,
>
> come sa chi per lei vita rifiuta
> (72)
>
> as he [Cato] knows who renounces life for it.

A verse so explosive that it pierces through four aligned targets: while it makes of Cato a Christian prophet, and of Dante an everyman-cum-evangelist, it turns Christ into a suicide, and Moses into a guerrillero. [We would not be surprised to find Che Guevara in this line of fire. I wonder sometimes if among the many lead bullets that transfixed his body in that forsaken corner of Bolivia there wasn't also the figural shot, mandating him to fulfil the story of the dead-and-therefore-immortal revolutionary.] Of Ulisse, however, this verse makes the selfish (or clever) one who dodges the bullet of figuralism to be differently (really?) free, to fall outside of the margins of the page, out of the boundaries of the *mare oceanum*, off the cliff of salvation history, down the drain of the universe's vortex.

Truly truly a man of many turns is Dante's Ulysses, but not one of return.

MNOGO RAZ‡

A question arises in support of Ulisse, though: is going back a good thing? Is it wise to look back, have retrospection, re-read, re-turn? In the Western imagination there is a ghostly shade who begs to disagree. [No, not Lot — I ain't going for yet another grit-and-gore story from the Bible.] Orpheus, the very figure of the poet. Orpheus and his lyre, an ancient cyborg that moves stones and tames wild animals, even leaving the otherworld speechless. His story, most elegantly told by Virgil in the fourth book of the *Georgics* (452–527), is about an inevitable turning back.

His young bride Eurydice killed by a snake bite, his inconsolable pain, his song softening even the laws of the abyss. The gods allow Orpheus to lead Eurydice out of Hades, but he must not turn to look at her. The slow ascent away from death, they are almost out when he is seized by a sudden insanity ('dementia'), worthy of forgiveness, Virgil bitterly remarks, if only the gods could forgive ('ignoscenda quidem, scirent si ignoscere Manes'; *Georgics* 4, 489). It is such a minute infraction, almost a conditioned reflex. Let us bring this to ourselves, to an afternoon walk with a loved one. If they fall out, even momentarily, from

---

‡ The title of this subchapter, if you were wondering, comes from Charles Aznavour interpreting a Roma-Russian song about violins bringing back memories of one's youth. 'Mnogo raz' means 'many times', 'over again', but the tragic thrill in the voice of this child of Armenian refugees questions this meaning. The sonority of the voice pronouncing 'over and over again' makes it sound like 'never again'. 'Forever' and 'never' have the same vibration, it seems.

our visual field, how many times do we check, almost instinctually, that they are still with us? Of course, they are still with us, but that infinitesimal suspense is excruciating. It is a strange vertigo, an emptiness, the mouth of Erebus gaping microscopically in front of us. Italian poet Eugenio Montale describes the loss of his wife: 'Ho sceso, dandoti il braccio, almeno un milione di scale | e ora che non ci sei è il vuoto ad ogni gradino' (I used to give you my arm to help you through the stairs, says the poet to his very near-sighted wife now dead. I must have done that one million times, without ever realizing that, now that you are no longer with me, the void awaits me at every step; my translation).

You lost us Orpheus, you crazy fool! Cries Eurydice while a thick night takes hold of her ('ingenti circumdata nocte'; *Georgics* 4, 497). Orpheus despairs, and sings, and shuns the human company. A mob of infuriated women lynches him. His severed head, thrown in the river, still sings her name: Eurydice, Eurydice, Eurydice.

> tum quoque marmorea caput a cervice revulsum
> gurgite cum medio portans Oeagrius Hebrus
> volveret, Eurydicen vox ipsa et frigida lingua,
> a miseram Eurydicen! anima fugiente vocabat:
> Eurydicen toto referebant flumine ripae.
> (*Georgics* 4, 523–27)

> And even when Oeagrian Hebrus rolled in mid-current that head, severed from its marble neck, the disembodied voice and the tongue, now cold for ever, called with departing breath on Eurydice — ah, poor Eurydice! 'Eurydice' the banks re-echoed, all along the stream (translation by H. R. Fairclough).

Ovid, you have guessed, expands, expands, and then expands some more, and then interlaces — the story of

Orpheus covering book 10 and the beginning of book 11 of the *Metamorphoses*, his story becoming that of the stories he sings. Importantly, Ovid fills a large Virgilian gap and outs Orpheus, explaining that the women were infuriated at his preference for the love of young men. Ovid's story ends with the lightest of touches, though. After being quartered by the Maenads, with severed head floating and all, Orpheus ends up in the otherworld, and finds his Eurydice. They hug and walk about, and there is no fear: he turns and looks at her all the time, just for the sake of it. Just like our afternoon walk.

> Umbra subit terras, et quae loca viderat ante,
> cuncta recognoscit quaerensque per arva piorum
> invenit Eurydicen cupidisque amplectitur ulnis;
> hic modo coniunctis spatiantur passibus ambo,
> nunc praecedentem sequitur, nunc praevius anteit
> Eurydicenque suam iam tuto respicit Orpheus.
> (*Metamorphoses* 11, 61–66).

> The poet's shade fled beneath the earth, and recognized all the places he had seen before; and, seeking through the blessed fields, found Eurydice and caught her in his eager arms. Here now side by side they walk; now Orpheus follows her as she precedes, now goes before her, now may in safety look back upon his Eurydice (translation by G. P. Goold).

Like Ulysses, Orpheus is yet another multilayered figure for the 'Western Spirit', if such a thing exists, and if it is not a brand of cigarettes. (I later checked: Western Spirit is a site for cycling adventures, and a football club in Australia. For once, the internet has amused me.) The elements of his story — song, power over nature, loss, journey, the otherworldly dimension, bisexuality, cruel death, and redemption — make him a pliable and open character.

Importantly, Orpheus has syncretic powers; he stands at the wobbling cusp of disciplines (music, literature, philosophy), of east and west, cult and religions, sexuality and, interestingly, race.

Since antiquity the crux of the figure of Orpheus is, very simply put, the joining of song with divinity, of poetry with theology. Is Orpheus a visionary who through his lyre unlocks the secrets of the universe, or is he merely an entertainer?

He is, variously,

- Turned into a poet-philosopher, and later into a poet-theologian (*poeta theologus*), with mixed reactions from philosophers, Plato in particular, who can never decide whether this is a good thing or a bad thing (mostly a bad thing, though).

- Wrapped up in mystery in late antique texts known as the 'Orphyc Hyms', and in ancient religion under the confusing label of 'Orphism', a literary/philosophical cult that displaces him somewhere between Egypt, Greece, and Rome, enmeshed with music, maths, and astrology, connected variously to Moses (of whom he is allegedly a disciple), Zoroaster, and Pythagoras, to be the figurehead of one of the many mystery sects budding at the time of early Christianity. Even Augustine, the defender of the flimsy early Christian orthodoxy, mentions with some respect the 'poet-theologians' Orpheus, Linus, and Musaeus (*De civitate dei* 18, 14).

- [One wonders what would have happened if Orphism had prevailed among the many Middle Eastern cults of which Christianity was one: would we be speaking Greek? Would heterosexuality be the infraction to the norm? Would we kill others in the name of Eurydice?]

- Abused by Christian allegory (Orpheus becomes a figure of Christ in the medieval re-reading of the *Metamorphoses*), and then abused again by some Christian thinkers, disdainfully denying him the status of theologian.

- Enthusiastically embraced by Renaissance philosophers — at that eventful intellectual juncture when the world looked, for one split second, one and many, when mysteries seemed to be the key to a more logical future. The great Neoplatonist philosopher Marsilio Ficino praises Orpheus for his *furores*, the insanity that makes one leap forward, that cracks open the doors of the beyond. Our own Pico della Mirandola includes Orpheus in the final syncretic orgasm of his *Oration*, where Christianity, Judaism, Eastern cults, maths, and cabbala all take flight together.

- Reinterpreted and reinvented many times in literature and music and more. In 1948, a pivotal collection of black poetry was prefaced by Jean-Paul Sartre's essay 'Black Orpheus', shaping the notion of *negritude* as perpetually entangled with poetry (so flawed and, oh, so beautiful — like Orpheus's backward gaze). In 1959, the film *Orfeu Negro* stirred enthusiasm and controversy. [It was the kind of film that was shown as an art, avant-garde, even revolutionary film in the leftist *cineforum* in my hometown. 'Cinefora', may god have them in their glory, were small independent movie theatres with a screen that buzzed before turning on, crackling audio, and unthinkably uncomfortable wooden chairs that shaped

> your ass into a square. I miss them though. I miss my youth, where ideals and creeds were also square. I miss Eurydice.] Today it is considered a naïf if not flatly colonial repitching (by nobody other than a white European male) of the ancient story of love and loss in contemporary Brazil. The final music score, though, *Samba de Orfeu*, still moves me. Samba you can't control or indict.

Dante hardly mentions Orpheus. A convoluted and textually unstable passage in the *Banquet* (2, 1, 2–4) employs the beginning of the eleventh book of the *Metamorphoses*, where Ovid talks about Orpheus moving trees, wild beasts, and even stones with his song (11, 1–2), to explain the notion of 'allegory of the poets' — literature being a beautiful tale under which wisdom is hidden. It sounds plain, but it is a controversial passage that seems to resist modern understanding.

One quick mention in Limbo, the area of hell where the 'just' pagans dwell, places Orpheus within a list of ancient philosophers, just one step away from his sidekick Linus; they are the only imaginary characters in the list (*Inferno* 4, 130–44). None of these instances are particularly out of line with the classical and medieval literary or philosophical reflections on Orpheus.

Strangely, though, there is no other mention of Orpheus in the *Comedy*, which allows us to speculate wildly, because the whole point is that Dante is Orpheus, and he does have a Eurydice — Beatrice, the *fil rouge* of his life-as-work. It begins with a historical woman, a young Florentine named Beatrice (Bice) Portinari (1265?–1290?), of whom we know very little (she married well and died young — what else does history care about a medieval woman?), whose existence and essence are entirely subsumed into Dante's fiction.

Lovers at first sight, in love forever; they met as children and then as youths, Dante tells us, and I have loved-and-sung her ever since. A creature of his early secular love poetry, Dante employs her as the material, erotic, and moral compass for arranging his first poetry into a little booklet called *Vita Nova* (*The New Life*), then tries to bury her in an allegorical grave in the *Banquet*, then resurrects her as the initiator of his journey and guide to the last leg of the *Comedy*, heaven, where Virgil cannot go because he is a pagan. Many still today interpret Beatrice solely as 'faith', or 'theology', or 'wisdom', which makes things easy, and also very Christian (possible), but also very boring (unacceptable). To me, Beatrice is a multilayered patchwork — historical woman, lyric creature, personification, allegory — a bride of Frankenstein's monster trailing the underworld with her tattered trousseau of genres and styles. Dante-Orpheus holds her tight. Strolling the underworld with her, he clenches her hand, never lets go, grips her with the revitalizing lift of literature, armours her with the energy of love poetry against the deadly bite of allegory. In the space of writing, she is forever alive, forever renewed. Forever *nova*.

The image of Dante-Orpheus works in both the secular and religious route of interpretation. It is ironic that one of the essays that mostly contributed to the modern Christian interpretation of Beatrice is called *A Journey to Beatrice* (playing with the idea that the *Comedy* is a journey to god). It was written in the fifties by Charles Singleton, our cautious translator. Strip it of allegory and you get the classical story of Orpheus. In the Christian allegorical route, you have guessed it, we have to postulate a figural reading of Orpheus. By now, reader, you know how to go down that lane if you wish, with this mini-chart: Orpheus = Christ, everyman, Dante; Eurydice = the human soul, faith, Beatrice.§

Like Orpheus, then, Dante goes in search of his dead beloved in the otherworld. No wait: she goes in search of him, because he, the idiot, as soon as she departed this vale of tears, turned to other women (= poetic creatures or doctrinal interests), leaving her to worry for him in heaven, forcing her to appear in his sleep to shake him up from bad visions or wet dreams, and even to go to that stinky hell to ask that snob Virgil to help him. And now I even have to dress up like a little Madonna (no, not that one, unfortunately), to descend and meet him in that loud, cheaply allegorical earthly paradise, all covered in a veil that trips

---

§ If you are feeling lazy, *voilà*, the ready-made allegorical meal of an early commentator of the *Comedy*; you only need to put it through the microwave of translation (peel or pierce the film of allegory before putting in the oven): 'Allegorice Orpheus est vir summe sapiens et eloquens. Euridice, sibi dilectissima, est anima eius rationalis, quam summe amat usque ad mortem, Aristeus pastor est virtus, quae naturaliter sequitur animam, sed illa fugiens per prata et flumina, idest delectamina, mordetur a serpente, idest fallacia mundi, et sic moritur moraliter et descendit ad Infernum, idest ad statum viciorum. Sed Orpheus vadit ad Infernum pro recuperatione animae suae, sicut similiter Dantes ivit, et placavit omnia monstra Inferni, quia didicit vincere et fugare omnia vicia, et supplicia viciorum. Sed Dantes, numquam respexit a tergo, quia nunquam redivit ad vicia more canis, sed Orpheus, quia non servavit legem datam, perdidit omnino animam suam, et sic fuit error novissimus pejor priore' (Benvenuto da Imola, commentary on *Inferno* 4, 141). In short: allegorically Orpheus is a man [now that is not much of an allegory], wise and eloquent, Eurydice is his beloved rational soul, and Aristaeus is virtue, who naturally pursues the soul [and this is bizarre, and shows you the limits of certain allegorical reading. In Virgil's tale, Aristaeus, here equated to virtue that naturally follows the soul, is, there is no other word for it, a rapist: in the frantic attempt to flee from him, Eurydice is bitten by a snake and dies]. The meadows and rivers where she runs are the pleasures of the world, and the snake that bites her is the world's deception. So; she ends up in hell, the state of vice. Like Orpheus, Dante descends to hell to rescue his soul, but unlike Orpheus he does not look back, so he is much better etceteraetcetera.

me at every step, to reproach him and make him confess all his escapades. He will cry, and say he didn't know, that he doesn't remember, that I am his only love, and I will have to abuse him verbally some more, and then pardon him, and then take him to my new place, and explain everything — he is not very bright, I am afraid, my lad, but I still love him ... men, men, men; those adorable rascals. This is what Beatrice, a stunningly postmodern character who talks back to her author, says when she meets Dante at the top of Purgatory, throughout cantos 30–33 (my translation, of course). This is, in other words, a more feminist, more ironic, if not straightforwardly comical, version of the story of the loss and retrieval of the female beloved. And a reversal as well; now it is the departed female who comes to rescue the lost male lover. Dante and Beatrice are a profoundly vernacular version of Orpheus and Eurydice.

The homoerotic diversion is also in place: the one time in which scholars think Dante might be mentioning the tale of Orpheus is when he mourns not Eurydice/Beatrice, but actually Eurydice/Virgil. It is the truly sorrowful moment in earthly paradise when the traveller has to let go of his beloved classical poet-guide, and all the beautiful poetry that they have devised together, in order to meet and welcome his Christian Beatrice. Luckily, Dante does so cross-dressed as Dido, evading quick heteronormative fixes.

Please let me linger on this rich scene. On the one side, we have Beatrice, infuriated, tapping her little foot on the chariot dragged by a griffin on which she just appeared. (Yep, they made me do that as well, they also gave me a cortege of embarrassing allegorical figures; later they will fire in the special effects, and transform the chariot into some crazy sci-fi creature with heads and horns, and then make it the set of a porn film, with a giant abusing a naked prostitute. Stop looking and laughing, you righteous pricks: the actors have to earn their wages, and I have vowed to do anything for him.) On the other side, we think we have dear Virgil to help make sense of this mess, but we do not:

> volsimi a la sinistra col respitto
> col quale il fantolin corre a la mamma
> quando ha paura o quand'elli è afflitto,
>   per dicere a Virgilio: 'Men che dramma
> di sangue m'è rimaso che non tremi:
> conosco i segni de l'antica fiamma.'
>   Ma Virgilio n'avea lasciati scemi
> di sé, Virgilio dolcissimo patre,
> Virgilio a cui per mia salute die' mi;
>   né quantunque perdeo l'antica matre,
> valse a le guance nette di rugiada
> che, lagrimando, non tornasser atre.
> (*Purgatorio* 30, 43–54)

> I [says Dante] turned to the left with the confidence of a little child that runs to his mother when he is frightened or in distress, to say to Virgil, 'Not a drop of blood is left in me that does not tremble: I know the tokens of the ancient flame.' But Virgil had left us bereft of himself, Virgil sweetest father, Virgil to whom I gave myself for my salvation; nor did all that our ancient mother lost keep my dew-washed cheeks from turning dark again with tears.

Virgil ... Virgil ... Virgil ... Eurydice ... Eurydice ... Eurydice

The name of Virgil is uttered like an echo in the same way in which Virgil's Orpheus (actually, his severed head) repeated the name of Eurydice in Virgil's own *Georgics*. Virgil, who is at the same time mother and father, the sweetest parent of all, becomes, at once, poetry and loss.

Notice the utter sense of despair in the last lines. Instead of describing Eden as a beautiful, happy place, Dante calls it 'the place that Eve (the ancient mother) lost for the human kind', and he goes on to say ... not even this lost place (and now regained but I don't give a damn) could prevent me from mourning the departure of Virgil. Notice the adjective 'atro' — a classicizing way to say dark in a menacing, deadly way. For a moment, the loss of Virgil and the loss of Eden are one. Notice the literal translation from the fourth book of the *Aeneid*. 'Agnosco veteris vestigia flammae' (4, 23) says Dido when she is falling in love with Aeneas. I recognize the signs of the ancient flame, says Dante when he sees Beatrice again. About to find his mortal beloved transfigured into Christian blessedness, Dante inhabits the voice of an African queen who committed suicide, a mad heroine of love and death, and sings the immortal words of his beloved master, Virgil-Eurydice.

Earlier in this canto, Dante had inscribed another powerful Virgilian line. A miracle of literature that explains, in one magical shot, the meaning of nostalgia and all the forces that are at work in it.

Beatrice appears in a beautiful, if a tad mawkish, cloud of flowers (he is a darling, my Dante, but a little cliché). She is surrounded by voices that sing for her fragments of poetry, sacred and profane (more than surrounded I feel stretched between all those intertexts ... if I inhabit them all I become a strange creature, both male and female, young and old, pagan and Christian ... They say that's allegory. To you, reader, it may look like a supremely sophisticated bondage, but to me it feels more like a tight bra).

One such intertextual rope sung by the heavenly choir is the only Latin quotation from his beloved Virgil (it is always between them men!): '*manibus*, oh, *date lilia plenis*' (*Purgatorio* 30, 21). This brings us to the sixth book of the *Aeneid*, Virgil's own descent to the underworld. Aeneas visits Hades in order to learn the future of his colonial (sea journey + military campaign) enterprise: the founding of the great city of Rome. His father, Anchises, shows him rather triumphally the future glories of the Roman empire (*Aeneid* 6, 756–892). Yet, all triumphs are based on loss and sorrow, says Virgil through the tragic figure of Marcus Claudius Marcellus, Augustus's nephew, who died at the age of nineteen in 23 BCE. Aeneas sights a handsome youth with shining arms ('egregium forma iuvenem et fulgentibus armis'; 6, 861), BUT ..., a tragic adversative is inscribed in his forehead: he is sad, his eyes dejected ('SED frons laeta parum et deiecto lumina vultu'; 6, 862). His head is circumfused by a dark, tragic night ('nox atra'; 6, 866; remember Dante's tragic dark, 'atro'?). Anchises tries to explain how promising this young man was, the great things he would have done, if only ... if only the gods could forgive, as the story of Orpheus puts it, if only we could imagine an illogical, ungrammatical future in which 'if you were able to break the harsh destiny, you will be Marcellus' ('si qua fata aspera rumpas | tu Marcellus eris'; 6, 882–83). BUT the gods do not pardon, we know that. Anchises' voice breaks, his tears pouring out like flowers ... you will be Marcellus. Give handfuls of lilies! ('tu Marcellus eris. manibus date lilia plenis'; 6, 883). He goes on, bitterly: 'so that I may at least scatter purple flowers and offer useless funereal gifts and vows' (6, 884–86; my translations). [Marcellus is, in other words, the Orphic moment in an otherwise Homeric, information gathering, *nekyia*.]

Dante employs this mournful line to celebrate Beatrice. He turns half a Latin hexameter (the classical epic verse in which the *Aeneid* is written) into one Italian hendecasyllable, with the mere insertion of a particle ... oh ... an interjection, somewhere between a word and a breath, belonging to no language and to all, expressing wonder, fear, sadness, or happiness, depending on how we pronounce it. The linguistic dress of an exclamation mark. Oh! Try and voice it: just an inhale and exhale, no effort from our throat or mouth involved, it is the smoothest piece of sound. In this spirit (breath, whiff, sigh, or even blast, or all the synonyms for respiration and 'soul' you can think of) lives poetry. With this spirit, Dante locks together the classical and the medieval otherworld, a Roman teenager of imperial descent and a young, unknown, Florentine, bourgeois woman, the pagan funerary purple lilies and the Christian white lilies of resurrection. And no; this line does not celebrate the linear, figural triumph of the Christian over the pagan world. Rather, it celebrates nostalgia at its best. Two lines in one, written by two canonical poets, together defy canon. A strange hermaphrodite, in terms of both politics and gender, binds together the imperial male surrounded by a halo of sorrow and the Christian female returning in glory. Two youths, beloved and dead. No triumph, imperial or religious, can make up for their loss, and their return.

Oh

Who utters this interjection? The heavenly choir pronounces it in the fiction of the poem. One clever commentator has interpreted this as the moment when Virgil disappears and Beatrice appears. I love this interpretation: the wave of one magic wand, abracadabra! We also might reasonably imagine Dante-character saying 'oh' (oh-my-god, oh-shit at once) at this cross dissolve. To me, it is us readers uttering 'oh'! Like the audience of a magic show, like children at the circus while the aerialists are flying over our heads on invisible trapezes. Amazed, full of excitement, we witness poetry jumping off into the void, holding together a wholeness that exists only in its immaterial dance, a wholeness suffused with sorrow.

Oh!, we say, for that speck of eternity surrounded by a sea of loss that poetry has brought to us.

I know one Orpheus. A poet who lost his loved one. They had the same name: Nicola and Nicolas. When Nicolas departed, almost hieratically, Nicola went in search for him with words alone. A prose diary, and one poem a day, weaving an impalpable net of words and visions, daily observations and little anecdotes, patiently taking the temperature of his mourning every day, making the bed of his sorrow every night. Everything but memories, because on that fragile net the two lovers still meet 'for real', Nicolas's non-ghostly shade and Nicola's ghostly body. They converse, they even touch each other. There is the occasional quarrel.

He is tired, he says. I don't blame him. He made himself a fiction in his dead husband's story. I have seen him knocking for two years at the gates of Hades, humbly, duly, stubbornly, singing only his sweet spouse, as the days were coming and going: 'te, dulcis coniux, te solo in litore secum | te veniente die, te decedente canebat' (*Georgics* 4, 465–66).

Manibus, oh!, *date lilia plenis*.

6. All In One Place

They are everywhere, so swollen a symbol of danger and allure that we hardly notice them any longer; so overwritten that it is both daunting and hollow to sit and type about them. The logical challenge of the trans-species. How they turned from half birds to half fish. How they moved places across the seas. Why did they become the prime image of the treacherous feminine, beautiful and lethal, or a heteronormative story of sorrow and sacrifice. When does 'the feminine' stop being so terribly banal? How the hell did they end up on the fire engine and attached to the ubiquitous 'nee-naw, nee-naw' of children's books, whereby hordes of toddlers and parents are actually delighted to hear a sound that signifies someone's life is in danger (as a matter-of-factsy acquaintance of mine once pointed out to me)?

This morning, the good news is twofold.

ONE is the voice. We tend to forget that the original sirens' allure and danger is set not in their beauty, the voyeuristic long red hair that barely covers their exposed breasts in depictions that have become mainstream, but in a treasure set much deeper in their chest. The voice, song, poetry. The opposite of the nee-naw: a sound so sweet, so cuddly, so soothing and exciting that it takes hold of all your senses, that it makes you forget the rest. Vibrations that drip and distil slowly in your heart, that swell your being with comfort. Clear harmony (*Odyssey* 12, 44 and 183), sound of honey (12, 187) that fills you with the pleasure and the joy of listening.

Of hearing what? Your story, is their answer:

> δεῦρ' ἄγ' ἰών, πολύαιν' Ὀδυσεῦ, μέγα κῦδος Ἀχαιῶν,
> νῆα κατάστησον, ἵνα νωιτέρην ὄπ' ἀκούσῃς.
> οὐ γάρ πώ τις τῇδε παρήλασε νηὶ μελαίνῃ,
> πρίν γ' ἡμέων μελίγηρυν ἀπὸ στομάτων ὄπ' ἀκοῦσαι,
> ἀλλ' ὅ γε τερψάμενος νεῖται καὶ πλείονα εἰδώς.
> ἴδμεν γάρ τοι πάνθ' ὅσ' ἐνὶ Τροίῃ εὐρείῃ
> Ἀργεῖοι Τρῶές τε θεῶν ἰότητι μόγησαν,
> ἴδμεν δ', ὅσσα γένηται ἐπὶ χθονὶ πουλυβοτείρῃ.
> (*Odyssey* 12, 184–91)

> Come hither on your way, renowned Odysseus, great glory of the Achaeans; stop your ship that you may listen to the voice of us two. For never yet has *anyone* rowed past the island in *their* black ship until *they have* heard the sweet voice from our lips; instead, *they have* joy of it, and *go their* way a wiser *person*. For we know all the toils that in wide Troy the Argives and Trojans endured through the will of the gods, and we know all things that come to pass upon the fruitful earth.

And in your story, everything is contained. All In One Place. [Maybe they can actually read at Apple but have decided to call the app Ulysses and not Siren for marketing reasons. Starbucks already claimed the siren, after all.]

You know the tale: Odysseus fills with wax the ears of his companions, has them tie him hand and foot to the mast, and orders them to row and not pay attention to his pleas; nay, at the acme of the paroxysm, when the sirens' song is most attractive and his desire peaks, they are instructed to bind him tighter. Sounds stranger than expected when you tell it this way.

This is, indeed, a strange story of bonds, pleasure, and knowledge: the fullness of pleasure (τερψάμενος, *terpsamenos*, suggesting the satisfaction of pleasure, *jouissance*) and an increased comprehension (πλείονα εἰδώς, *pleiona eidos*, knowing more things) are bound together in the same line, and they are logically followed by the tale of Odysseus's past (the war of Troy), in turn connected with universal knowledge. The sirens promise, in other words, pleasure as the centre that interconnects the circles of 'me' and 'everything'. Not only it is a good story to hear; it is also mine.

If I were to rewrite the sirens, I'd be a (female) drug lord who puts on the market a drug called Siren that does precisely that, lulls you with the vibe of your story, enhanced with pleasure and comprehension (it is a good story, and you own it). The shores of the sirens' island, the streets of a post-apocalyptic city lined with grotesquely dead drug fiends, 'great heap of bones of moldering men, and round the bones the skin is shriveling' (*Odyssey* 12, 45–46). Ambulance and police sirens shrieking through the endless night, dirty with orange streetlights and toxic fumes. The hero, a rugged policeman who has his best friend, a coarse snitch, inject him with a wax that hinders the drug, and so manages to take a shot of the Siren without dying, all written in a gritty and snappy language ready to be shot in black and white ... I have no future as a blockbuster novelist, as you plainly see, but I do think the concepts of drug and addiction, not beauty and attraction, are what best explains the ancient sirens. Some kind of vocal heroin that squares the circle inside. A sound not yet heard. There is something left to wonder in this trite tale.

SECOND. Dante's siren is, thankfully, a rather special creature, which proves my author is a timeless genius (always a boost to the morale). We meet her in canto 19 of the *Purgatorio*, just at the end of a long and complex speech on love and desire that takes hold of the centre of the second canticle (parts of cantos 16 and 17, and canto 18). After the mechanics of passion seem to be explained, she appears in the traveller's dream like a malignant figure, as proof that matters of love are not entirely clarified or obvious. Like those thrillers of the nineties, where the killer you had presumed dead returns after the final credits to terrify the audience in an open-ended micronarrative. You thought it was over, it might happen again ... it might happen to you.

At the start of canto 19, Dante both plants an old story and makes it new. This siren has no wings or fish tail, but she is a version of a staple universal misogyny: the theme of the enchantress turned hag. Children's fables and folktales, epic poems, novels, and film: whatever your pleasure is, sooner or later you will encounter an evil woman whose beauty is magic, often due to a spell or a potion. Beauty (maleficent, feminine beauty) is only as deep as the skin and hides all sorts of horror and disgust. An ancient philosophical and moral theme crosses history all the way to modern psychoanalysis and our popular culture. My favourite take on the shallowness of female beauty is that of the medieval monk Odo of Cluny (tenth century).

> Nam corporea pulchritudo in pelle solummodo constat. Nam si viderent homines hoc quod subtus pellem est [...] mulieres videre nausearent. Iste decor in flegmate, et sanguine, et humore, ac felle, consistit. Si quis enim considerat quae intra nares, et quae intra fauces et quae intra ventrem

> lateant, sordes utique reperiet. Et si nec extremis digitis flegma vel stercus tangere patimur, quomodo ipsum stercoris saccum amplecti desideramus? (*Collationes* 2, 9).

> Bodily beauty resides solely in the skin. If men were able to see what is under the skin [...] they would throw up at the sight of women. Their beauty is made of phlegm, blood, humours, and gall. If we consider what is concealed in the nostrils, in the mouth and in the bowels, we find it is just garbage. And if we do not suffer to touch phlegm and faeces even with our fingertips, why would we want to hug a sack of shit? (my translation).

Beauty and youth, say Odo & Co., are just deceptive ornaments of an intrinsically sinful and constitutionally corruptible body. Beauty, like body (and even more quickly than body), is perishable and subject to decay. In the traditional narrative of the enchantress turned hag, then, external beauty becomes a sorcery that holds the unsuspecting male hostage to some kind of evil plot. Until … until he pierces her (so banal it pains me to write it); he penetrates her, tears the plot open, sometimes by sheer mistake. He has both rational and under-the-belt tools to do so. Horror unleashes, but it also fizzles out, and we all know what happens. Luscious hair turns sparse and grey, the skin wrinkles, we catch a glimpse of a toothless mouth and a flaccid belly, fluids of all kinds erupt.

So, what about the genius of your poet and yesterday's boost, you might ask?

He flips the story around. He starts with the hag.

The siren that appears in the traveller's dream is not a mythical figure, or a seductive woman: she is 'just', and yet much more realistically, an ugly woman; crippled, perhaps disfigured by disease, covered in rags, stench emanating from her womb. A poor woman, like the many beggars Dante saw in Florence or on the roads of Italy. Much more tragic and shocking, much less domesticated.

I was recently reminded of Dante's siren when I saw an etching by young Rembrandt at the Ashmolean Museum in Oxford: the portrait of a poor woman, her genitals on show, her eyes devoid of sparkle, both grotesque and true; the tragic reality of abject poverty (Figure 6).

Dante's siren appears in a dream.

> una femmina balba
> ne li occhi guercia, e sovra i piè distorta,
> con le man monche, e di colore scialba.
> (*Purgatorio* 19, 7–9)

a woman, stammering, with eyes asquint and crooked on her feet, with maimed hands, and of sallow hue.

It is the gaze of the poet that makes her beautiful and attractive. It erases her flaws and colours her with the shade of beauty and youth, and, importantly, it unties her tongue, and releases the song.

> Io la mirava; e come 'l sol conforta
> le fredde membra che la notte aggrava,
> così lo sguardo mio le facea scorta
>   la lingua, e poscia tutta la drizzava
> in poco d'ora, e lo smarrito volto,
> com' amor vuol, così le colorava.
>   Poi ch'ell' avea 'l parlar così disciolto,
> cominciava a cantar sì, che con pena
> da lei avrei mio intento rivolto.
> (*Purgatorio* 19, 10–18)

ALL IN ONE PLACE

Figure 6. Rembrandt van Rjin, Etching, 1631.

> I gazed upon her: and even as the sun revives cold
> limbs benumbed by night, so my look made ready
> her tongue, and then in but little time set her full
> straight, and colored her pallid face even as love
> requires. When she had her speech thus unloosed,
> she began to sing so that it would have been hard
> for me to turn my attention from her.

This transformation allows the siren to find her ancient song, full of pleasure and fulfilment.

> 'Io son', cantava, 'io son dolce serena,
> che ' marinari in mezzo mar dismago;
> tanto son di piacere a sentir piena!
>   Io volsi Ulisse del suo cammin vago
> al canto mio; e qual meco s'ausa,
> rado sen parte; sì tutto l'appago'.
> (*Purgatorio* 19, 19–24)

> 'I am', she sang, 'I am the sweet Siren who leads mariners astray in mid-sea, so full am I of pleasantness to hear. Ulysses, eager to journey on, I turned aside to my song; and whosoever abides with me rarely departs, so wholly do I satisfy him'.

Wait a minute! Another twist on the story of Ulysses? Indeed. One single siren. Ulysses' journey deviated by her. No wax, or mast, or ropes. Yet, the aspects of sweetness, pleasure, and fulfilment are the same. Dante, who (remember remember) did not read Homer, has another stunning Homeric intuition, and emphasizes the plenitude of the pleasure deriving from the siren's song: she is so 'full of pleasure' ('di piacer [...] piena') that she completely satisfies the sailors who listen to her ('tutto l'appago'), as per the Homeric τερψάμενος, fulfilment here being again the tricky 'purgatorial' mix of appeasement and payment ('appago', from 'pagare', to pay, see chapter 4). A clever dissension from the unread *Odyssey* is the radius of attraction: while Homer's sirens claim that the sailors depart from them appeased and more knowledgeable, Dante's siren, more honestly, states that they do not leave her.

The hinge of the Dantean twist is a sibylline construction in line 22, where one could read either 'With my song, I turned away Ulysses, who was keen on his journey' or 'I turned Ulysses away from his journey, making him keen to hear my song'. The hinge of this twist, the hinge of all twists, is desire. Desire is, aptly, 'vago'; so vague and sophisticated an adjective that we cannot quite pin it to one meaning: desirous, enamoured, adventurous, wandering, and more. So, did she twist Ulisse's route after he had committed to his new journey in the Atlantic, or is she the lure that hijacked the *nostos* and sent him flying beyond Hercules' pillars? In this second interpretation, she might then be the seducing (and ultimately illusory) image of 'virtue and knowledge' that takes hold of our hero and erases his every other desire, which would dovetail well with the story we have heard in hell. This would also concur with a couple of ancient upmarket readings, in which the sirens are not a matter of lust and seduction, but the attraction of knowledge itself.

So says Cicero. In his moral work *De finibus bonorum et malorum* (5, XVIII, 48–49), while celebrating the powers of the human mind, Cicero extolls the love of knowledge as the most complete and exclusive desire of all, and he wonders whether the song of the sirens might be precisely that: not so much the sweetness of their voice, nor the unheard variety of their song, but the hit of knowledge itself. A great man like Ulysses tangled in the net of a silly song? Impossible. They must have promised knowledge, and of the best kind, not the amateur's piecemeal and superficial one, but the 'big stuff'. For Cicero, that meant being able to 'enter' the nature of all things ('intrandum [...] rerum naturam') through which we can get to know ourselves (5, XVI, 44). [I wonder whether it is still true two millennia later.]

> Vidit Homerus probari fabulam non posse si cantiunculis tantus irretitus vir teneretur; scientiam pollicentur, quam non erat mirum sapientiae cupido patria esse cariorem. Atque omnia quidem scire cuiuscumquemodi sint cupere curiosorum, duci vero maiorum rerum contemplatione ad cupiditatem scientiae summorum virorum est putandum (*De finibus* 5, XVIII, 49).

> Homer was aware that his story would not sound
> plausible if the magic that held his hero immeshed
> was merely an idle song! It is knowledge that the
> Sirens offer, and it was no marvel if a lover of
> wisdom held this dearer than his home. A passion
> for miscellaneous omniscience no doubt stamps
> *one* as a mere dilettante; but it must be deemed
> the mark of a superior mind to be led on by the
> contemplation of high matters to a passionate love
> of knowledge (translation by H. Rackham).

Enmeshed ... dearer than home ... some of Dante's Ulisse is already there. Ulysses, it seems, had started taking off already in antiquity.

The sirens are learned for Ovid as well; they are the *doctae sirenae*. Ovid makes them the wise friends of Proserpina, her companions in the fateful moment when she was abducted by Ades while picking flowers. He wonders whether this is the sirens' only fault; being the witnesses to a dark and tragic crime:

> vobis, Acheloides, unde
> pluma pedesque avium, cum virginis ora geratis?
> an quia, cum legeret vernos Proserpina flores,
> in comitum numero, doctae Sirenes, eratis?
> quam postquam toto frustra quaesistis in orbe,
> protinus, et vestram sentirent aequora curam,
> posse super fluctus alarum insistere remis
> optastis facilesque deos habuistis et artus
> vidistis vestros subitis flavescere pennis.
> ne tamen ille canor mulcendas natus ad aures
> tantaque dos oris linguae deperderet usum,
> virginei vultus et vox humana remansit.
> (*Metamorphoses* 5, 552–63)

> But, daughters of Acheloüs, why have you the feathers and feet of birds, though you still have maidens' features? Is it because, when Proserpina was gathering the spring flowers, you were among the

number of her companions, ye Sirens, skilled in song? After you had sought in vain for her through all the lands, that the sea also might know your search, you prayed that you might float on beating wings above the waves: you found the gods ready, and suddenly you saw your limbs covered with golden plumage. But, that you might not lose your tuneful voices, so soothing to the ear, and that rich dower of song, maiden features and human voice remained (translation by G. P. Goold).

Proserpina's story is one intolerable composite of tragedy and symbol. A girl abducted by the hideous older man. The loss of Eden. Embodiment, the human ex-perience, death, rebirth. Hypnotic pomegranate seeds — juicy, putrid, the colour of blood. Winter and summer. [The girl now spends half the year in Hades with her husband and half the year on earth with her mother. She does not seem to mind, but we do.] They were there, the sirens, witnessing the abduction. Speechless, song-less. It always amazes me how Ovid, who has no restraint in pushing stories at their most disturbing acme, and in forcing his readers onto some very uncomfortable spots, sometimes allows himself a surprising light touch, as is the case with the sirens (and with Orpheus, as we have seen in the previous chapter). Ovid's sirens are no monsters, just inconsolable friends. They do not stop travelling (like Ulisse), they do not stop searching their lost companion, and the merciful gods turn them into colourful winged creatures, with oars-like wings. But they let them retain their lovely voice, and their beautiful song, a soothing, rather than provoking, sound ('canor mulcendas natus ad aures').

Dante's siren might then hint at the Ciceronian lust for knowledge, or at the restless and canorous journey at sea of Proserpina's friends. But, let us face it, she is not upscale, or elite; if she is a twisted figure for the desire for knowledge that has turned Ulysses from his journey, she is a pretty vulgar one. If anything, she could be a figure for the dissemination of learning gone wrong — a frequent theme in ancient and medieval times, a theme in which the image of the beautiful woman turned horrid is at home, with other writers featuring Muses stripped naked by inept and ignorant readers, or Philosophy prostituted at the brothel.

Moreover, the classy references still do not fully explain why Dante's old maimed little lady would have turned Ulysses away from his journey, whatever that is. She does not, however, turn Dante-traveller away from journeying in purgatory, but it takes a bit of action to save him. Somewhat as passive as Homer's Odysseus at the mast, Dante-traveller is at the centre of an equally sadistic play. With a further twist on the theme of the enchantress-turned-hag, a (holy) woman intervenes to chase the (evil) woman away.

A woman from heaven rushes in and orders Virgil to comply with the traditional male act and uncover the hag; to reveal, with a theatrical gesture, the horror emanating from her womb, a revolting stench (Odo is cheering here) that wakes our dreamer up:

> Ancor non era sua bocca richiusa
> una donna apparve santa e presta
> lunghesso me per far colei confusa.
>   'O Virgilio, Virgilio, chi è questa?'
> fieramente dicea; ed el venìa
> con li occhi fitti pur in quella onesta.
>   L'altra prendea, e dinanzi l'apria
> fendendo i drappi, e mostravami 'l ventre;
> quel mi svegliò col puzzo che n'uscia
> (*Purgatorio* 19, 25–33)

> Her mouth was not yet shut when a lady, holy and alert, appeared close beside me to put her to confusion. 'O Virgil, o Virgil, who is this?' she said sternly; and he came on with his eyes fixed only on that honest one. He seized the other and

> laid her bare in front, rending her garments and showing me her belly: this waked me with the stench that issued therefrom [therefrom? As with the previous 'therewithin', sometimes this translation baffles me. Therefrom my ass! A facetious friend of mine would say].

Shortly after, Virgil explains that 'the ancient witch' (*Purgatorio* 19, 58) is an image for *cupiditas*, the composite of the 'sins of passion' (lust, gluttony, and avarice) that are purged in the higher terraces of purgatory. A fast and plain allegorical reading is ready on your plate: Passion, ugly and disgusting, looks momentarily beautiful and seduces the Christian, but then Reason (the old, dull explanation of the role of Virgil), instructed by Faith, shows that Passion actually stinks.

But this accounts only for part of the story. To me the dream of the siren, coming as it does after the poem's grand and nuanced explanation of the nature of love, divine and human alike, also represents the fallibility, subjectivity, and ultimate catastrophe of the experience of love. How to be in love is to gild an otherwise opaque object with the fine dust of our desires, like the gaze of the poet does. The siren represents the instability of beauty, not its inherent dishonesty; a beauty that is in the eye of the beholder in many more, and much more tragic, ways than we think.

The siren also represents the allure and the danger of the magnificent textuality that is borne in the encounter of fallible love and unsteady beauty. The siren can be read, in other words, as poetry. (In line with the nature of the ancient sirens as voice, this siren could represent the form of the text, its exterior ornament, its seductive call.) There is too much technical faffing around her: two poets, one making her up and giving her a beautiful voice only to be then seduced by her, the other tearing the siren's clothes apart and displaying her horror again. Even her initial ugliness can be almost wholly related to the poetic art. Her stammering ('balba'; 19, 7) suggests poor fluency, her squinting ('guercia'; 19, 8) hints at the eyes, the main engine of the process of love and the chief image of love poetry, her limping ('sovra i piè distorta'; 19, 8) could allude to crooked metrical feet, and her pale complexion ('di colore scialba'; 19, 9) to a lack of rhetorical colours. The gaze of the beholder/lover/poet rectifies all these flaws, constructing an image of female beauty and beautiful poetry, making her tongue fluent, setting her straight and giving her a rhetorical make up, creating a visual/textual attraction that absorbs all the beholder/reader's desires.

It takes another poet to uncover her. The tearing of her clothes by Virgil to expose the horrid materiality of her body is an act of violent reading; the stripping away of rhetorical layers in order to unveil the substantial ugliness of her content.

What about the 'other' woman in this story of textuality? I am not sure, I must admit. She works better in the allegorical reading of 'sin-and-salvation'.

Unveiling, undressing, uncovering, denuding: you won't be surprised to hear that these are images for reading and interpretation, and they have been around forever, from the Bible to our days. And it is sexist, there is no way around it. Roland Barthes, an intellectual whom I otherwise much admire, compares reading to a striptease in *Pleasure of the Text*; an accelerated one, in fact, where the spectator rushes on stage to fast-forward the denudation, to help the stripper out of her costume.

Really, Mr Barthes? Besides the obvious complaint about the objectification of the female body, this is an utterly empty and boring metaphor for a large part of the reading humanity. I can assure you that the last thing I think about when I open a book is the Chippendales. In addition to vulgar, it sounds plainly wrong to me. The desires and pleasures of reading are much more sophisticated and fluid, I think.

What about the other woman in this story of reading-as-stripping, then? Does she make the striptease scene of reading somewhat more feminist? A female reader who incites the male interpreter to strip the female text: is this some kind of premodern burlesque? In my research on women-as-text I have oftentimes encountered female texts stripping and reclothing themselves, but rarely such a crowded stage. Are the woman text (the siren) and the woman reader (the holy lady) reclaiming for themselves the act of stripping and interpretation?

For a daughter of an older, even primitive, form of feminism [if I have to declare myself, I suppose my politics are still second wave, and my intellectual appreciation somewhere at the beginning of the third], this is a truly complicated issue. The-object-becomes-subject-and-subverts-an-imposed-order kind of trick has its appeal but does not quite convince me. There is a sadness to it that I cannot but notice. A sorrow, a rift, the tears of those for whom it was no play.

My staple anecdote on the topic is the following. Some years ago, the object-turned-subversive-subject thing trickled down to the gym I was a member of. Suddenly, pole dancing was marketed as a great, fun, and empowering way to keep fit for women. So they set up classes, and planted a pole in 'my' yoga studio. ('My': I wonder whether this whole story, and my own aversion to sex-positive feminism, revolves around a petty resentment at expropriation.) And then, to my puzzlement and amusement, a shutter went up. Not sure where the problem was: embarrassment from the inside or voyeurism from the outside. A cheap, plastic venetian blind. Beige. Never mind sadness: that soulless thing had no tears to cry.

The curtain closes very fast on the *Purgatory*'s burlesque too, but the siren (sirens, in the plural) makes a quick comeback later in earthly paradise, when Dante is trashed by his departed beloved. 'Next time, when you hear the sirens, don't be such a sissy', indignant Beatrice screams. [Is she telling me that I am a wimp Ulysses? Wonders Dante with a downcast face.] At this point (*Purgatorio* 31, 45), the formidable allegory come alive is tracing a damning bi(bli)ography of her lover/poet — a twin accusation of betrayal and rubbish writing. We soon understand what the siren/s stand for ... the call of lyric poetry perhaps, a narcissistic cutie we met a long time ago, the devastation of our Eden, a lethal self-destructive furore, the day justification kicked in for both why and how we carried ourselves in matters of love, an embarrassing attempt at rationalizing it all, someone at the window we once fell in love with for the gentle way they looked at us [*voilà*, belatedly a list of Dante's other works, heavily translated by 'life']. 'Still', says Dante, 'desire, desires, all previous, all future illusions turned ugly are the wings to my flight of writing.' 'I may be a limp Ulysses', he continues, wondering if this is a good time to raise the gaze at her [it is not], 'but I listened to all them sirens without the need of wax or ropes' [stop here, we plead]. 'You are one of them too', he ventures, with a half sly, half contrite smile. [He should not have contradicted her. Let us leave it at that.]

Still, the journey of writing is the *Comedy*'s great Ulyssean adventure, one with which Dante identifies entirely, sirens and all. Following an image old as literature, Dante envisions his poetry as a navigation in perilous, untravelled waters.

PAPER BOATS

>Si je désire une eau d'Europe, c'est la flache
>Noire et froide où vers le crépuscule embaumé
>Un enfant accroupi plein de tristesses, lâche
>Un bateau frêle comme un papillon de mai.

>If I want a water of Europe, it is the black
>Cold puddle where in the sweet-smelling twilight
>A squatting child full of sadness releases
>A boat as fragile as a May butterfly.
>(translation by Wallace Fowlie)

>I want none of Europe's waters unless it be
>The cold black puddle where a child, full of sadness,
>Squatting, looses a boat as frail
>As a moth into the fragrant evening
>(translation by Samuel Beckett)

If you can imagine a sixteen-year-old writing these lines then you can understand literature at its rawest, and most rare. You can hold poetry in your hands if you can envisage the miracle of childhood sadness (not trauma or tantrum, not displeasure or fear, not need or frustration: sadness). And if you can weigh in your fingertips the lightness of the paper boat, then you will find a moment of stillness in the midst of vortexes, waves, and nimbi. The frailty of the butterfly's wings, the chilling touch of the puddle, the balmy evening, Europe; these are adornments, but of the most sophisticated kind.

It is an old saying that the poet is a child. It is said about many poets, it has been said even about the very adult-looking Dante (by Umberto Saba, whose version of Ulysses I quoted earlier on). Most likely, the poet is a child who knows sadness. A child who needs readers his same age and mood.

[Sad children — I was one — are not always sad. Like everyone else, they have moments of elation and laughter. They cry often, but this is not the point. They are shy, and nervous. They are independent, but not self-sufficient. A slow fire is consuming, or sustaining, them.]

Arthur Rimbaud's *Le Bateau ivre* (of which, above, I quote the second-last of twenty-five stanzas, I add, nervously balancing grand entrance vs the minimum requirements of academic rigour) is my favourite poem (irrelevant until it also is or becomes yours) and an offshoot of Dante's Ulisse. An illegitimate, unacknowledged, non-procreated offspring, that is.

It is just the boat this time, no captain, helmsman, or sailor. Rimbaud's vessel shakes crews and anchors off, breaks away from berths and ports. Exhilarated, hallucinated, free. The boat says 'I' and roams free in the great blue poem of the sea.

> Je me suis baigné dans le Poème
> de la Mer, infusé d'astres, et lactescent,
> dévorant les azurs verts
> (stanza 6)

> I bathed in the Poem
> of the Sea, infused with stars and lactescent,
> devouring the azure verses.
> (translation by Fowlie)

There are some Coleridge-style zombies, Homeric curiosity, and Vernian abysses-minus-octopi. Knowledge, as in Dante, is one of the rewards: of storms, vortexes, and currents, of evenings and dawns, and of the fallible perception of humans ('Et j'ai vu quelque fois ce que l'homme a cru voir!'; at times I have seen what *humans* thought *they* saw). The boat, you have guessed, has wings — it wishes to show them to his children-readers:

J'aurais voulu montrer aux enfants ces dorades
Du flot bleu, ces poissons d'or, ces poissons chantants.
— Des écumes de fleurs ont bercé mes dérades
Et d'ineffables vents m'ont ailé par instants.
(stanza 15)

I should have liked to show children those sunfish
Of the blue wave, the fish of gold, the singing fish.
— Foam of flowers rocked my drifting
And ineffable winds winged me at times.
(translation by Fowlie)

Ulisse's speech begins with 'When I was' ('Quando ...'), the *bateau*'s speech begins with 'As I was' ('Comme ...'). The *bateau*'s speech is immersive. This poem *is* the siren, it is the addictive sound that tells you everything about yourself, and then leaves you shaking, fragile, frustrated, and wanting for more. It ends, you have guessed, in disaster. The *bateau* wishes dissolution ('Ô que ma quille éclate! Ô que j'aille à la mer!': O let my keel burst! O let me go into the sea!, stanza 23; translation by Fowlie), a tempestuous dissolution, perhaps, like the one that sank Ulisse's boat. But it doesn't come. There is no merciful (?) god here. [It is only after re-reading Rimbaud that I have contemplated that Dante's 'other' who sends the deadly vortex might be actually compassionate.] The *bateau* dreams of being folded like paper and pensively abandoned on the dark puddle of Europe (stanza 24), but it might end up back where it fled from, into its worst nightmare: the society of men (this is intended on my part), that of commerce, war, imprisonment.

Je ne puis plus, baigné de vos langueurs, ô lames,
Enlever leur sillage aux porteurs de cotons,
Ni traverser l'orgueil des drapeaux et des flammes,
Ni nager sous les yeux horribles des pontons.
(stanza 25)

> No longer can I, bathed in your languor, o waves,
> Follow in the wake of the cotton boats,
> Nor cross through the pride of flags and flames,
> Nor swim under the terrible eyes of prison ships.
> (translation by Fowlie)
>
> Steeped in the languors of the swell, I may
> Absorb no more the wake of the cotton-freighters,
> Nor breast the arrogant oriflammes and banners,
> Nor swim beneath the leer of the pontoons.
> (translation by Beckett)

Dante's poetry *is* a ship, but the poet firmly holds the helm, and steers it skilfully in untravelled seas away from vortexes. In the story of writing, then, Dante is Homer's Ulysses, not his own: he travels, encounters, faces dangers, ends up underwater a couple of times, risks losing his crew, and comes back to his Ithaca, to his desk with the instruments of writing laid out. In the *Banquet,* Dante describes his writing as a boat that calmly sails; the wind of his desire (style, language, writing) inflating the sail of his reason (content, thought, subject matter).

> lo tempo chiama e domanda la mia nave uscir di porto; per che, dirizzato l'artimone della ragione all'òra del mio desiderio, entro in pelago con isperanza di dolce cammino e di salutevole porto e laudabile nella fine della mia cena (*Convivio* 2, I, 1).
>
> time calls and requires my ship to leave port; thus, having set the sail of my reason to the breeze of my desire, I enter upon the open sea with the hope of a smooth voyage and a safe and praiseworthy port at the end of my feast.

This would be one of my favourite passages in Dante were it not for its absurd conclusion involving dinner, which just proves what I have always suspected, that the guy cannot write prose.

In the *Comedy*, unsurprisingly, the metaphoric use of navigation as writing is embedded at the beginning of each canticle. At the outset of *Inferno* there is, intuitively, a splendidly symbolic shipwreck, to which I shall return. On its arrival in *Purgatory*, the little ship is, as we have seen, on a safer course:

> Per correr miglior acque alza le vele
> omai la navicella del mio ingegno,
> che lascia dietro a sé mar sì crudele
> (*Purgatorio* 1, 1–3)

> To course over better water the little bark of my genius now hosts her sails, leaving behind her a sea so cruel

These lines are as plain as they are metaphorical: this well-constructed, sound, stable image *is* a solid ship. Having crossed with suffering the dirty, slow, dangerous water of hell, Dante's text — seen in the phase of ideation ('ingegno'), not of material writing — can now lift its sails, its navigation more dynamic and yet tranquil. End of turbulence, good weather ahead. The seat belt signal is off.

I love the way medieval illuminators capture this metaphor, flatten it, and yet reveal it. Now, the discourse of medieval manuscript illumination is endlessly entertaining. When I venture into it, I experience a childish pleasure. This is due no doubt to my limited expertise in the field (which is always a good gateway to pleasure), but also to the fact that medieval art is infantile, especially so when it is applied to the *Comedy*, a comic text of a serious nature: illuminations manage to catch and expose the child in Dante. Ultimately, the utterly hilarious fact is that the two media, text and image, do and do not properly communicate, no matter how they (and we) try.

With medieval illuminations we typically deal with different artists (writer, scribe, and illuminator/s), with stock, even recyclable images that are, however, idiosyncratically diverse, with different skills applied at different times, with different trades, and with different publics that are permanently linked on one fragile page as they try and construct together one awkward 'meaning', only to be dismembered again by modern editions (in which, as well as illumination, also the great variance of a medieval manuscript is obliterated) and by disciplinary boundaries (art historians study illuminations and historians of literature or of language study the text).

In the next few pages, then, I propose we form a playgroup: a child author, an infantile art, an immature academic, and a child reader, if you do not mind to become so momentarily. I hope you share with me the conclusion that infantilization is not always a bad thing (once you do it yourself and don't let the evil other — the heteronormative Parent — do it to you: aha!, the fun already begins; I have appropriated appropriation).

The illuminations that give me the most childish delight are the so-called 'decorated' or 'historiated' initials. The initial letter (of a book, of a section, in the case of the *Comedy* of a canto or a canticle) is traced as a frame, inside which some kind of veduta of the text that we are about to read is inscribed. A pale trace of decorated initials is retained in modern books, with the initials of chapters printed in larger font or different type. In medieval times, all sorts of layers were embedded in such illuminations: language (the letter) becomes matter (the frame), and is then flattened into painting (the letter-frame is painted on the page) to enclose the visual rendering of a piece of text that is written next to the frame and that the historiated initial frames in turn. It is thoroughly delectable when, instead of

Comicia la ſa parte dela comedia di date
alleghieri di fireçe. nella quale parte ſi
purgano li comeſſi peccati zuitij dequali
luomo ε coféſſo τ pentuto cōammo diſati
ffaçione. τ contiene. xxxiij. canti.
Qui nel primo canto ſono quelli che ſpera
no diuenire quando che ſia alebeate genti.

PEr correr miglior
acque alça le uele
omai la nauicella
delmio ingegno
che laſcia dietro aſſe
mar ſi crudele.

Et cantero di quel ſecondo regno
doue lumano ſpirito ſi purgha
τ di ſalire al ciel diuenta degno
Ma qui la morta poeſi riſurgha
o ſante muſe poi che uoſtro ſono
τ qui caliope alquanto ſurgha
Seguitando elmio canto conquel ſono
Dicui lepiche miſere ſentiro
lo colpo tal che diſperar perdono
Dolce color doriental çaffiro
che ſaccoglieua neſſereno aſpecto
dal meçço puro inſino alprimo giro
A ghi occhi miei ricomincio dilecto
toſto chio uſci fuor delaura morta
che mauea contriſtati liocchi eſpecto

V idi preſſo di me un ueghio ſolo
    degno di tanta reuerença inuiſta
    che piu non dee a padre alcun figliuolo
L unga la barba τ di pel bianco miſta
    portaua iſuo cavelli ſimigliante
    dequai cadeua alpecto doppia liſta
L i raggi deſſequattro luci ſante
    fregiauan ſi la ſua faccia dilume
    chio lueda come ſol foſſe dauante
C hi ſiete uoi chencontro alcieco fiume
    fuggita uete la pregione etterna
    diſſel mouendo quelle honeſte piume
C hi u a guidati oche uiſu lucerna
    uſcendo fuor della profonda nocte
    che ſempre nera fa lauaſſe inferna
S on le leggi dabiſſo coſi rocte
    ce mutato in ciel nuouo conſiglio
    che damnati uenite ale mie grotte
L o duca mio allor midie dipiglio
    τ con parole τ comani τ concenni
    reuerenti miſe legambe el ciglio
P oſcia riſpuoſe alui dame nonuenni
    donna ſceſe dalciel perliquai priegh
    dalamia compagnia coſtui ſouenni
M a dache tuo uoler chepiu ſiſpiegh
    dinoſtra condicion comella ε uera
    eſſer nonpuote ilmio chatte ſi niegh
Q ueſti nom ide mai lultima ſera
    ma perla ſua follia le ſu ſi preſſo
    che molto pro tempo auolger era

a particular piece of text, the image of the author is encased in the very initial that he/she (you can't catch me) first traced or dictated as the initial (indeed) manifestation of their 'genius' and inspiration. Rules explained, let us play this game. It is repetitive, free of care, and amusing.

The initial P of Purgatory becomes a circular frame, is filled with water, and a boat is placed in it. Often, it looks like a badly traced brown shell. Dante, after all, writes of a little boat, but this is too much of a reduction; a nut-shell (aha! It is easy when you let go). Two oversized figures, representing Virgil and Dante, are often chatting the crossing away (Figure 7).

It is fascinating to see the way the decorated initial takes up the entire page, flustering it with banners and flame-like gold (Rimbaud, what are you doing in my playgroup? Your 'drapeaux' and 'flammes' have stuck with me from the previous page, so vivid was your drawing of that final image). A heavy, over-productive, overbearing alphabet in drag, the dress-up party of language. (Notice the little stylized, 'meaning-less' dragon on the top, its face merging into the decorative leaf.)

Of this kind of rough, nut-shell representation, one of my favourites is the depiction that displays a bit of subdivision of labour, with Virgil at the oars and Dante at the sails (Figure 8). You see what I mean when I say 'they (the illuminators) don't get it': Virgil is not supposed to be in the picture — this is Dante-writer, not traveller, sailing on the boat of his poetic genius. Well, what do you do with Virgil, then, how do you make him cross to purgatory? (silly! They didn't cross the sea; they climbed over Lucifer's willy! giggle). Unless it takes an older poet, the tradition of poetry perhaps, to row the new poet's boat ahead, whilst the sea is contained by but also exceeds the frame of the letter; the bottom of the letter P becoming another hull caressed by

Figure 8. Firenze, Biblioteca Medicea Laurenziana, Plut.40.13 (detail).

Figure 9. Firenze, Biblioteca Medicea Laurenziana, Conv.Soppr.204, 96r (detail).

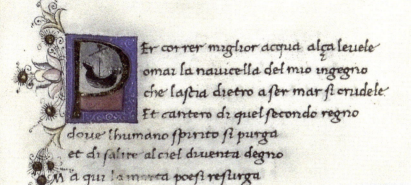

Figure 10a. Firenze, Biblioteca Medicea Laurenziana,
Plut.40.20, c. 78r (detail).

the wave — a blue wave morphing into a blue flower, 'foam of flowers rocked my drifting' … Arthur; would you please stop disrupting my game? — the belly of the P an inflated wing. The vessel of language, perhaps. The new poet's sail transgresses the frame of the letter, rising from the centre of the boat, where it lies somewhat lowered, to be lifted outside of the constraints of the P, in an imaginary non-sky. Did we put on wings in the mad flight, perhaps?

Sometimes the boat is by itself. Alone and personified. And navigating. *Le bateau* itself. In one early fifteenth-century illumination (Figure 9), while the detail of the ship becomes sharper — we have a mast, a crow nest, mainsail and jib, ropes and ladder, and the hint of an actual deck — the human presence is lost. The not-so-little bark is now sailing by itself. Is it drifting? And where?

The one in Figure 10 (a and b) truly embodies *le bateau* for me; there is something strangely desperate in this image. The water is cold, the hull dark, the sails, although unfurled, are tattered in my imagination. There is an ominous mist

Figure 10b. Firenze, Biblioteca Medicea Laurenziana, Plut.40.20, c. 78r (smaller detail).

rising from the sea; sea and sky fade into each other in a flat grey palette. The P is severe, grim, like the border of mourning paper. Even the inevitable flowers look like they are grieving in their gold and black suit. A sense of decay, and of profound undoing. A ghost ship — you got it, Charlie: the Black Pearl! Or: the only illuminator who actually read the text with a bit of curiosity and depicted the boat of the poem just before it enters the 'better waters' of the second canticle, still trapped in the gloom of so cruel a sea of hell.*

One last one, then the game is over (for today). The illustration of the Egerton codex (Figure 11a). An illuminated initial (the pink P on the bottom) is enclosed in an oddly shaped square P and features a double Dante.

In the foot of the P, Dante is writing in his study. Next to his desk, a stylized image of a starry sky — or is it the lactescent poem of the sea with its azure verse storming in? Well done, Artie, your poem has now become an illumination on the page of my memory, as you plainly see. Dante writes himself writing, the two little men are plainly the same, they are making the same gesture within the same

---

* One child has momentarily left the group and sits pensive on a step. An air of melancholy around her. What is she pondering? No, not the Black Pearl as that raucous Charlie says; nor the clever illuminator, as our group's leader is telling us (she acts all sweet, babytalk and all, but she thinks she is smarter than us). In this illumination there is a candid reader, she thinks, who knew about exile, and of hearts in the storm, and of another little boat of writing tossed in dark seas. 'Cumque sit hibernis agitatum fluctibus aequor, | pectora sunt ipso turbidiora mari. | quo magis his debes ignoscere, candide lector, | si spe sint, ut sunt, inferiora tua. | non haec in nostris, ut quondam, scripsimus hortis, | nec, consuete, meum, lectule, corpus habes. | iactor in indomito brumali luce profundo | ipsaque caeruleis charta feritur aquis | improba pugnat hiems indignaturque quod | ausim scribere se rigidas incutiente minas. | vincat hiems hominem! sed eodem tempore, | quaeso, ipse modum statuam carminis, illa sui.' (Ovid, *Tristia* 1, XI, 33-44) [and though the sea is shaken by stormy billows my breast is more turbulent than the sea. And so, kindly reader, you should grant me the more indulgence should these verses be — as they are — poorer than your hopes. They were not written, as of old, in my garden or while you, my familiar couch, supported my frame. I am tossing of a winter's day on the stormy deep, and my paper is sprayed by the dark waters. The vicious storm battles, indignant that I dare to write whilst he is brandishing against me his stern threats. Let the storm vanquish the man; but at the same time that I end my verse, let him, I pray, reach his own end (translation by G. P. Goold)].

Or maybe it is only me, she thinks. Why do I always have to be so sad and so different? Why is my heart always stormier than the storm? Well, she thinks with a sigh, time to rejoin the group.

Figure 11a. British Library, Egerton MS 943, f.63r (detail).

activity, and the corresponding pages are full of characters. On top, however, Dante's room has become the sea. He is on the boat, he is actually the captain, his study now turned in the quarterdeck.

[Check this kaleidoscope out, friends: a page carries a letter that is a painting, in which a page with letters is depicted, in which … reminds me of those endless nursery rhymes. In Italian, we have a very funny one: 'C'era una volta un re | seduto sul sofà | che disse alla sua serva | raccontami una storia | la storia incominciò | "C'era una volta un re | seduto sul sofà ..."' (Once upon a time there was a king | sitting on the sofa | who said to his maidservant | tell me a story | the story began | 'Once upon a time there was a king | sitting on the sofa ...') and on you go for as long as you want. This is a comic version of the frame of the *Thousand and One Nights*, incidentally. The death-defying power of story.]

The image of Dante's writing projects the image of Dante's writing. Dante-writer is most likely writing the poem, but what is Dante-captain doing? Recording coordinates on the logbook? Jotting down observations on the new land? Or is he retiring in his innermost self, dreaming of verses to write? Remember this is the 'boat of my genius', and scholars tell us that the mind was viewed like a boat in those times, and the quarterdeck like the place of the mind's highest faculties.

Either way, this image is stunning, isn't it? But a bit grown up, unless you realize the inanity of the two giant oars (I hope I am not missing some crucial info on medieval boat-making) and the silly face of the figurehead, here confusingly placed under the quarterdeck near the stern — looks a little like the mangy wolf in Little Red Riding Hood, doesn't it? Too bad it is not a mermaid.

In the very distance, almost invisible, a light stroke of paint appears to signify 'land', with a tall dark shade, almost a pillar of smoke ... the mountain dark in the distance ('la montagna bruna per la distanza'; *Inferno* 26, 133), Ulisse's sighting of the mount of Purgatory, perhaps?

One last bit of fun before the bell rings. The two Dantes, when you look at them closely, are not exactly the same. Dante 1 (Figure 11b), lost in the imaginary starry sky, seems

Figures 11b and 11c. Dante 1 and Dante 2.

to be captured in the moment of conception — he even looks like he is sucking the end of the pen, as we children do when we draw, his eye fixed on a point beyond the page. Dante 2 (Figure 11c) on the background of the sea seems instead to be writing, his eye intent, the pen more firmly on the page. Who is dreaming of the other? Maybe I am the dreamer, and the bell is ringing, we have to get in line.

Hey, psst, Charlie: do you know what my computer did just now when I was playing cut and paste with the images? … Shush, children! … it labelled my Dante 2 as 'a picture containing text, old, dirty … description automatically generated'. So rude: I am going to tell on it.

Had Derek Walcott seen this page in the Egerton manuscript, he would perhaps have explained it like this:

> Mark you, *he* does not go; he sends his narrator;
> he plays tricks with time because there are two journeys
> in every odyssey, one on the worried water,

the other crouched and motionless, without noise.
For both, 'I' is a mast; a desk is a raft
for one, foaming with paper, and dipping the beak
of a pen in its foam, while an actual craft
carries the other to cities where people speak
a different language, or look at him differently
(*Omeros*, LVIII, ii)

ARE WE THERE YET?

The next time that the Ulysses theme and the boat of the poem appear in the *Comedy*, it is both much more explicit and much more conceptual. This time, Dante places us readers on little boats, and himself on the flagship. We are a fleet.

It is the beginning of the second canto of *Paradiso*, where things start being intellectually challenging: philosophy, theology, science. Many readers are tempted to let go. Dante prefaces this difficult canto with a second proem, a properly oratorical one that actively engages the audience:

> O voi che siete in piccioletta barca,
> desiderosi d'ascoltar, seguiti
> dietro al mio legno che cantando varca,
> tornate a riveder li vostri liti:
> non vi mettete in pelago, ché forse,
> perdendo me, rimarreste smarriti.
> L'acqua ch'io prendo già mai non si corse;
> Minerva spira, e conducemi Appollo,
> e nove Muse mi dimostran l'Orse.
> Voialtri pochi che drizzaste il collo
> per tempo al pan de li angeli, del quale
> vivesi qui ma non sen vien satollo,
> metter potete ben per l'alto sale
> vostro navigio, servando mio solco
> dinanzi a l'acqua che ritorna equale.
> Que' gloriosi che passaro al Colco
> non s'ammiraron come voi farete,
> quando Iasón vider fatto bifolco.
> (*Paradiso* 2, 1–18)

> O you that are in your little bark, eager to hear, following behind my ship that singing makes her way, turn back to see again your shores. Do not commit yourself to the open sea, for perchance, if you lost me, you would remain astray. The water which I take was never coursed before. Minerva breathes and Apollo guides me, and nine Muses point out to me the Bears. You other few who lifted up your necks betimes for bread of angels, of which *human beings* here subsist but never become sated of it, you may indeed commit your vessel to the deep brine, holding to my furrow ahead of the water that turns smooth again. Those glorious ones who crossed the sea to Colchis, when they saw Jason turned plowman, were not as amazed as you shall be.

The elements of this proem are as disparate as they are convergent.

Two groups of readers, both placed in the range of the familiar ('you'); those who have a solid philosophical background and those who don't. I think Dante here is challenging, rather than excluding, the less equipped reader: what would be the point of saying to one's reader 'now stop reading, please'; if not to mean, please read on, just beware this is a little trickier, and more exciting than before. I know this is difficult and you are getting a little impatient, but stay with me, please.

One little boat (remember the many times Ulisse used the word 'small'?), and by implication a more solid boat, on which the better, more erudite readers are. And then there is the poet's boat, commanding the fleet. You have noticed the oddity of the image of a vessel that 'crosses singing'. Luckily, the end of line 3, 'cantando varca', is of such perfect sonority, has the most appealing sequence of consonants and vowels that we forget, or forgive, the logical awkwardness, one may say the ridicule, of a singing boat — even the fearless *bateau* would not claim that much. Unless this boat has become the siren.

Safe shores are still in sight, yet there are chances of getting lost in the high sea (incidentally; 'smarrita', lost, is one of the first words of the entire *Comedy*).

Untravelled waters and a pantheon of Greek divinities, weirdly placed at the outset of a Christian heaven: Minerva, goddess of wisdom, Apollo, god of poetry, and all nine Muses to allow for a bit of stylistic variation (or are they perhaps 'new' Muses? The word 'nove' means both new and nine).

The bread of angels, manna in the Bible — that delicious, moist food that fed the Israelites in the desert during the Exodus, and that can be interpreted, as you can imagine, as all sorts of nurturing backup from above. While addressing his readers in the unfinished *Convivio*, Dante explained that at his banquet one would eat no less than the bread of angels (or, rather, crumbs of it), and described it as human knowledge. It may mean the same in this proem, especially because the canto that follows is heavily technical, complete with hard science and experiments, but for those to whom the idea of a secular Dante causes an onset of urticaria it is to be understood, at least, as theology. Amen, you cannot fight all battles. I wonder which antihistamine they take to alleviate the part with all the Greek deities.

The 'high salt' is a very classical image for the sea; in it, Dante traces the stubbornly precise picture of the wake of the boat leaving a foamy V sign on the surface of the sea, until the water becomes 'equal' again.

And, for our amazement, another story of sea navigation, trespassing, and conquest comes on stage: the story of Jason and the golden fleece, systematized in the third century BCE in Apollonius Rhodius's *Argonautica*, lavishly narrated by Ovid in the seventh book of the *Metamor-*

phoses, and widely popular in the ancient and medieval world. We, the readers, will be more amazed in reading Dante's *Paradiso* than were the Argonauts witnessing the deeds of their leader. [The reference to Jason turned ploughman is a little masterpiece: 'bifolco' is a very low-key word for ploughman, so much so that in modern Italian it signifies a rough farmer and, by extension, a rude person. Here, however, it depicts Jason's most complicated feat — ploughing a field with fire-breathing oxen, only to sow it with dragon teeth, and then to kill the warriors that sprouted from them. Dante, in other words, sows his vernacular realism into the furrow of the classics (in this case, Ovid, *Metamorphoses* 7, 115–21). No wonder readers are amazed by the creature that is sprouting.]

The story of the Argonauts is a tale of navigation in unknown parts of the world (although this is east rather than west) and of successful return. It is, therefore, an 'odyssey' as well as a proper story of conquest and colonization, complete with a powerful (foreign, female) other — the stupendous, horrendous Medea, the woman-in-love, magician and murderer, who commits 'what no Greek woman' would ever dare to do (this is Euripides; this is Athens, spellbound and frightened by the 'barbarians', by otherness, by the dark cry of the soul). Here is the delicious detail I prefigured in chapter 4: in the quote above Dante calls the Argonauts 'glorious' — theirs is the proper modern story, then!

In addition to the difficulty posed by an uncontrollable female character, I feel the fallacy of the story of Argo lies in the presence of a feeble hero (Jason), surrounded by too many Alpha-types (the Argonauts, including Heracles and, you won't believe this, Orpheus); in the vanity of the quest (Jason is sent to retrieve the fleece by his uncle, king Pelias, for the sole reason that he lost a sandal, and a fortune teller had foretold that a single-shoe wearer would bring misfortune); in the excessive materiality of the object of the quest, an actual fleece made of gold; and in some weak storytelling. Weak is not bad in my books, but Apollonius is a scholar and a librarian, and he has the frailty and hesitation of his trade, which makes him overcompensate. Take Orpheus, for instance. Apollonius makes pre-Eurydice, young, bold Orpheus one of the Argonauts for the sole purpose of having someone on board the Argo who can out-sing the sirens (*Argonautica* 4, 891–919). It is not clear whether Orpheus is a better singer than the sirens, but he is definitely louder. In the *Argonautica*, the tragic story of the sirens is told in a quasi-comic mode. The 'virgin' sirens are rather weak, passive; their keyword is 'languor', a torpid, idle yet content state (I told you: drugs are the gateway to understanding the sirens), their song is enchanting yet delicate (λείριον, leirion; lily-like), their voices relentless but fading, while Orpheus, turned into some kind of football choir leader, stretches his lyre as he would a bow and bangs and bangs on 'the rapid beat of a lively song' (4, 907; translation by Willliam H. Race), a deafening and rumbling noise, buzzing in his companions' ears. Eventually, only one man is lost to the sirens, but merciful Aphrodite saves even him. Don't get me wrong: the *Argonautica* is a beautiful story; but sometimes it feels too loud, perfunctory, and latex; a bit like an Avengers movie.

Dante has mixed feelings towards this story. He places Jason in hell, among the seducers (well done him! The way Jason treated women is unacceptable), here he compares us, his readers, to the Argonauts (nice! Can I be Heracles?), and later ... be patient and you will be amazed.

The Ulyssean elements in the proem of *Paradiso* 2 are clear: the speech to the crew; untravelled waters; ocean; trespassing ('cantando varca', similar to Ulisse's 'varco folle'; his mad track); a classical setting; a passion for knowledge (philosophy/theology); a little scuff with the *Convivio* (the 'Ulyssean', i.e., failed, philosophical moment in Dante's career, as many believe) over the bread of angels; a small oration; and water that closes over both Ulisse's ship and the wake of Dante's boat.

The metatextual elements are also plain: we are the readers, the text is a boat. Dante-poet *is* Ulysses giving us, his sailors, a little speech in order to make us even more eager to follow him in his textual journey. The distinction between weak and smart readers is flattery in disguise. Those who keep on reading are the smart ones, by definition. The fact is; we all keep on reading. I have still to meet a reader who has taken Dante's advice and quit after this proem (Macareus, if you are there somewhere, please give us a sign). If this small oration were pronounced in hell, someone could call it fraudulent. But we are in paradise, and the good Christian god is all ears.

Intriguingly, desire and orality mark this journey — we are 'desirous' to 'listen', and the boat of the text sings ('cantando', the prime verb, if you remember, of the epic proem: for good material reasons, in ancient times writing and speaking, reading and listening, were often synonyms). Trespassing is textual, and the untravelled waters are a daring new topic (heaven, and the vision of god). Minerva (knowledge) is the wind in the sails, Apollo (poetry, inspiration) takes the helm, and the Muses (poetic genres) provide the map. The bread of angels is the subject matter (philosophy/theology), and some readers (those on the sturdier boat) have chewed on it before. [Here too navigation and dinner are brought together in the same image, as in the prose of the *Banquet* quoted above, but I hope you agree with me that this floating restaurant is less irritating, or more sophisticated.] We need to follow the poet closely, lest the sea (the untravelled topic) closes over us and we lose track of what is going on. But it is going to be amazing! We are going to be astonished, enthused, entertained. I'm on board.

The enormous untravelled waters are the white page in front of the writer. Here Dante goes all bombastic, but I sense some trepidation on his part, and we feel it in the readers' boat too. Later on in the poem, we often have the impression that our navigator is exhausted. [I wonder if he wants to turn around and go back home, or if, like Macareus, he is tempted to say: I stop here.] When hitting a particularly difficult point of his writing, he even admits that his flagship might not be that grand. Endearingly, the point in question is the description of the heavenly smile of his beloved Beatrice; such an enamouring and indescribable crease that 'the sacred poem is forced to jump' (*Paradiso* 23, 55–69). Dante comments that this part of the navigation 'is no voyage for a little bark, this [topic, the smile] which my daring prow cleaves as it goes, not for a pilot who would spare himself' ('non è pareggio da picciola barca | quel che fendendo va l'ardita prora, | né da nocchier ch'a sé medesmo parca'; 23, 67–69). Or; see it another way, we realize we are all on board a dinghy (or, at best, a small catamaran); it is choppy, risky, but fun.

Whoever has attempted sustained writing — and it need not be a novel, or an epic poem; think an essay, a letter to a friend, a report — knows that there is truth in the sailing simile. The beginning of a new piece of writing, however small, is a momentous event. One feels scared, exposed, and fragile. Unfit for the challenge, with your little frail paper boat. That fragility, you feel it in the skin. But at your fingertips there is excitement, amazement, concentration ... in we go. Often, you might have noticed, it starts very humbly, with buying a notebook, sharpening your pencil (there was loads of sharpening going on in the middle ages), acting compulsively towards the environment around you. Although writing and characters differ widely across history and around the world, the basics are the same: a (normally) flat surface, a hand-held pointed object, with different degrees of sharpness (from chisel to paintbrush) and, in most cases, a dark liquid. A hand that follows docilely the train of thoughts. She knows how to type, doesn't she? I hear a whispered concern — either for my age or for my sanity. Yes yes, I am aware of my modernity; the technology may be different, but the ideology of page and ink is the same, for now at least. A surface and a sign. An incision that no matter how small modifies the universe of human communication: no wonder Dante calls the wake of his boat 'solco' (furrow), which we would expect more on a field than on the sea. A furrow in the sea is an evanescent yet stubborn sign, a gurgling foamy bubble, a grappling cluster of scribbles. It is an impossibility.

Italo Calvino imagines the end of his novel, *The Baron in the Trees* (*Il barone rampante*, 1957), as the return of writing to nothingness. The metaphor, in this case, is that of an unravelling forest:

> [Ombrosa] era un ricamo fatto di nulla che assomiglia a questo filo d'inchiostro, come l'ho lasciato correre per pagine e pagine, zeppo di cancellature, di rimandi, di sgorbi nervosi, di macchie, di lacune, che a momenti si sgrana in grossi acini chiari, a momenti si infittisce in segni minuscoli come semi puntiformi, ora si ritorce su se stesso, ora si biforca, ora collega grumi di frasi con contorni di foglie o di nuvole, e poi si intoppa, e poi ripiglia a attorcigliarsi, e corre e corre e si sdipana e avvolge un ultimo grappolo insensato di parole idee sogni ed è finito.

> [Ombrosa, the location of the adventures of the Baron,] was an embroidery, made on nothing, that resembles this thread of ink, as I've let it run for pages and pages, full of erasures, of references, of nervous blots, of stains, of gaps, that at times crumbles into large pale grains, at times thickens into tiny marks resembling dotlike seeds, now twists on itself, now forks, now links knots of sentences with edges of leaves or clouds, and then stumbles, and then resumes twisting, and runs and runs and unrolls and wraps a last senseless cluster of words ideas dreams and is finished (translation by Ann Goldstein).

Bring this to the image we are working with, the sea, and writing is tracing the crest of the waves, now white and foamy, now a bluer ripple. It is guessing the colour of the sea at a certain hour, it is marvelling at the sudden dart of a fish or caressing the dark liquid fin of a dolphin. It is stabbing the page with the inexistent line between the sea and the sky.

Did she say that it was the second proem of the *Paradiso*? Yes, yes, and now that you ask, the first is even weirder, and frames the question of inspiration and writing in an even more potent way. It is a little long, so please allow me a bit of summary. At the beginning of the last section of his work (*Paradiso* 1, 1–36), Dante tells us:

- My topic is the glory of God (1–3)
- I went all the way to heaven (4–6)
- had a ball, but don't remember what happened (7–9)
- will try to write what I can (10–12)
- [the juicy part] (13–21)
- will try to write what I can (22–24)
- I really want the poetic laurel (25–27)

- nobody gets it (the laurel) (28–30)
- it is fucking hard (to get the laurel), so I am trying, without succeeding, to impress some laurel-dispensing arse by repeating *ad nauseam* the word laurel and making incomprehensible poetic references to it (31–33)
- maybe there will a better writer than me (34–36)

The juicy part is the following invocation to Apollo. The Greek god of poetry is here turned into a cruel master within a sadomasochistic game. Dante wishes to be (dis)possessed by poetic inspiration, he wants the god to penetrate him and inspire him, like he skinned the satyr Marsyas.

>   O buono Appollo, a l'ultimo lavoro
> fammi del tuo valor sì fatto vaso,
> come dimandi a dar l'amato alloro.
>   Infino a qui l'un giogo di Parnaso
> assai mi fu; ma or con amendue
> m'è uopo intrar ne l'aringo rimaso.
>   Entra nel petto mio, e spira tue
> sì come quando Marsïa traesti
> de la vagina de le membra sue.
> (*Paradiso* 1, 13–21)

> O good Apollo, for this last labor make me such a vessel of your worth as you require for granting your beloved laurel. Thus far the one peak of Parnassus has sufficed me, but now I have need of both, as I enter the arena that remains. Enter into my breast and breathe there as when you drew Marsyas from the sheath of his limbs.

The story, you have guessed, is narrated by Ovid in the sixth book of the *Metamorphoses* (6, 382–400). Marsyas, the usual mortal (in this case a satyr, a lower divinity) equipped with enough *hybris* to challenge the god at making music, is defeated and punished by being skinned alive. The Ovidian tale, albeit gruesome, is not particularly innovative or strange, but what Dante does with it is. Not only does he place this story at the outset of the last, most Christian, allegedly 'chaster' part of his poem, but he also reverses Marsyas's punishment into desire. The poet is passive: he is the vessel ('vaso') of poetic inspiration and wishes the god to enter his chest ('entra') and violently inspire him. And he is liking it. Whereas Ovid's Marsyas asks Apollo with a disconsolate voice: 'why do you tear me from myself?' ('quid me mihi detrahis?'; *Metamorphoses* 6, 385), Dante begs the god ... 'tear me from myself!'; get me out of this body, hurt me, break me free of this constraint, and yet subjugate me profoundly to and into this body of mine, make me yours, make me a divine breath of poetry. Talk about being scared, and fragile, at the outset of writing. And feeling it in the skin. And embracing your fragility.

Do I see the word 'vagina' on the page? Yes, yes, you do, but fortunately (or unfortunately), it does not mean vagina (it does not mean that until a couple of centuries later), but 'guaina', or sheath. Yet the image of Apollo extracting the Satyr from the sheath of his limbs (instead of, more intuitively, taking the skin off his body) is reminiscent of a rather deviant fantasy of a violent birth, where Dante is both the woman in labour and the foetus.

OF FRAUD AND FICTION

In addition to the Argonauts and the siren, another figure articulates the marine metatextual links between Dante and Ulysses. Earlier in the journey, the reader meets Geryon, an enigmatic infernal monster that ferries Dante-traveller and Virgil to the lower part of hell, the circle of fraud. Drafted on the fading trace of a minor character of Greek mythology, Geryon is a superb Dantean invention, through which the poet ponders the short distance between fraud (in a moral and religious sense) and fiction (in a literary sense). Geryon is a textual vessel, and like the siren he is both ugly and beautiful.

The link was first observed by Teodolinda Barolini, in a fine essay entitled 'Ulysses, Geryon, and the Aeronautics of Narrative Transition'. The aeronautics in question follow from the fact that while Ulisse's navigation looks like a flight, the trip on Geryon's shoulders to reach the circle of fraud is described as navigation through the air.

Geryon, Dante tells us, is the very image of fraud. He is made of three different species: a human head, the body of a lion, and the tail of a serpent or a scorpion. In plain allegory: fraud first seduces, then attacks, and ultimately annihilates. And it stinks.

> Ecco la fiera con la coda aguzza,
> che passa i monti e rompe i muri e l'armi!
> Ecco colei che tutto 'l mondo appuzza!
> [...]
>   E quella sozza imagine di froda
> sen venne, e arrivò la testa e 'l busto,
> ma 'n su la riva non trasse la coda.
>   La faccia sua era faccia d'uom giusto,
> tanto benigna avea di fuor la pelle,
> e d'un serpente tutto l'altro fusto;
>   due branche avea pilose insin l'ascelle;
> lo dosso e 'l petto e ambedue le coste
> dipinti avea di nodi e di rotelle.
>   Con più color, sommesse e sovraposte
> non fer mai drappi Tartari né Turchi,
> né fuor tai tele per Aragne imposte.
> [...]
>   Nel vano tutta sua coda guizzava,
> torcendo in sù la venenosa forca
> ch'a guisa di scorpion la punta armava.
> (*Inferno* 17, 1–3, 7–18, and 25–27)

> Behold the beast with the pointed tail, that passes mountains and breaks walls and weapons! Behold him that infects all the world! [...] And that foul image of fraud came onward, and landed his head and his bust, but it did not draw his tail onto the bank. His face was the face of a just man, so benign was its outward aspect, and all his trunk was that of a serpent; he had two paws, hairy to the armpits; his back and breast and both his sides were painted with knots and circlets. Tartars or Turks never made cloth with more colors of groundwork and pattern, nor were such webs laid on the loom by Arachne. [...] All his tail was quivering in the void, twisting upward its venomous fork, which had the point armed like a scorpion's.

On the pattern of the ur-fraudulent beast, Genesis's snake, Geryon is stitched together through the best of biblical and medieval horror writing: locusts with human faces, tempting snakes, destructive large scorpions and lions with hairy armpits. But Geryon is also attractive. In addition to the outward benign appearance of his face, his back is adorned with the splendour of textiles, so rich and complex that Dante dwells on the intricacies and exoticism of its embroidered circlets. The good old merchant, savouring the finesse of rare cloths, is always around the corner.

The connection between the art of weaving and textuality is as old as literature itself. (My Penelope ... she wove and unwove my story day after day, and I exist only in the dry and sharp sound of her loom.) Not by chance, Dante mentions here Arachne, the weaver turned spider from the *Metamorphoses* (6, 1–145), another minor but resilient alter ego of his, whom he later places as an example of pride in purgatory, calling her mad in her challenge to the divine text ('folle'; *Purgatorio* 12, 43) — like himself (*Inferno* 2, 35), like Ulisse (*Inferno* 26, 125).

Whether this is a matter of weaving, embroidery, textile painting, or a combination of these arts, the issue of poetic beauty is both at the heart and on the surface of Geryon-as-text. Geryon's beauty is presented as something complicated, knotted ('nodi'), twisted ('rotelle'), heavily embroidered, and colored. Very much like the siren's fake adornment, this is an artistic, textual beauty. The comparison with textiles shows that poetic beauty is woven into the very 'stuff' of the text, coloring both the groundwork and the pattern. [Here, in the 'Tartar clothes', is the one faint allusion to the voyage of Marco Polo I mentioned before. Polo dwells at length on the beauty and complexity of Asian textiles. Maybe Dante is suggesting that fiction is not fraudulent in itself, but the trade, marketing, and merchandizing we make of it is. Off point and full of assumptions, the tutor in me writes in the margins.]

So incredibly strange is this beast that Dante-poet prefaces it with an even stranger address to the reader.

> Sempre a quel ver c'ha faccia di menzogna
> de' l'uom chiuder le labbra fin ch'el puote,
> però che sanza colpa fa vergogna;
>   ma qui tacer nol posso; e per le note
> di questa comedìa, lettor, ti giuro,
> s'elle non sien di lunga grazia vòte,
>   ch'i' vidi per quell'aere grosso e scuro
> venir notando una figura in suso,
> maravigliosa ad ogne cor sicuro
> (*Inferno* 16, 124–32)

> To that truth which has the face of a lie *people* should always close *their* lips so far as *they* can, for through no fault *of theirs* it brings reproach; but here I cannot be silent; and, reader, I swear to you by the notes of this Comedy — so may they not fail of lasting favour — that I saw, through the thick and murky air, come swimming upwards a figure amazing to every steadfast heart

The trick is as clever as it is clear:

Geryon, the beautiful/ugly monster that I am describing is fraud = a lie that looks like the truth.

My poem, the beautiful/intriguing monster that you are reading, is the exact opposite = a truth that looks like a lie.

In other words, as Barolini puts it, Geryon 'is both the poem and its antithesis'. What remains to be seen, though, is whether this is a defence or a condemnation of fiction. Whether fiction is fraud (the lie that looks like the truth) or a mysterious type of truth (that looks like a lie but is not).

The strangest part of all is Dante's reaction. Confronted with an unbelievable, 'fictional' truth, he takes an oath on his poem. One usually did so on the Bible or a sacred text. One still does that, as I discovered not long ago while serving on jury duty, half horrified at the Christian-centric nature of UK tribunals, and half exhilarated at the continuing power of the book as a material object. Dante, however, takes the oath on his own book. Now; that takes guts. And (talk about fragility and excitement), not on his book as a stable, written, bound, 'sacred' object, but on an oral, poetic, even musical image of his work: he talks about the 'notes' of his *Comedy* — invoking here for the first (of a handful) of times the (probable) title of his poem. Like the book that 'trespasses singing' at the beginning of paradise, this is an aural book, yet it has the power of a durable, authoritative object. We-the-readers are placed in the jury's stand, and entrusted with the task of verifying Dante's words and upholding their fame.

Oscillation between beauty and ugliness, reference to textual beauty and ornateness, tension between fraud and fiction, a text of daring making and of complex reading: like the siren, then, Geryon is a statement on writing. However, the beautiful-ugly woman/poetry, animated by the eager, or lustful, gaze of her author/dreamer, adds a twist to the already intricate discourse of textuality and intertextuality: the role of the ever elusive, never illusive, present moment of falling in love.

We are in a dream, though, and maybe sirens are also the image of the writer. A beautiful voice confined into an ugly body. A honey-sweet sound trapped inside, which trumps every other quality or talent. The hypnotizing call to write and write and write, as if it were a blessing, or a curse. Is Dante the ugly woman, grotesquely made beautiful by a couple of rhymes and figures? Is he the vulgar (as in vernacular), outcast, shamed peasant woman squatting on a country road? Is Homer the terse, unbreakable, mellifluous, imageless voice that belongs to no one? Is there a scared and bold little girl in Ovid? Is Apollonius the muted siren's voice or the loud Orpheus? (that would be *so* Apollonius).

TIED AT THE MAST

Some ten or fifteen years ago, I saw an exhibition about 'wonders of the sea' or something like that, of which I remember little or nothing (I went to see it with someone I fancied a lot). But I do remember her, a strange little siren, an ugly, desiccated, crinkly little creature in a glass case. I have later learned that she is a specimen of a larger kind known as the Fiji or Feejee mermaids (Figures 12 and 13).

Of various sizes and shapes, these curiosities were manufactured in the east, especially in Japan, throughout the eighteenth and nineteenth centuries and sold to gullible travellers. One such siren made quite an appearance in Dickensian London in 1822 and was then exhibited in

Figure 12. The Feejee mermaid on show at the Harvard Museum.

Barnum's American Museum. They were made by grafting an ape's torso onto a large fish tail, sometimes by messing with the ape's own skeleton and sometimes with the help of a wooden or papier mâché structure, and they were often embellished with human hair and horn nails. One German mermaid apparently vaunts the upper body of a human foetus.

This strange creature has stuck in my mind for years, strangely rising from the hazy, elapsed context of the exhibition I saw her in. She reminds me of several things.

She reminds me of Dante's siren: a poetic object tragically stripped of its external beauties. Is she the ugly core of poetic language?

Figure 13. Specimen of the Feejee mermaid found in the Museum of Natural History in Milano. Is this the one I saw? It does remind me of Geryon's 'just man face', but with a smirk.

    She reminds me of Geryon: like him, she is a patchwork of different animals, a unified body constructed by grafting three species. Is she fraud or fiction?

    She reminds me of fraud in a commercial sense: she was made to deceive customers and sold well beyond her price.

    As the sole memory of an enamored afternoon at the museum, she reminds me of an unconsummated, still thrilling, somewhat literary infatuation. I felt like I was swimming through the cases, trying to catch a reflection of my beloved in the glass. I am not sure why my memory retained this and no other object from the exhibit. Maybe our heads got to touch momentarily as we were trying to examine this curiosity? Or did I just linger there by myself, listening to the old sound emanating from inside of me, promising a sweet wholeness if only I could make him mine? That All would fall back In One Place?

I still wonder whether the love that exists without ever being — the love that resides in a stretch of desire and nothing else, the paper love of the troubadours, perennially displaced in a pale blue distance that one day, without you noticing, turns into absence — is the perfect form of love, or whether it is the old, seducing siren's song that keeps calling, the drug that keeps the pilgrim on the trodden journey, making it look untravelled. Or whether, tied to the mast, I had just then realized that there was no sound for me to hear, only silence from the desiccated yet familiar mouth of all the consummated loves, the water closing over the great sea of my fictions.

Colophon

In the medieval book craft, scribes sometimes left a sign or a personal note at the end of the book. This manuscript was copied by so-and-so, at such time, in such place. Sometimes they complain of exhaustion, cold hands, or tired eyes. They may pray or ask for a prayer from the reader. In ancient and medieval times, authors too lingered often on the end of their text. Go, my song, to the most beautiful lady. Farewell, my little book, make sure you don't get lost in your wanderings around the city. Reception is a sea voyage; watch for storms, my tiny little vessel. Alas, I was so different when I started writing this songbook. Look at you! my poetry collection, so pretty and polished, just now smoothed by dry pumice …

It is a form of control, for sure, but it also opens a door for the readers, welcoming them in a small but cosy room where we sit together before travelling in opposite directions, before time ravages this precious moment in which the vulnerability of the text lies open. When the scribe or writer pauses to appreciate with quasi-parental admiration the sheer materiality of their work; and bids it a farewell that is not nostalgic, because this separation is in the order of things; a bit hurried, like that of the sweet friends at the dock, and a bit teasing, like the mask of a comic character that is placed for a short instance into a serious, sentimental role; to thine own self be true, my little book! When readers realize that, well, they have been readers throughout; they have made this knot of meaning too; that, whether pleased or displeased, they have mapped this little journey with their own coordinates.

Dante closes his poem with the most cunning signpost. Each of the three sections of the *Comedy* ends with the word 'stars' ('stelle').

> E quindi uscimmo a riveder le stelle.
> (*Inferno* 34, 139: and thence we issued forth to see again the stars.)
>
> puro e disposto a salire a le stelle.
> (*Purgatorio* 33, 145: pure and ready to rise to the stars.)
>
> L'amor che move il sole e l'altre stelle.
> (*Paradiso* 33, 145: the Love which moves the sun and the other stars.)

Stars seen again after emerging from the claustrophobic darkness of hell (sounds like there is light at the end of the tunnel, but the mere fact that there are stars means that it is night, that there is darkness outside of hell too); stars ready to be reached from the top of purgatory by a pure [now this is the one word that gives me hives] and eager traveller [last time I felt like that, I was, what?, fifteen maybe?]; stars that are for a split second around me in the freefall ending of paradise (talk about a cliffhanger ... without us even noticing, Dante depicts himself falling from the heavens after the vision of god). The repetition of this crystalline word gives the appearance of order and stability to those who crave it, but it is, in fact, an echo, not a recapitulation;

a fragment, not a segment; ding … tinkle little star … tintin — never has the sound of a bell been so sly, tolling the desire of the readers/sailors.

'Stars, stars, stars … this is all I see in this darn southern hemisphere!', Ulisse bursts out laughing.

If I ever imagine a colophon for my Dante, I find a rather mysterious signature encrypted at the end. Call me Ishmael, this writer says.

Did you ever wonder what happened to Ulisse's crew? I mean, we have been talking about him all the time. What about the poor fellows who followed him in the mad flight? Ulisse's speech posits that the mad flight is plural — it marks indeed the switch from singular to plural: from now on, when they start pointing west, they are 'us' ('noi'). What happens to them, do they just die, and nobody talks about them anymore?

Not quite. Or at least not in my reading. At the beginning of his poem, Dante features himself (or better, his soul) … like a sailor, who has survived a shipwreck and is washed ashore:

> E come quei che con lena affannata,
> uscito fuor del pelago a la riva,
> si volge a l'acqua perigliosa e guata,
>   così l'animo mio, ch'ancor fuggiva,
> si volse a retro a rimirar lo passo
> che non lasciò già mai persona viva.
> (*Inferno* 1, 22–27)

> And as *one* who with laboring breath has escaped from the deep to the shore turns to look back on the dangerous waters, so my mind which was still fleeing turned back to gaze upon the pass that never left anyone alive.

One of them has survived! As far-fetched as this idea might be (that the character Dante at the beginning of the *Comedy* is staged as one of Ulisse's crew), these lines never fail to remind me of that other amazing beginning.

   'Call me Ishmael.'

They remind me of that other terrifying and immense story of navigation, search, trespassing, and writing; of an obsessed captain and of a punitive divinity rising from the sea and causing a vortex that sinks a ship. Ishmael, you remember, emerges from the final whirlpool in a (very eschatological) coffin, floating back to safety and story. Likewise, thrown up by his immense story, the lonely poet washes ashore. Dante's prologue, snatched from the middle of the unread *Odyssey*, is the future's epilogue. (Odysseus too was the only survivor of a shipwreck, reaching the safe shore of storytelling on the Phaeacian island, after Poseidon sent a vortex-like storm to destroy his raft; book 5).*

The textual shipwreck might not be that lonely after all, though. Earlier in this book, I invited you to inhabit the underwater perspective to fully understand the close of the episode of Ulisse ('until the sea closed over us'). The impatient reader among you might have noticed already another

---

*   The literary tradition does indeed squirt out a shipwrecked poet and his work. Or so they say ... that in 1559 Luís Vaz de Camões was shipwrecked at the mouth of the Mekong River. The poet was apparently able to swim to safety, his only salvaged property being the *Lusíads*. I wonder whether the poet rescued the poem or vice versa — we can see him either clasping his manuscript while trying to swim, or using it as a raft. I am not sure whether he is more an Odysseus or an Ishmael: yet the fact that the writer of a version of the *Odyssey* should survive shipwreck swimming with/on his text is literature telling its own story on life. The book is soaking wet, though ('Cantos que molhados | vêm do naufrágio triste e miserando'; canto 10, 128). The legend also says that Camões's beloved died in the shipwreck.

point in the poem where Dante places us at the bottom of the sea. At the very end of *Paradiso*, in the course of the vision of god — an unwieldy, difficult piece of writing where the exhausted poet is trying every trick on his exhausted readers, to keep us in there for yet another canto — Dante invokes in one compact tercet the 'shadow of Argo', his own lethargic stupor (I told you ... drugs), and amazement ('ammirare'), recalling the Ulyssean proem to *Paradiso* 2: while in that occasion Dante's readers were going to be as amazed as Jason's crew, this time divinity itself is amazed when they see Argo's underside from bottom of the sea.

> Un punto solo m'è maggior letargo
> che venticinque secoli a la 'mpresa
> che fé Nettuno ammirar l'ombra d'Argo
> (*Paradiso* 33, 94–96)

> A single moment makes for me greater oblivion than five and twenty centuries have wrought upon the enterprise that made Neptune wonder at the shadow of the Argo.

Neptune, the god of the sea: you are free to interpret him as Odysseus's vengeful Poseidon, Dante's angry god, or Ishmael's ferocious sea creature — although now, whoever they are, they are just chilling on the seabed looking up at the keel of the boat that looks like a line of a shadow, of a darker blue than the water surrounding it. Readers are amazed too when we are set on such a stunning roller coaster that from the heavens takes us precipitously to the bottom of the sea, while the poet secures his writing by inserting a thin dark line ('ombra'; shadow), or script, on the all-blinding luminosity of the page of the vision of god. Writing, the literary tradition even, is the otherness that makes divinity visible.

Do not worry, though, we are not sinking. The poet's roller coaster will propel us to the surface again with a big, foamy splash, still jolted from having been whirled by the great vortex of literature, the grand attraction of poetic language.

'Now I have to put up even with whale hunters and the Southern Pacific. And with Argo' — Ulysses shrugs and tuts — 'those pumped-up heroes.

And with readers' — a hint of stroppy indecision lifts the sides of his mouth into a faint smile.

'This one; she has yet to learn that I sail solo.'

~

Ashore, the sea throws up refuse. Organic and inert. Algae, dead fish, the odd starfish, torn rope, plastic bottles.

Amber is not for us southerners. Rather, small pieces of glass from broken bottles, a faded green or blue, smoothed by the waves, they glimmer like poor gems on the shoreline (I collect them anyway, at least they do not cut anymore). Or drops of oil from faraway boats that look under the midday sun like shining black pebbles, absorbing light and attention as the ancient velvety nights at Alcinous's court, but just before you reach for them, they turn into soft, slimy matter (our parents used to apply gasoline with a cotton ball to get them off from our feet). Humble seashells. And pebbles, of course, of enamouring shades: rosy, green, verdigris, perfect white and perfect black, or with veins of impossible colours; iridescent like fish when you stroke them in the shallows. (At home, they all look like a dull and sad grey, but my best friend, the one with the dolphin tattoo and an inveterate optimist, has taught me to regild them with nail polish.) And so our stories go.

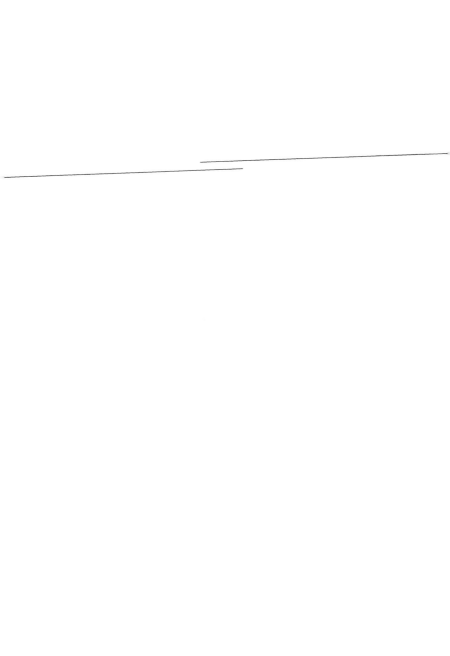

A Narrated Bi(bli)ography Preceded by a Postface and Interspersed with Notes that Lack Superscript. Also Illustrated, for that Matter. With the Addition of a One-word Glossary.

The premise of this book, which I have come to call affectionately 'Ulissino', little Ulysses, is real. The canvas was, initially, a university lecture on *Inferno* 26 that I have performed for the last many years in the context of my courses on Dante's *Inferno*. Its expansion is due, indeed, to the Ulyssean curiosity left 'therewithin'. The writing sprang forth bubbling and fizzing during a term of sabbatical leave, very much in the shape in which you read it.

The only plan I sensed and pursued was the merging of fragments, shards, flakes, and splinters: polished pieces of literature, memories of reading, bits of scholarship (some of them discarded as untenable in my waking life), attempts at theorizing, and raw fragments of me placed themselves on the page, like guests who do not know each other entering a familiar living room; like when you invite best friends from different lives who have yet to meet, but have heard of each other and are well inclined already. There is a little uneasiness ('I thought she was taller from your extolling praise', 'did not expect him to wear glasses, so keen you said he was') and the occasional friction, but soon they mingle, and you can leave the room.

The poetics of this book, if there is one, is a poetics of the fragment, or of the fragmentary: the imperfect matching, the seams, cracks, and wounds that are ultimately the poetic word's territory.

If there is a theory in this little book, it is a theory of 'personality'. It states that the literary endeavour and the literary pleasure are personal, at times even eccentrically so (they are not, however, individual, or random, or private). And so is literary scholarship.

Personality was not planned. It happened; for instance, when children's songs popped up in the *lectura*, while I was leisurely and somewhat aimlessly transcribing the manuscript of my university lecture on *Inferno* 26, or when the foamy wake of the *Bateau ivre* frothed into an old illuminated initial. These doodles of my memory, like the irreverent monkeys on medieval manuscripts (see chapter 4), were here to stay. Like those images in the margins, they are not comic or dramatic interludes. They are proper glosses. And I have come to think that they are not marginal.

This way to interpretation is personal, and experiential (Ulisse asks that much from us with his insistence on the importance of 'experience'), but it also forms communities of readers that are less definite, more intangible, and more surprising than the ones we may be used to (the academic, the historical, the national, the political, that of gender, et cetera).

The theory of personality entails that interpretation is plural and often unexpected. It is not linear and can be anachronistic. That there is no such thing as a standard voice of interpretation, that sometimes the role of the interpreter is just that of bringing two objects into the same space and creating a relaxed atmosphere where they can talk and illuminate each other. That it is ok, indeed interesting, sometimes important (nay, necessary), and ultimately unavoidable, to bring one's life, one's 'human stain' to bear on scholarship and interpretation. In this little book, I have often put my lives on the line of interpretation; the academic, the teacher, the student, the parent, the daughter, the friend, the lover, the sad child — together they have, I believe, cast unusual lights on the texts that I am reading.

The theory of personality also states that to study is to desire, and to learn is to love, and it hurts, but it is also the locus of pleasure. Minus the hurt, this is what Augustine thought of the process of knowledge ('appetitus [...] rei cognoscendae, fit amor cognitae'; the desire for the object that you have yet to know becomes the love of the known object; *De Trinitate* 9, 12, 18; my translation). 'Love hurts', though. I fully understood this *dictum* when I saw it tattooed in large gothic letters, blurred by time and leaking into the ageing skin, slightly reddened by sweat, on the large forearm of a female bus driver at the Saint Aldate's stop in Oxford. I wish I had thanked her for more than the ticket she sold me: more at length, more profusely, for the lesson on the meaning of literality she taught me. I am also thankful that the bus driver interpreted Augustine, and Augustine shed light on the bus driver. They would not have met without my journey. The journey is the place of pleasure.

Creative scholarship, post-scholarship, punk scholarship? I am not sure what to call the 'methodology' of this book. It certainly aims at exposing the beauty and the limits of disciplines and discourses that take themselves very seriously and sometimes refuse to enter in conversation with one another. Intimacy is little Ulisse's critical tool.

The most consistent aspect of this little book is the reflection on reading, which is both my most beloved activity and my current scholarly interest.

At the heart of my little Ulysses are literary texts that relate, in different ways, to its main protagonist, canto 26 of Dante's *Inferno*. There are multiple designs (layouts, drawings, patterns) and sketches (splashes, drafts, squirts, spatters, spurts, dabs, and stains), infatuation with language, and amazement at the folly of writing. There are, you have noticed, three main writing personas: the academic, itself made of a consummate literary scholar, a repentant philologist, a tentative philosopher, an amateur historian, and an amused art historian; the passionate reader, who pre-exists the academic and hopefully will survive it; and the creative writer, a newborn character, both defenceless and demanding, brimming with life, yet still in nappies. They are at once listening to and trying to capture a concerto of voices around them, the sombre melody of literature and the vibrant cacophony of 'life'. There is a consistent comic vein that is explained, I hope, by the quote from Rabelais, and by Dante's own understanding of the comic as 'polytropy' (plurilingualism and pluristylism roaming free).

There are several internal references, not all of them visible to the naked eye. There are textual encounters that will mean different things at different times to the diverse people who will read this book. Homer greets Dante in an anachronistic space–time, a long-forgotten piece of scholarship encounters the dodo in an impossible resort, a pop jingle enters an invective by means of rhythm alone, Janis Joplin meets Plutarch at the Canaries (or is that Eden? They are both irremediably earthly; I cannot imagine them either in heaven or hell). Emily Dickinson goes shopping. Sinatra waltzes with Beatrice while Orpheus plays the lyre. A bird flies on the page of history. The splish-splash of the sea laps the prose.

You might not be interested in all the voices and all the fragments that make up this little book. I hope I have made it clear that this text does not need to be read continuously or linearly. Not even left to right for that matter. Feel free to skip (but remember Boccaccio).

As I reflect post-factum on my operation, a further memory surfaces.
 That of a clever and quirky student of mine, who, after tests, or exams, or even at the end of the year, would knock energetically at my office door and walk in with a spring in his step demanding to do what he called the *post-mortem* (of an essay, of the exam session, even of the entire year). The first time I heard this expression, I was horrified: on a good day it reminds me of Rembrandt; on a bad day of unfathomable incisions. For Ferdi, I realized this after a couple of years, the *post-mortem* meant not so much to analyse his performance on a given aspect of academic life, but also to put the seal on it (or, to zip it in one of those large freezer bags, like in the movies) and to proclaim it done. After the *post-mortem*, Ferdi used to be unusually calm, and I rather shaking. The *post-mortem* of this book would be identifying what I have done in the different chapters — stripping them of their 'life', so to speak, and putting them under the microscope of justification. As academics, we normally place this at the beginning, safely zipping the decay of a finished book into its synopsis.
 Chapter 1. I do textual analysis, close reading, the main literary skill that I have, and that I owe to the Anglo-American part of my formation, with a huge debt of gratefulness.
 Chapter 2. I do intertextuality as I declare. The use of the term intertextuality refers to a vigorous conversation among scholars in the second half of the last century. [I do not know why I get a hit every time I write 'last century'. My intellectual formation is history, it has a sepia patina.] The

intertextuality I care for is infinite, intricate, and expansive. It is not linear (from text a to text b) but involves all texts in a strange form of 'presentness'. It is irresistibly connected to memory, pleasure, and personality.

I also hint here and elsewhere at the thorny issue of 'the canon'. It is a very critical question these days, which scholars, educators, and students are debating with ferocious earnestness. I take a comic shortcut to this very serious theme, as a way of saying; I see the problem, I am engaging, I do not believe in quick fixes. [For a more mature take on the question, one with which I broadly concur, see 'Marginality and the Classics: Exemplary Extraneousness' by Marco Formisano, the introductory essay to the volume *Marginality, Canonicity, Passion*, ed. by Formisano and Christina Shuttleworth Kraus (Oxford: Oxford University Press, 2018).]

Chapter 3 is, generally speaking, theme based. I search in fits and starts for the past and present of two very loaded themes — 'virtue' and 'knowledge'. I ask, and do not answer, a troubling question. What is it to be human?

In this chapter, I also trace the mobile outline of the question of 'modernity' that is the tormented protagonist of the next chapter. The modernity that went up in flames in the Lagers, that is. In a way, Dante's Ulysses and Levi's Ulysses are the entrance and exit ways (or; thresholds) to this issue. Levi's Ulysses says that after the Shoah language, literature, and 'reality' are forever tainted. Dante's Ulysses says that things were pretty bad even earlier on. In this conversation I hope there emerges a glimpse of a better present. One is left to wonder what Homer's Ulysses would have to say.

Chapter 4. After a lot of gutting, and cutting, and miasmas I found, you will be surprised, a skeleton of the historical-philological formation of my past. If you see me today, you will hardly believe that in my early twenties I was a manic philologist, memorizing names and numbers of codices, and working at transcribing manuscripts. There was a romantic, or psychopathic, aspect to it, though: every year I would bring a red rose to the funeral statue of the poet I was philologizing. Not sure whether to say 'I love you' or 'I am sorry'.

This chapter also asks: what happens when the imagination of literature becomes the reality of 'progress'? Is there any sort of capricious intertextuality between these two planes?

Chapter 5. Orpheus rescues me from these conundrums, proclaiming: only loss is real. Nostalgia is the only map of journeys and lives. The narrator of this chapter is, I suppose, the medievalist in me, who joins forces with the nervous traveller to embark, very physically, on a rather imaginary journey: that of the pilgrimage of interpretation. We went on foot, with packsacks, and picnic, and water bottles. We walked and chatted, got some blisters on our feet, lost our way, and ended up all the way to Eden, to meet an angry allegory, who told us to go back to the start and re-read. Parts of this chapter, especially the one on pilgrimage, figural reading, and desire are fragmented and full of stops and starts: this has to do with the creaking and banging movement of the train of allegory.

Chapter 6. With the sirens, these badly sung beautiful singers, I toy with literary theory, in particular with gender theory applied to literature, and I give into one of my guiltiest pleasures: visual studies. I also engage with writing's discourse on writing — metatextuality, litteralogy, fantawriting, truefiction? — whatever you want to call it, it is the writer's sweat stain on the page, sometimes mixed with a drop of blood from a paper cut.

Finally — what am I doing now, meta-scholarship? meta-myself? the anatomy of the anatomy? — this last little chapter understates the question of objectivity in literary studies. Modern epistemology and even physiology maintain that knowledges are situated and embodied, yet the Grail of objectivity looms large, often encupped in some dry, make-believe apparatuses of authority. The answer of this little book, if any, to the disintegration of the concept of objective truth in scholarship and otherwise, is not, however, 'to each their own truth'. It is: patience, close reading, and irony.

The bibliography, the most barren and scorched part of a book, is also always a biography. Before turning into a lifeless alphabetical list in which it is impossible not to *live* [NB: typo, but of a curious kind] ... not to *leave* typos and inaccuracies, these were organisms that the scholar consumed and excreted, loved and sometimes hated, ignored or accepted as inevitable. There are tears, and fears, and sneezes; tummy and head aches, passions and betrayals, kilometres of underlining, and countless folded 'dog ears'. The whole 'back matter' (what a great name) — bibliography, index (publishing's most endangered species), perhaps glossary — the ever so serious ticket to authority, is also the most idiosyncratic and genuine part of a book. Pliny the Elder, the punkiest of scholars, boldly placed the back matter at the front of his *Historia Naturalis*: the first book is a maddening long index and bibliography of each subsequent book. If you manage this, Pliny seems to say with a smirk, you can read the next thirty-six.

As you can imagine, a great deal of scholarly effort has gone into the writing of this book. Some of it is part of my training, my research, and my many years of teaching Dante. In my academic monographs — *The Syntax of De-*

sire: Language and Love in Augustine, the Modistae, Dante (Toronto: University of Toronto Press, 2007), *The Wings of the Doves: Love and Desire in Dante and Medieval Culture* (Montreal: McGill University Press, 2012), *Imagining the Woman Reader in the Age of Dante* (Oxford: Oxford University Press, 2018), and the one I was supposed to complete when Ulissino took over, provisionally entitled *Reading and Writing in Dante* (Somewhere: ACertain University Press, one day) — and in my articles that I will not list, you will find, with tons of footnotes, some of the ideas that I express here. If I look back at all the books and articles I have written, I realize that they were never impersonal.

I first heard the chiming of the cheeky voice of the amused scholar-narrator when I was commissioned to write a book on women in Dante for a large-scale publication on the occasion of the recent Dante anniversary — *Beatrice e le altre. Dante e le figure femminili* (Rome: Gedi-La Repubblica, 2021) — and I have listened to it ever since.

In this book you will find some old knowledge that I no longer can tell how I have developed. Some is new knowledge that I have acquired recently reading excitedly, voraciously, and sometimes bulimically. I have picked up and dropped books, imperiously demanded interlibrary loans [they make you fill this strange bit: 'not needed after': NOW for Christ's sake!] and then forgot they were there. I have downloaded the same articles twice and let two files with the same name butt eternally like two rams in the 'Save as' option. I have bought volumes on a whim, and then left them open on the table to never read later.

The 'theme of Ulysses' in literature and culture has been explored in many studies. Of these, three are particularly famous and inspiring.

W. B. Stanford, *The Ulysses Theme: A Study in the Adaptability of a Traditional Hero* (Oxford: Blackwell, 1954) is a gentle, old-style, erudite take on Ulysses, particularly the classical heritage. In it, you will find an intriguing quote on the relation between scholarship and creative writing: 'accident, ignorance, misunderstanding or carelessness — fatal faults in a work of scholarship — may lead a creative author to valid new conceptions of the traditional myths' (p. 3). And one remarkable piece of creative writing, in which Stanford imagines the conversation between Homer and Virgil in Dante's Limbo (Dante actually does place the two together in his Limbo, the area of hell dedicated to the great souls of antiquity). It is worth reading: 'Virgil could have answered the *poeta sovrano* [this is what Dante calls Homer in *Inferno* 4, 88]: "Homer, poetry as well as war has its *ineluctabile fatum* [here he is quoting *Aeneid* 8, 334]. You know this, you who praised the virtues of the Achaeans to please the Greek princes for whom you sang. Did you not represent the Trojans as having begun the war for the sake of an adulterous prince? Did you not say that the Trojans broke their solemn oath at the Truce? I had my prince and my people to please, as you had yours. But I did not slander your Odysseus — and surely you, subtle master of epic, know it. You will find no comment of mine on him in any line of my poem. Indignant Aeneas speaks of him in the manner of a defeated soldier. Perfidious Sinon traduces him. But surely you see that I transferred the chief burden of odium from your Odysseus (whom your fellow-countryman Euripides did not spare) to Sinon, who never appears in your poems. Sinon is my real villain, not Ulysses"' (pp. 133–34). [Fuck you, Virgil, my Homer answers, still from within Dante's Limbo.]

Piero Boitani's *The Shadow of Ulysses: Figures of a Myth* (Oxford: Clarendon, 1994) is a vast and passionate journey in various embodiments of Ulysses, especially in the literature of the modern era. In this book you will find a chapter on Dante and one on Renaissance navigators and their poets (where I first encountered Magellan's winged Victoria), and pages on Levi and Melville.

Edith Hall, *The Return of Ulysses: A Cultural History of Homer's Odyssey* (Baltimore, MD: The Johns Hopkins University Press, 2008) offers a much needed global, postcolonial, and feminist take on the theme.

For a survey of critical positions on Ulysses from antiquity to yesterday, see the volume *Odysseus/Ulysses* (New York: Chelsea, 1991) — part of a series on *Major Literary Characters*, all volumes of which were edited by the bard of the Western canon himself, Harold Bloom. Guess the ratio of white male heterosexual characters to, well, 'the rest' in this series.

This is not the first time that the story of Ulysses inspires a half academic half personal take, which goes to show that of all characters, Odysseus is, indeed, 'us'. I am currently enjoying Daniel Mandelsohn's *An Odyssey: A Father, a Son and an Epic* (New York: Collins, 2017).

Like Odysseus, Dante's Ulisse too has been put through the relentless machine of scholarship, from which I list here the handful of essays that are dearest to me: Bruno Nardi, 'La Tragedia di Ulisse' (for which see later); several pages of Maria Corti's essays on Dante and Cavalcanti (*Scritti su Dante e Cavalcanti* (Turin: Einaudi, 2003)); John Freccero, 'Dante's Ulysses from Epic to Novel', in his *The Poetics of Conversion* (Cambridge, MA: Harvard University Press, 1986), pp. 136–51, from which I first learned, among other things, about the spiritual reading of the *nostos* and about Lukács's take on epic and the novel; Teodolinda Barolini, 'Ulysses, Geryon and the Aeronautics of Narrative Transition', in her *The Undivine Comedy: Detheologizing Dante* (Princeton, NJ: Princeton University Press, 1992), pp. 48–73; Gary

Cestaro, 'Is Ulysses Queer? The Subject of Greek Love in Inferno XV and XXVI', in *Dante's Plurilingualism: Authority, Vulgarization, Subjectivity*, ed. by Sara Fortuna, Manuele Gragnolati, and Jürgen Trabant (Oxford: Legenda, 2010), pp. 179–92; and Lino Pertile, 'Ulisse in chiesa', in his *Dante popolare* (Ravenna: Longo, 2021), pp. 181–200, and the forthcoming *Ulysses and the Limits of Dante's Humanism. Ulisse o dei limiti dell'umanesimo dantesco*. As friendship between books and scholars wants, this book too is affectionately called *Ulissino*.

One of the sweet martyrdoms of scholarship is to make an exciting textual discovery only to find out, later, that it had been discovered already. What a fitting punishment for the scholar of Dante's Ulisse. Past the pillars of Gibraltar, there is nothing new, it seems. This has happened at least twice with this book. The first time was when I thought I had discovered the figure of Macareus from Ovid, only to find him, still a refusenik, in an essay by Michelangelo Picone on Dante and the Classics ('Dante, Ovidio e il mito di Ulisse', *Lettere italiane*, 23 (1991), pp. 500–16). The second time, I was giving the last hurried touches to the *lectura*, and suddenly remembered Diomedes in the flame in Homer's *Doloneia*, a point that I later found in an essay by Piero Boitani ('Dante and the Three Traditions', in *Dante and the Greeks*, ed. by Jan M. Ziolkowski (Washington, DC: Dumbarton Oaks Medieval Humanities, 2014), pp. 265–71). More of my brilliant ideas may have been written already. It is humbling to be reminded how scholarship is a more infinite book than the literature it writes about. Still, I remain a practitioner of the 'write now — read later' formula.

I mentioned already my fondness for Charles Singleton's translation of Dante. The correlative item in the classical world is, for me, the LOEB classical library. I used to dream that I became so rich that I was able to buy the whole thing in one shot, all the green and all the red books. And a custom bookshelf for it. I fantasized about casually piloting my guests toward the library: 'aah ... you own the entire LOEB.' With a modest smile and the softest of voices I would answer: 'Indeed ...'. That dream buried like many others, I still cherish the LOEB's inspired blandness: most of the translations from the classics in this book are taken from there.

In some cases, I have attempted my own translation.

INCIPIT

If you chose to be reader-student and you are in need of more information on Dante and the *Comedy*, there are various resources you can use — I am fond of the *Cambridge Companion to Dante*, edited by Rachel Jacoff and first published in 1993, where some of the best Dante scholars of that generation gathered to make Dante accessible to an Anglo-American audience. The recent *Oxford Handbook of Dante* (2021), which I have co-edited with Manuele Gragnolati and Francesca Southerden, is rather successful, I think, in communicating the complexity of Dante's *oeuvre* and the manifold ways in which it can be read. The *Introduction* that I have co-written with Manuele and Francesca gives a sense of where I and some other scholars stand with regards to Dante's biography. A very clever take on Dante's life is found in Elisa Brilli's and Giuliano Milani's *Dante's New Lives: Biography and Authobiography* (London: Reaktion Books, 2023).

As the editor of the *Handbook*, I encountered the amazing quote by Osip Mandelstam as the epigraph to Ted Cachey's essay on 'Traveling/Wandering/Mapping' (pp. 416–30). Recently, I have learned an even more amazing detail about Mandelstam; that he always brought a pocket size copy of the *Comedy* with him, for the fear of being suddenly arrested and separated from it. Now that is a powerful statement. Whether it speaks of the death-defying power of literature, or the madness of writers, I do not know. But the statement is still here. We are still reading it. Still imagining that pocket, that small volume, and that hand clasping nervously at it.

'Not consolation, no. Consolation is not for books and readers' is a reference to the famous ending of Derek Walcott's 'Sea Grapes': 'The classics can console. But not enough', which I gloss with Rainer Maria Rilke's *The Notebooks of Malte Laurids Brigge* (1910). It goes like this: 'O night without objects. O blind window to the outside, o diligently locked doors; these are features that date from long ago, inherited but never fully understood. O silence in the stairwell, silence from the rooms next door, silence high above on the ceiling. O mother: unique one, who hid away all this silence once, when I was a child. Who takes it upon herself and says, "Don't be afraid, it's me"' (translation by Robert Vilain).

CHAPTER 1

In the *lectura* of canto 26 and throughout the text, for those textual details that are not the fruit of my invention, I owe a lot to the countless *lecturae* and commentaries on the canto. Many commentaries are easily available through a helpful electronic resource, the *Dartmouth Dante Project*, a rather monumental digitization of 75+ commentaries, ancient and modern alike.

Fireflies: my late-blooming childish excitement for these coleopters aptly called *Lampyridae* derives not only from my obdurate city-dwelling nature, but also from the fact that there are very few fireflies these days in Italy and, I suppose, in many parts of the world. Wiped out by pesticides. Pier Paolo Pasolini lamented their death in a fiercely political newspaper article in 1975 ('Il vuoto di potere in Italia', *Corriere della Sera*, 1 February).

CHAPTER 2

The *Odyssey*, the *Aeneid,* and the *Metamorphoses* would be a welcome pre-read to this chapter. But then again — who does pre-read these days? There is beauty also in synchronicity. On the *Odyssey*, Virgil's works, and Ovid's *Metamorphoses*, I went bareback, I promise. Just the raw texts and some good Italian and English translations. I had no other choice, or desires.

Emily Wilson's translation of the *Odyssey* (New York: Norton, 2018) — where the *pulytropos* becomes 'complicated' — deserves a special mention: it is bold and innovative.

Ulysses App: when I went back to check the robotic quote, it had disappeared. I swear to god, reader, it was there. Forgive me god, for I am a sloppy writer, and do not keep track of my quotes. The new blurb is as disturbing as the first, although more mellow: 'Powerful features and a pleasant, focused writing experience combined in one tool, made for people who love to write and write a lot — this is Ulysses.' All the while symbols such as #, &, and ∩, just imperceptibly mutilated, float through the page, as if it were snowing. Later on, we are even reminded of the beauty of the PDF ('After you're done writing, Ulysses can turn your texts into beautiful PDFs, Word documents, ebooks and even blog posts'), but still no clue as to why the app is called Ulysses (https://ulysses.app/).

The conversation on intertextuality is still ongoing and relevant. The voices that are dearest to me are, as mentioned above, rather last-century; for instance those of Julia Kristeva, *Desire in Language: A Semiotic Approach to Literature and Art* (New York: Columbia University Press, 1980), and Gerard Genette, *Palimpsests: Literature in the Second Degree* (Lincoln: University of Nebraska Press, 1997). On poetic memory and poetic craft, I am still mesmerized by T. S. Eliot's 'Tradition and the Individual Talent', in his *The Sacred Wood: Essays on Poetry and Criticism* (New York: Knopf, 1921), pp. 42–53, where the idea of 'presentness of the past' comes from. I still read with passion G. B. Conte, *Memoria dei poeti e sistema letterario* (Turin: Einaudi, 1974), and, of course, the little gem I quote in the text: Giovanni Nencioni, 'Agnizioni di lettura', *Strumenti critici*, 2 (1967), pp. 191–98 [although sometimes I think I am more attached to the title and the beginning than to the article itself].

My little library of rewritings is made of the following. Well, Dante and Joyce; Walcott, *Omeros* (1990); Atwood, *Penelopiads* (2005); Kazantzakis, Οδύσσεια (1938), which I read in the beautiful Italian translation by Nicola Crocetti (2020), itself a rewriting, I believe; and Chaudhuri, *Odysseus Abroad* (2014). Chaudhuri's essay 'For the Joy of Joyce' (https://theamericanscholar.org/for-the-joy-of-joyce/) details an intriguing and open conversation with one of the Ulysses now considered 'canonical', and shows that the canon is only canonical if we make it so.

The 'sadistic dictature of language' is an expression found in an essay by Leo Spitzer, 'Speech and Language in *Inferno* XIII', *Italica*, 19 (1942), pp. 77–104. I ended up not talking more at length about Leo Spitzer (1887–1960, author of *Classical and Christian Ideas of World Harmony* and several studies on medieval literature and Dante), Er-nest Robert Curtius (1886–1956, author of several essays, and of the classic *European Literature and the Latin Middle Ages*), and Eric Auerbach (1892–1957, author of *Mimesis*). These three scholars have many things in common. They lived in the same period, they were German-language scholars (one a Jew from Vienna, the other Alsatian, the third a German Jew), they were philologists. They shared a similar fate: opposers or critics of the Nazi regime, two were exiled, and moved to the United States after a fascinating stopover in Istanbul, and one retreated into scholarship. They shared a similar secularity and encyclopaedic knowledge. They were erudites, the last of a kind [still seen in the wild (or is that a zoo?) in certain universities, the least commercially-minded ones, but threatened by extinction]. They shared a similar love for the classics and a belief in the moral role of great literature. I am not sure their positions are still tenable in today's world, but literary studies would not exist without them and without their isolation, resistance, and erudition.

For the *nostoi*, see a recent volume on *The Returning Hero: Nostoi and Traditions of Mediterranean Settlement*, ed. by Simon Hornblower and Giulia Biffis (Oxford: Oxford University Press, 2018). For the philosophical and then religious readings of Homer, see Robert Lamberton, *Homer the Theologian: Neoplatonist Allegorical Reading and the Growth of the Epic Tradition* (Berkeley: University of California Press, 1986) and Jean Pepin, 'The Platonic and Christian Ulysses' (1982), reprinted in *Odysseus/Ulysses*, pp. 228–48.

CHAPTER 3

On Pico della Mirandola, Poliziano, and the lights and shadows of the literary Italian Renaissance, see Nicola

Figure 14.

Gardini, *Rinascere. Storie e Maestri di una idea italiana* (Milan: Mondadori, 2019).

This is my mum just after the war (Figure 14). Decisively looking at the future ahead. She was formidable, fearless, and uncompromising. I hope she still is, now that her mind has been engulfed by the shadow of dementia. I hope she still reads and has memories of long snowy slopes and a tiny trail of young people climbing on sealskins. I hope the Elysian Fields look like the mountains of her youth.

Dante-and-Levi is a much-treated topic: for an updated view see Tristan Kay, 'Primo Levi, Dante, and Language in Auschwitz', *MLR*, 117 (2022), pp. 66–100. On the complexities of the role of Dante in Levi's times and his work, see Lino Pertile, 'Dante and the Shoah', in the *Oxford Handbook of Dante*, pp. 651–67.

CHAPTER 4

Bruno Nardi's 'La tragedia di Ulisse' was first published in 1937 in the journal *Studi Danteschi*, 20 (1937), pp. 5–15. This is Italy at its most obscure, knee-deep in the slime of Fascism, the racial laws about to be promulgated, a destructive war looming. The indefatigable medievalist — to my knowledge not a proponent of the regime, but neither a vocal opponent — tries to untangle a thread, at least, of the modern tragedy.

I went recently in the Taylorian Library here in Oxford to double-check this essay, reprinted in the collection *Dante e la cultura medievale* (Bari: Laterza, 1942). I randomly picked up one of the two copies, and then put it back: I hate readers who underline and gloss library books. I am so pedantic that I erase other people's underlining, do my own, and then erase it before I return books (which is probably more damaging for the paper, and a great loss for those scholars who in 5023 will try to study the 'pre-future' reader's response on those strange printed objects collected in places called, we think, libraries [or perhaps toilets, as one historian will have suggested comparing signs found in the post-apocalyptic sites of the Bodleian Library and the Bibliothèque Nationale de France]). Just to tell how compulsive I am about this, I recently had a panic attack when my first-ever Kindle sent me a message, as I was scrolling through a random page of a book, saying that '356 readers have underlined this passage'. Anyway, the other copy seemed more virgin, so I checked it out. At home, what a surprise! In an otherwise untouched book, an All-Hell-Is-Shit reader had glossed only the essay on Ulisse. An old-style handwriting, belonging to someone who clearly read Italian fluently, my guess is more a scholar than a student. Whenever Nardi talks about the *Odyssey* or the fact that Dante placed a great deal of admiration into his Ulisse, the marginal comments are as follows: 'rubbish', 'rubbish', 'dishonest'. The grand final statement about Dante discovering the discoverer is glossed as 'silly' (possibly later, the same or similar hand with a different pencil adds an arrow pointing to 'silly' and the comment 'and uptight'). The note that follows is marked as 'bollocks'. I could not stop laughing for an entire afternoon thinking about my reluctant philological encounter with this ungracious reader. I will make copies, and maybe even pictures. But then, I think, I will erase the marginal comments, as I usually do.

Modernity … us. Adorno and Horkheimer in their *Dialectic of Enlightenment* (1944) take Odysseus as the image for the power and shortcomings of modernity, of the perennial double bind of progress and destruction; of reason sabotaging its own achievements. I argue that Dante's Ulisse is even more so — but more in a self-destructive kind of way, and that Dante might have foreseen such a double bind from the margins of his mad intertextual tangent.

Citation, citationality, iterability — these are (or were?) hot topics in literary and critical theory. They bring to mind especially Derrida (*Margins of Philosophy*, *Marges de la philosophie* (Paris: Éditions De Minuit,1972)) and Butler (*Gender Trouble* (New York: Routledge, 1990)) and a whole turn-of-the-millennium optimism in the possibility of shaking up the structures of language and power. Of revolution and resistance being inbuilt into language and speech. *Mais où sont les neiges d'antan?* I sometimes wonder, crying the optimism of the 1990s, of a younger me.

On the birds of paradise, I enjoyed an illustrated essay by Nathalie Lawrence: 'Fallen Angels: Birds of Paradise in Early Modern Europe' (https://publicdomainreview.org/essay/fallen-angels-birds-of-paradise-in-early-modern-europe). Viewed as versions of the phoenix or veritable 'angels', these rare South Asian birds were actually a much-coveted object of hunt and trade.

This little, humble pigeon also deserves a place in my bibliography (Figure 15). It stares, perplexed, at the dreadful monument of Dante that was placed in Santa Croce in Florence on the occasion of the sixth centenary of his birth in 1865, portraying a surly, warlike, dominating Dante, a tamer of eagles (where eagle = empire). They even put the laurel on him, which he never received in life because he refused to write in Latin and clung to his lowly vernacular. 'This is all wrong', my little winged vindicator thinks, as he is about to besmirch and beshit the august composition. 'Who are you, colossal Accipitridae?', it wonders, 'And why are you both (you and the human) so pissed off? I haven't started yet.'

Michael Camille's *Image on the Edge: The Margins of Medieval Art* (Cambridge, MA: Harvard University Press, 1992) is a precious text, on medieval art but also on the medieval mind, I think. It begins like this: 'I could begin, like St. Bernard, by asking what do they all mean, those las-

Figure 15. Dante's monument in Florence.

civious apes, autophagic dragons, pot-bellied heads, harp-playing asses, arse-kissing priests and somersaulting jongleurs that protrude at the edges of medieval buildings, sculptures and illuminated manuscripts? But I am more interested in how they pretend to avoid meaning, how they seem to celebrate the flux of "becoming" rather than "being"' (p. 9).

On the Franklin expedition, I have read mostly essays and novels and the random website: I started with Atwood's *Strange Things: The Malevolent North in Canadian Literature* (1995) followed by Richler's *Solomon Gursky Was Here* (1989). After the chapter was done, I read Dominique Fortier's *Du bon usage des étoiles* (2008), to which I am grateful for a beautiful story and for reconnecting me to reading in French.

Gog and Magog and the gates of Alexander are medieval concepts best enjoyed through the reading of the medieval *Roman d'Alexandre*. Medieval Alexander is an explorer in his own way and has touches of Dante's Ulisse.

The Hereford *mappa mundi* is navigable online at <https://www.themappamundi.co.uk/>. For portolan charts, see Tony Campbell, 'Portolan Charts from the Late Thirteenth Century to 1500', in *History of Cartography*, ed. by J. B. Harley and David Woodward, 6 vols (Chicago: University of Chicago Press, 1987–), I: *Cartography in Prehistoric, Ancient, and Medieval Europe and the Mediterranean* (1987), pp. 371–463. I first encountered the T-O map in figure 5 on the website 'mapping the world' by Hanna Vorholt, published by the British Library (https://www.bl.uk/medieval-english-french-manuscripts/articles/mapping-the-world).

A good way to approach the figure and writing of Marco Polo in the new millennium is the volume *Marco Polo and the Encounter of East and West*, ed. by Suzanne Akbari and Amilcare Iannucci (Toronto: University of Toronto Press, 2008).

My 'standard Polo paragraph' is a mix of two paragraphs in chapters 50 and 52 of one Italian edition (Milan: Rizzoli, 1998), but then Polo's text is so variable that editions differ greatly. Polo's text is very much on the move like his journey. Wherever it lands, it takes up local languages and mores, but remains unsteady to the end.

The charge of Orientalism was brought to Dante by Edward Said in, well, *Orientalism* (New York: Pantheon, 1978), not without reason. In this matter, however, I prefer the more balanced approaches of recent scholars. See for instance the essays on 'The Mediterranean' by Karla Mallette and 'The East' by Brenda Deen Schildgen in the *Oxford Handbook*, pp. 368–82 and 383–98.

The documents on the brothers Vivaldi are nicely published by the Genoese state archive (http://www.archiviodistatogenova.beniculturali.it/index.php?it/252/ugolino-e-vadino-vivaldi). Of the various essays that treat their expedition, the clearest one is by Jill Moore, 'The Expedition of the Brothers Vivaldi: New Archival Evidence', in *Spain, Portugal and the Atlantic Frontier of Medieval Europe*, ed. by José-Juan López-Portillo (London: Routledge, 2016), pp. 1–18 (the Latin transcription of Jacopo Doria's *Annales* is found on p. 14). I read the *Libro del conoscimiento* in the edition and translation by Nancy F. Marino (Tempe: Arizona Center for Medieval and Renaissance Studies, 1999).

Dante's *Monarchia* is not my forte. I struggle to enjoy it. Of late, a brilliant essay by Claude Lefort, brought to life again by some of my equally brilliant colleagues, has changed my mind on Dante's political modernity (*Dante's Modernity: An Introduction to the 'Monarchia'. With an Essay by Judith Revel*, ed. by Christiane Frey, Manuele Gragnolati, Christoph F. E. Holzhey, and Arnd Wedemeyer, trans. by Jennifer Rushworth (Berlin: ICI Press, 2020)).

The classic study on medieval purgatory is Jacques Le Goff, *La naissance du Purgatoire* (The Birth of Purgatory) (Paris: Gallimard, 1981).

Manuele Gragnolati's *Experiencing the Afterlife* (South Bend, IN: Notre Dame University Press, 2005), his *Amor che move* (Milan: Saggiatore, 2013), and *Possibilities of Lyric* (Berlin: ICI Press, 2020), co-written with Francesca Southerden, have deeply influenced Dante studies of the new millennium with powerful reflections on bodies, embodiment, language, desire and its various forms, and non-linear readings.

The book I make fun of at the end of this chapter is J. L. R. Anderson, *The Ulysses Factor: The Exploring Instinct in Man* (London: Hodder and Stoughton, 1970). For the NASA website: <https://www.jpl.nasa.gov/missions/ulysses>.

CHAPTER 5

'Five senses …': I first encountered the quote by J. C. Lewis in the *Very Short Introduction to Memory* by J. K. Foster (Oxford: Oxford University Press, 2019).

The notion of recapitulation is crucial to John Freccero's *Dante: The Poetics of Conversion*. See especially the essay 'The Significance of Terza Rima' (pp. 258–71), but the whole book is one of a kind. John was my graduate teacher and dissertation supervisor, and my early work is imbued with the veneration I had for him. He was the most charming lecturer I have ever met. He would sit with his copy of Singleton's facing translation, blank with the exception of the occasional underlining, and talk for two hours without one hesitation. The only times when he snapped from this lecturing trance was when he was remembering his own teacher, Charles Singleton. His voice shaking just imperceptibly, he used to say 'I wish I could talk now to Singleton and discuss with him how my interpretation of this point is different from his'. Then he looked at us —

young people confused as to why one would like to resuscitate their magister to prove them wrong — sighed, smiled, and went on. John Freccero passed away as I am writing this book, in November 2021. And I, who have deviated from his interpretations, as one ought to do to become one's own scholar and to honour one's teachers properly, who have stopped venerating him, and even keeping in touch, wish now I could discuss points of divergence with him. And tell him that I miss him.

'Figura' is the title of a famous essay by Eric Auerbach, where you will find the story of this concept from antiquity to the Christian interpretation, as well as the two little goats from Leviticus 16. 7, still bleating and trembling as they await sacrifice, and pages on Dante's Cato and his role as *figura*. For a critique of figural reading, see Carlo Ginzburg, *La lettera uccide* (The Letter Kills) (Milan: Adelphi, 2021).

'Desire is now' is a beautiful definition of Christian religious blessedness from Caroline Walker Bynum's *The Resurrection of the Body in Western Christianity* (New York: Columbia University Press, 1995), p. 339, here glossed with my highest authority on emotions, Tina Turner ('Paradise Is Here', from the album aptly entitled *Break Every Rule*, Capitol Records, 1986).

On the various mutations of Orpheus in antiquity and the middle ages, see John Friedman, *Orpheus in the Middle Ages* (Cambridge, MA: Harvard University Press, 1970). 'Orphée noir' is Sartre's preface to the *Anthologie de la nouvelle poésie nègre et malgache de langue française*, ed. by Léopold Sédar Senghor (Paris: Presses universitaires de France, 1948). The film *Orfeu Negro* is now available on YouTube, and it does look dated without the tough love of the *cineforum*'s wooden seats.

The Virgil/Eurydice pattern in earthly purgatory was noticed already by Renaissance commentators and picked up by Robert Hollander in *Il Virgilio dantesco: tragedia nella Commedia* (Florence: Olschki, 1983). Occasionally, scholars point out the Orphic pattern in the Beatrice/Dante story. The standard interpretation — to which I am allergic, as you know by now — is that, you have guessed, Dante either damns or corrects Orpheus, like all other ancient myths, because he has god on his side.

Now a *memoir*, not a memory, Nicola Gardini's novel *Nicolas* (2022) has tied the departed beloved to literature. Indissolubly.

CHAPTER 6

I learned about the theme of the enchantress turned hag from Barbara Spackman's 'Inter ursam et musam moritur: Folengo and the Gaping Other Mouth', in *Refiguring Woman: Gender Studies in the Italian Renaissance*, ed. by Juliana Schiesari and Marilyn Migiel (Ithaca [talk about a dream publishing place!], NY: Cornell University Press, 1991), pp. 19–34. I have learned many things from Barbara, who was my graduate teacher too. Most importantly, the subtle relations between gender and rhetoric, and how to unveil a misogynist discourse. More intimately, the power of engaged scholarship and that we are allowed to dislike some canonical writers.

A very learned and original take on the long and complex history of the representation of the sirens is Agnese Grieco, *Atlante delle sirene* (Milan: Saggiatore, 2017).

The most enlightening essays on medieval illuminations are those by Michael Camille. For the illuminated Dante, see the recent collection called *Dante visualizzato*, ed. by Rossend Arqués and Marcello Ciccuto in five volumes: the reference to the quarterdeck of the mind comes from the essay by Anna Pegoretti, 'Un Dante "domenicano": la *Commedia* Egerton 943 della British Library', in the first volume (Florence: Cesati, 2017), pp. 127–42. To childishly enjoy the images, do roam the sites of the British Library, Bodleian Library, French National Library, and the Illuminated Dante Project.

It is immensely entertaining to skewer Geryon with the double fork of fraud and fiction. It is delightfully modern to try and figure out where Dante places himself in this equation — does he really claim he is 'non-fiction'? or is he messing with us? It stopped being fun and became very worrying the day I was flipping through a newspaper and saw Ameca, the robot with a human face (Figure 16) whose benign appearance raised the temperature of my internal malaise until I realized that he (they?) had the Dantean 'face of a just man' and looked exactly like the medieval representation of Genesis's serpent with a human face, on which images of Geryon are patterned. I only later realized that Ameca might be the English sound translation of *amica*, the Latin and Italian word for female friend. I tried watching a YouTube video on Ameca but it was prefaced by a mandatory McDonald's ad, so I quit. 'This is all wrong!' I erupted. 'From Genesis to now.'

The silence of the siren is the core of Kafka's rewriting of the myth, as I realized after I wrote my chapter. I had not thought of Kafka's short story for a long time until I found it mentioned in an article by Clayton Koelb, 'Kafka and the Sirens', in a volume called, simply, *Homer*, ed. by Katherine Callen King (New York: Routledge, 1994), pp. 191–208, on which I stumbled by chance while looking for something else in the library. Internet notwithstanding, I still believe in chance encounters in library aisles. [There is more to this chance encounter with Kafka, but I will tell you another time.]

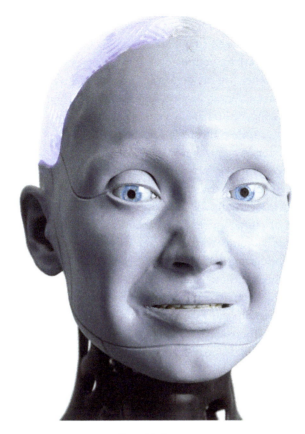

Figure 16. Ameca.

ONE WORD GLOSSARY

'We'. You have noticed that I use freely this pronoun throughout the book. Who are we? Readers may ask. 'Us', is the short answer. Let us (oops!) begin with what 'we' is not. It is not, clearly, the *plurale maiestatis*, the 'royal we', pasted there to say that there is more to 'us' than to you because my name is on the cover.

It is also not, hopefully, a 'universalizing we', although sometimes I fear I stray unintentionally into it, and retrospectively ask for your pardon. It is creepy, even when it is benign, when 'we' are the kind of people 'we' know and like — liberal, tolerant, pacifist, feminist, tree-loving, organic-purchasing, flexitarian. In a couple of cases, I have noticed the universal 'we' through re-reading, but I have left it there, as a testimony of how easy it is to slip.

Sometimes it is the 'didactic we' that we teachers use in the classroom to denote (in earnest, I believe) a shared space for learning, full of desire for knowledge. I hear this type of plural applies to preachers as well (ouch!). But, look at it another way, it also applies to aerobic teachers (a category from which I am excluded by reasons of physical clumsiness, although I am no stranger to the sweaty and euphoric collectivity of a group galvanized by the exhortation 'let us firm up those buttocks, now, together!'). It applies wherever there are walls and a shared activity perhaps? It may be kind, pedagogic, and enthusing but it is also gated, I realize now.

I hope my 'we' is more porous than that. I hope it addresses, without identifying it, a community of passionate and curious readers. I think it is called a 'narrative (?) we', and it implies this kind of spiel: 'we are in the same boat' (well, Dante says something similar in the second proem to *Paradiso*, as 'we' have seen), 'but I am no captain. We are all rowing or sailing. We ain't getting nowhere. But it is good to be together.' It reminds me of another boat that Dante imagined to navigate with his readers-friends and their lovers. A magic little vessel, lost like Ulisse's, but not in a threatening way. No shipwreck (or Eden) in sight, only capricious pleasure, and a bunch of 'us', perhaps captured and absorbed in the present of reading.*[footnote in the back matter? Anarchy reigns – I need to wrap up soon]

Reading is an elite activity in only one sense — it is a choice. It is exclusive because it requires concentration and absorption away from 'things'. Its only real currency is curiosity. Its wealth, words. You do not have to be literate or educated to be a reader. This is the little that I have learned from studying the medieval practices of reading.

But sometimes it is only me and you. You, the reader whose eyes are scanning now this page, and whose hands are leafing this book (or who are listening to this, or scrolling on the computer, or ...). I do not presume to know you. Nor that you and I agree. But we are a 'we' in the moment of reading. Reading is some kind of solidarity.

Of you I know nothing but this mute message that sustains my journey.

And I am a recidivist, as one might have noticed. This is a quote from a poem. A poem about the sea, for that matter. Or better, a poem about the place and moment in which the river meets the sea, the end of Eugenio Montale's

---

*   'Guido, i' vorrei che tu e Lapo ed io | fossimo presi per incantamento | e messi in un vasel, ch'ad ogni vento | per mare andasse al voler vostro e mio; | sì che fortuna od altro tempo rio | non ci potesse dare impedimento, | anzi, vivendo sempre in un talento, | di stare insieme crescesse 'l disio. || E monna Vanna e monna Lagia poi | con quella ch'è sul numer de le trenta | con noi ponesse il buono incantatore: | e quivi ragionar sempre d'amore, | e ciascuna di lor fosse contenta, | sì come i' credo che saremmo noi' (Guido, I wish that you and Lapo and I could be taken by magic and placed in a boat that, whatever the wind, was carried over the sea wherever you and I chose to go, unhindered by tempest or any foul weather — our desire to be together in fact always increasing, living as we would in unceasing harmony. And with this, that the good wizard should give us for company lady Vanna and lady Lagia and her who stands on number thirty, there to talk always of love; and that each of them should be happy, as I'm sure we would be; translation by K. Foster and P. Boyde).

Delta (from the collection *Ossi di Seppia*, 1928). A poem of confluence. Of the 'confluence of alienness and intimacy', perhaps.

I could imagine my little Ulysses mouthing these words as it takes leave from me, and I from you. I hope you do not mind if I dedicate this quote to you. [I have sent this quote at least three different times to three different lovers, with mixed success at being understood. I hope you do not mind that, too.]

> Tutto ignoro di te fuor del messaggio
> muto che mi sostenta sulla via:
> se forma esisti o ubbia nella fumea
> d'un sogno t'alimenta
> la riviera che infebbra, torba, e scroscia
> incontro alla marea.
> Nulla di te nel vacillar dell'ore
> bige o squarciate da un vampo di solfo
> fuori che il fischio del rimorchiatore
> che dalle brume approda al golfo.

> Of thee
> I know nothing, only
> the tidings sustaining my going,
> and shall I find
> thee shape or the fumes of a dream
> drawing life
> from the river's fever boiling darkly
> against the tide.
> Of thee nothing is the grey hours and the hours
> torn by a flame of sulphur,
> only
> the whistle of the tug
> whose prow has ridden forth into the bright gulf.
> (translation by Beckett) [too bad for the 'thee']

Finally, now that I have reached the end of my little book, I think I owe myself a reflection on the meaning of reading, writing, and doing scholarship as a way of living and journeying together. These days, the part I read more eagerly in a book is where scholars, and sometimes writers, thank their dear ones (spouses, partners, friends, lovers, children, kind readers). 'This book would not exist without you' is the controlled way of saying 'forget about the book, *I* would not exist without you'. Thanks are, therefore, due to 'the Pantheon', the family and friends who write my life and whose life I read. I wish to thank by name the first readers of this book for their amazing kindness, support, and enthusiasm: Francesca Southerden, Manuele Gragnolati, Nicola Gardini, Christoph Holzhey, Marco Formisano, Maggie Kilgour, Craig Offman. I am also very grateful to the ICI Berlin Press editorial team: Louisa Elderton and Claudia Peppel, to Sean Wyer for the help with image copyright, and to Ilaria Fusina and Ray Charles White for reconstructing the cover picture from our shared memories.

Misreadings, mistakes, and errancy are mine — and Ulysses'.

This book is dedicated to my 'wings': **A** (Alessandro) and **L** (Lyubov) (L-)**I**.

A List of Primary Sources

IN ORDER OF APPEARANCE

Machiavelli, Niccolò, 'Lettera a Francesco Vettori' (10 dicembre 1513), in Machiavelli, *Opere*, ed. by Corrado Vivanti, 3 vols (Turin: Einaudi, 1997–2005), II: *Lettere* (1999), pp. 294–97

—— 'Letter to Francesco Vettori' (10 December 1513), in *Machiavelli and his Friends: Their Personal Correspondence*, ed. and trans. by James B. Atkinson and David Sices (DeKalb: Northern Illinois University Press, 1996), pp. 262–65

Augustine, *Confessionum libri tredecim*, in *Patrologia Latina*, ed. by J.-P. Migne, 221 vols (Paris: Migne, 1844–65), 32 (1845), 659–867

Alighieri, Dante, *'La Commedia' secondo l'antica vulgata*, ed. by Giorgio Petrocchi (Florence: Società Dantesca Italiana, 1966–68) <https://dante.princeton.edu/> [accessed 21 March 2023]

—— *The Divine Comedy*, trans. by C. S. Singleton (Princeton, NJ: Princeton University Press, 1975)

Swift, Edgar, and Angela Kinney, eds, *The Vulgate Bible: Douay-Rheims Version*, 6 vols (Cambridge, MA: Harvard University Press, 2010–13)

Homer, *Iliad*, trans. by A. T. Murray and William F. Wyatt (Cambridge, MA: Harvard University Press, 1924)

Tennyson, Alfred, 'Ulysses', in *The Poems of Tennyson*, ed. by Christopher Ricks (London: Longman, 1969), pp. 560–66

Alighieri, Dante, *Convivio*, ed. by Franca Brambilla Ageno (Florence: Le Lettere, 1995) <https://dante.princeton.edu/> [accessed 21 March 2023]

—— *The Banquet*, trans. by Richard Lansing (New York: Garland, 1990) <https://dante.princeton.edu/> [accessed 21 March 2023]

Homer, *Odyssey*, trans. by A. T. Murray and George E. Dimock (Cambridge, MA: Harvard University Press, 2014)

Ariosto, Ludovico, *Orlando Furioso*, ed. by Cesare Segre (Milan: Mondadori, 1976)
Roth, Philip, *The Human Stain* (London: Vintage, 2000)
Foscolo, Ugo, 'A Zacinto', in Foscolo, *Opere*, ed. by Franco Gavazzeni, 2 vols (Turin: Einaudi Gallimard, 1994–95), I: *Poesie e tragedie* (1994), pp. 17–18
Saba, Umberto, 'Ulisse', in Saba, *Tutte le poesie*, ed. by Arrigo Stara (Milan: Mondadori, 1988), p. 556
—— 'Ulisse', in *Songbook: The Selected Poems of Umberto Saba*, trans. by George Hochfield and Leonard Nathan (New Haven, CT: Yale University Press, 2012), pp. 492–93
Claudel, Paul, 'Sur l'Odyssée' (1947), in Homer, *Odyssée*, trans. by Victor Bérard (Paris: Gallimard, 1972), pp. 7–9
Augustine, *Epistula* 138, in *Patrologia Latina*, 33 (1845), 521–25
Virgil, *Aeneid*, trans. by Henry Rushton Fairclough and G. P. Goold (Cambridge, MA: Harvard University Press, 2014)
Baudelaire, Charles, 'Hymne à la beauté', in Baudelaire, *Œuvres complètes*, ed. by Claude Pichois, 2 vols (Paris: Gallimard, 1975–76), I (1975), pp. 24–25
Plotinus, *Enneads*, trans. by Stephen Mackenna and B. S. Page (London: Faber and Faber, 1966)
Augustine, *De doctrina christiana libri quatuor*, in *Patrologia Latina*, 34 (1845), 15–120
—— *On Christian Teaching*, trans. by R. P. H. Green (Oxford: Oxford University Press, 1995)
Cicero, *De finibus bonorum et malorum*, trans. by Harris Rackham (Cambridge, MA: Harvard University Press, 2014)
Horace, *Satires, Epistles and Ars Poetica*, trans. by Henry Rushton Fairclough (Cambridge, MA: Harvard University Press, 2014)
Seneca, *Epistula* 88, in *Epistles*, trans. by Richard M. Gummere, 3 vols (Cambridge, MA: Harvard University Press, 2014), II, pp. 348–76
Ovid, *Metamorphoses*, trans. by Frank J. Miller and G. P. Goold (Cambridge, MA: Harvard University Press, 1921)
Plato, *The Republic*, trans. by Benjamin Jowett (Mineola, NY: Dover Publications, 2000)
Pico della Mirandola, Giovanni, *Oration on the Dignity of Man: A New Translation and Commentary*, ed. and trans. by Francesco Borghesi, Michael Papio, and Massimo Riva (Cambridge: Cambridge University Press, 2012)

Pindar, *Pythian 8*, in *Olympian Odes, Pythian Odes*, trans. by William H. Race (Cambridge, MA: Harvard University Press, 1997), pp. 336–47

Petrarca, Francesco, *Triumphus mortis*, in Petrarca, *Triumphi*, ed. by Marco Ariani (Milan: Mursia, 1988), pp. 225–76

Levi, Primo, *Se questo è un uomo* (Turin: Einaudi, 2012)

—— *If This Is a Man / The Truce*, trans. by Stuart Woolf (London: Abacus, 1987)

Plutarch, *Life of Sertorius*, in *Lives*, trans. by Bernadotte Perrin, 11 vols (Cambridge, MA: Harvard University Press, 2014), VIII, pp. 2–75

Rabelais, François, *Œuvres Complètes*, ed. by Mireille Huchon and François Moreau (Paris: Gallimard, 2020)

Hesiod, *Theogony*, in *Theogony. Works and Days. Testimonia*, trans. by Glenn W. Most (Cambridge, MA: Harvard University Press, 2018), pp. 2–85

Richler, Mordecai, *Solomon Gursky Was Here* (London: Vintage, 1991)

Leopardi, Giacomo, 'Canto notturno del pastore errante dell'Asia', in Leopardi, *Canti*, ed. by Franco Gavazzeni and Maria Maddalena Lombardi (Milan: BUR Rizzoli, 1998), pp. 434–54

Augustine, *Enarratio in Psalmum 64*, in *Patrologia Latina*, 36 (1845), 772–85

Virgil, *Georgics*, trans. by Henry Rushton Fairclough and G. P. Goold (Cambridge, MA: Harvard University Press, 2014)

Montale, Eugenio, 'Ho sceso dandoti il braccio', in Montale, *Tutte le poesie*, ed. by Giorgio Zampa (Milan: Mondadori, 1977), p. 351

Benvenuto da Imola, *Comentum super Dantis Aldigherij Comoediam* <https://dante.dartmouth.edu/> [accessed 21 March 2023]

Odo of Cluny, *Collationes*, in *Patrologia Latina*, 133 (1853), 517–638, 556

Rimbaud, Arthur, 'Le Bateau ivre' / 'The Drunken Boat', in *Rimbaud: Complete Works, Selected Letters*, ed. by Seth Whidden, trans. by Wallace Fowlie (Chicago: University of Chicago Press, 2005), pp. 128–34

—— 'The Drunken Boat', trans. by Samuel Beckett, in Beckett, *Selected Poems 1930–1989*, ed. by David Wheatley (London: Faber and Faber, 2009), pp. 126–39

Ovid, *Tristia*, in *Tristia. Ex Ponto*, trans. by G. P. Goold and Arthur Wheeler (Cambridge, MA: Harvard University Press, 2014), pp. 2–261

Walcott, Derek, *Omeros* (London: Faber and Faber, 1990)

Apollonius Rhodius, *Argonautica*, trans. by William H. Race (Cambridge, MA: Harvard University Press, 2014)

Calvino, Italo, *Il barone rampante* (Milan: Mondadori, 2012)

—— *The Baron in the Trees*, trans. by Ann Goldstein (London: Vintage, 2019)

Melville, Herman, *Moby Dick, or, the Whale* (New York: Penguin, 1992)

Camões, Luís de, *Os Lusíadas*, ed. by Frank Pierce (Oxford: Clarendon Press, 1973)

Augustine, *De Trinitate libri quindecim*, in *Patrologia Latina*, 42 (1845), 819–1098

Walcott, Derek, 'Sea Grapes', in *Collected Poems 1948–1984* (London: Faber and Faber, 1986), p. 297

Rilke, Rainer Maria, *The Notebooks of Malte Laurids Brigge*, trans. by Robert Vilain (Oxford: Oxford University Press, 2016)

Alighieri, Dante, 'Guido i' vorrei', *Rime* LII, ed. by Michele Barbi, trans. by Kenelm Foster and Patrick Boyde <https://dante.princeton.edu/> [accessed 21 February 2023]

Montale, Eugenio, 'Delta', in Montale, *Tutte le poesie*, p. 125

—— 'Delta', trans. by Samuel Beckett, in Beckett, *Selected Poems 1930–1989*, pp. 120–21

Cultural Inquiry

EDITED BY CHRISTOPH F. E. HOLZHEY
AND MANUELE GRAGNOLATI

Vol. 1   TENSION/SPANNUNG
Edited by Christoph F. E. Holzhey

Vol. 2   METAMORPHOSING DANTE
Appropriations, Manipulations, and Rewritings
in the Twentieth and Twenty-First Centuries
Edited by Manuele Gragnolati, Fabio Camilletti,
and Fabian Lampart

Vol. 3   PHANTASMATA
Techniken des Unheimlichen
Edited by Fabio Camilletti, Martin Doll, and
Rupert Gaderer

Vol. 4   Boris Groys / Vittorio Hösle
DIE VERNUNFT AN DIE MACHT
Edited by Luca Di Blasi and Marc Jongen

Vol. 5   Sara Fortuna
WITTGENSTEINS PHILOSOPHIE DES
KIPPBILDS
Aspektwechsel, Ethik, Sprache

Vol. 6   THE SCANDAL OF SELF-CONTRADICTION
Pasolini's Multistable Subjectivities, Geographies,
Traditions
Edited by Luca Di Blasi, Manuele Gragnolati,
and Christoph F. E. Holzhey

Vol. 7   SITUIERTES WISSEN
UND REGIONALE EPISTEMOLOGIE
Zur Aktualität Georges Canguilhems und Donna J.
Haraways
Edited by Astrid Deuber-Mankowsky
and Christoph F. E. Holzhey

Vol. 8	MULTISTABLE FIGURES On the Critical Potentials of Ir/Reversible Aspect-Seeing Edited by Christoph F. E. Holzhey
Vol. 9	Wendy Brown / Rainer Forst THE POWER OF TOLERANCE Edited by Luca Di Blasi and Christoph F. E. Holzhey
Vol. 10	DENKWEISEN DES SPIELS Medienphilosophische Annäherungen Edited by Astrid Deuber-Mankowsky and Reinhold Görling
Vol. 11	DE/CONSTITUTING WHOLES Towards Partiality Without Parts Edited by Manuele Gragnolati and Christoph F. E. Holzhey
Vol. 12	CONATUS UND LEBENSNOT Schlüsselbegriffe der Medienanthropologie Edited by Astrid Deuber-Mankowsky and Anna Tuschling
Vol. 13	AURA UND EXPERIMENT Naturwissenschaft und Technik bei Walter Benjamin Edited by Kyung-Ho Cha
Vol. 14	Luca Di Blasi DEZENTRIERUNGEN Beiträge zur Religion der Philosophie im 20. Jahrhundert
Vol. 15	RE- An Errant Glossary Edited by Christoph F. E. Holzhey and Arnd Wedemeyer

Vol. 16 Claude Lefort
        DANTE'S MODERNITY
        An Introduction to the Monarchia
        With an Essay by Judith Revel
        Translated from the French by Jennifer Rushworth
        Edited by Christiane Frey, Manuele Gragnolati,
        Christoph F. E. Holzhey, and Arnd Wedemeyer

Vol. 17 WEATHERING
        Ecologies of Exposure
        Edited by Christoph F. E. Holzhey and Arnd
        Wedemeyer

Vol. 18 Manuele Gragnolati and Francesca Southerden
        POSSIBILITIES OF LYRIC
        Reading Petrarch in Dialogue

Vol. 19 THE WORK OF WORLD LITERATURE
        Edited by Francesco Giusti and Benjamin Lewis
        Robinson

Vol. 20 MATERIALISM AND POLITICS
        Edited by Bernardo Bianchi, Emilie
        Filion-Donato,
        Marlon Miguel, and Ayşe Yuva

Vol. 21 OVER AND OVER AND OVER AGAIN
        Reenactment Strategies in Contemporary Arts
        and Theory
        Edited by Cristina Baldacci, Clio Nicastro,
        and Arianna Sforzini

Vol. 22 QUEERES KINO / QUEERE ÄSTHETIKEN
        ALS DOKUMENTATIONEN DES PREKÄREN
        Edited by Astrid Deuber-Mankowsky
        and Philipp Hanke

Vol. 23 OPENNESS IN MEDIEVAL EUROPE
        Edited by Manuele Gragnolati
        and Almut Suerbaum

Vol. 24   ERRANS
         Going Astray, Being Adrift, Coming to Nothing
         Edited by Christoph F. E. Holzhey
         and Arnd Wedemeyer

Vol. 25   THE CASE FOR REDUCTION
         Edited by Christoph F. E. Holzhey
         and Jakob Schillinger

Vol. 26   UNTYING THE MOTHER TONGUE
         Edited by Antonio Castore
         and Federico Dal Bo

Vol. 27   WAR-TORN ECOLOGIES, AN-ARCHIC
         FRAGMENTS
         Reflections from the Middle East
         Edited by Umut Yıldırım

Vol. 28   Elena Lombardi
         ULYSSES, DANTE, AND OTHER STORIES

Milton Keynes UK
Ingram Content Group UK Ltd.
UKHW022114231123
433173UK00014B/205/J